LIVERPOOL FC
THE OFFICIAL GUIDE
2012

Sport Media
A Trinity Mirror Business

HONOURS

LEAGUE CHAMPIONSHIP (18)
1900/01, 1905/06, 1921/22, 1922/23, 1946/47, 1963/64, 1965/66, 1972/73, 1975/76, 1976/77, 1978/79, 1979/80, 1981/82, 1982/83, 1983/84, 1985/86, 1987/88, 1989/90

DIVISION TWO WINNERS (4)
1893/94, 1895/96, 1904/05, 1961/62

FA CUP WINNERS (7)
1964/65, 1973/74, 1985/86, 1988/89, 1991/92, 2000/01, 2005/06

LEAGUE CUP WINNERS (7)
1980/81, 1981/82, 1982/83, 1983/84, 1994/95, 2000/01, 2002/03

EUROPEAN CHAMPIONS CUP/UEFA CHAMPIONS LEAGUE WINNERS (5)
1976/77, 1977/78, 1980/81, 1983/84, 2004/05

UEFA CUP WINNERS (3)
1972/73, 1975/76, 2000/01

EUROPEAN SUPER CUP/UEFA SUPER CUP WINNERS (3)
1977/78, 2001/02, 2005/06

FA CHARITY SHIELD WINNERS/FA COMMUNITY SHIELD WINNERS (15)
1964 (SHARED), 1965 (SHARED), 1966, 1974, 1976, 1977 (SHARED), 1979, 1980, 1982, 1986 (SHARED), 1988, 1989, 1990 (SHARED), 2001, 2006

SCREEN SPORT SUPER CUP WINNERS (1)
1986/87

LANCASHIRE LEAGUE WINNERS (1)
1892/93

INTRODUCTION

Welcome to the **Liverpool FC : The Official Guide**, the essential club publication for 2012. As ever, we have aimed to provide you with the very best there is to celebrate about the club, both on and off the pitch, while keeping you in touch with what has happened in the previous 12 months.

The period has seen Jamie Carragher move up to second in the all-time appearance list behind club legend Ian Callaghan. Pepe Reina, again an ever-present in 2010/11, has continued to make his mark as one of the club's greatest-ever goalkeepers, while the return of Kenny Dalglish dominated LFC news in early 2011 – a fact duly noted in these pages.

The 2011/12 season kicked off with the squad looking in healthy shape to once again establish its place amongst the big players in the Premier League, with player movement in and out of Anfield ensuring the squad has increased in quality, and standard.

This edition of the Guide is packed with the most accurate information, statistics, results and LFC photography, which will hopefully enhance your experience. There is the usual mix of regular features blended in with new content for you to enjoy. There are pages celebrating Jamie Carragher and Pepe Reina's achievements, added content in The Manager section – while the For Club, For Country section includes content on the Copa America and LFC Youth Internationals.

Once again our gratitude to Ged Rea and Dave Ball, who have again been instrumental in providing up-to-date, accurate statistical information, while also making helpful suggestions to enhance the depth and quality of the Guide.

We hope you continue to find this publication of interest and a major reference point, balancing as it does the best of Liverpool FC in the past, present and future, whilst also utilising some of the best pictures available, celebrating the club's rich pedigree at home and abroad.

ABOUT THE CONTRIBUTORS

Ged Rea and Dave Ball are the statisticians for the official Liverpool FC matchday programme, and *LFC* weekly club magazine. Ged's Liverpool FC records are the most accurate available, while Dave is a key researcher for long-running BBC TV show *A Question of Sport*. James Cleary has overseen the editorial, design, research and writing of the publication.

Executive Editor: KEN ROGERS Senior Editor: STEVE HANRAHAN
Senior Production Editor: PAUL DOVE Senior Art Editor: RICK COOKE
Production Journalist: JAMES CLEARY
Sport Media Marketing Executive: CLAIRE BROWN

ISBN 978 1 9068 02783
Photographs: PA Photos, Trinity Mirror, Liverpool FC & AG Ltd
Printed and finished by KINT Ljubljana

CLUB CONTACT NUMBERS

Main Switchboard	0151 263 2361
Customer Services	0843 170 5000
International callers	+ 44 (0)151 907 9399
Ticket Office	0843 170 5555
International Ticket Office	+ 44 (0)151 907 9399
Mail Order Hotline (UK)	0843 170 1892
International Mail Order Hotline	+ 44 (0)151 907 9500
Club Store (Anfield)	0151 263 1760
Club Store (Williamson Square – City Centre)	0151 330 3077
Club Store (Liverpool One – City Centre)	0151 709 4345
Club Store (Chester)	01244 344608
Club Store (Belfast)	02890 319341
Conference and Banqueting (for your events at Anfield)	0151 263 7744
Corporate Sales	0151 263 9199
Community Department	0151 432 5689
Museum & Tour Centre	0151 260 6677
Membership Department	0843 170 5000
Public Relations (including all charity requests)	0151 432 5671
Press Office	0151 230 5721
Digital Media (online, TV and mobile)	0151 263 2361

BECOME AN LFC OFFICIAL MEMBER NOW.
To join, visit **www.liverpoolfc.tv/membership** or call 0843 170 5000.

SUBSCRIBE TO THE OFFICIAL **LFC PROGRAMME AND WEEKLY MAGAZINE**
To take out a subscription please call: 0845 143 0001

LIVE AND BREATHE LFC 24/7
Official Club Media

Online – visit the official club website at **www.liverpoolfc.tv** for breaking news,
views, match reports, interviews, statistics, history and more.

Watch goals, highlights, interviews, press conferences, reserve matches, classic matches and
listen to commentary of every game with a subscription to LFCTV Online – visit
www.liverpoolfc.tv/video

TV – the official TV channel (LFC TV) is broadcast every day from the heart of your club.
Available by satellite, cable and online on Sky 434 and Virgin Media 544
– visit **www.liverpoolfc.tv/tv**

Mobile – take LFC wherever you go. Download player animations, videos, games
and our new mobile apps or get the news as it happens with the club's text alerts – visit
www.liverpoolfc.tv/mobile

Visit the official online store at **www.liverpoolfc.tv/store**

CONTENTS

MANAGERS   12-23

A look back at the main men in charge – while also celebrating the return of The King. Complete with a statistical breakdown of Reds managers, as well as the former Liverpool favourites who have taken the leap into the managerial hotseat with other Football League clubs.

NEW CAMPAIGN   24-45

The complete squad list for the 2011/12, updated to include ins and outs at the end of the August 2011 transfer window. The section also includes a look at the management and backroom staff, the Summer Diary 2011 and 2011/12 fixtures for the first team, reserves and Academy.

THE 2010/11 SEASON   46-79

An in-depth review of the campaign, including day-to-day goings on, results, goalscorers, league positions and quotes. Six Of The Best offers the pictorial highlights, while there's a complete breakdown of player statistics and a season review for the reserves, Academy and Liverpool Ladies' 2011 FA Women's Super League campaign.

EUROPE   80-121

The 2010/11 UEFA Europa League Liverpool matches are documented, while the complete set of European results from 1964 onwards are updated. European club, player and manager records and statistics are also included, while the Classic European Season is the 1980/81 campaign, which saw the club lift the European Champions Cup for a third time.

FOR CLUB, FOR COUNTRY   122-133

A breakdown of the club's international players past and present, from the home nation representatives to further afield. There is also focus on the Copa America, other major international tournaments and the Youth Internationals the Reds have produced.

CLUB RECORDS   134-171

A compilation of LFC achievements – both from the team and individually, from the Complete First-Team Record through to Away Goalscorers in the Premier League. Recent achievements by Pepe Reina and Jamie Carragher are also noted, as well as the complete Premier League Players' Record – from Agger to Ziege.

OPPOSITION   172-183

A run through the Reds' Premier League opponents in 2011/12, with team factfiles including away travel information and the Reds' leading league goalscorers against each side.

ESSENTIALS   184-208

The official off-field club information, compiled for fans to get to know LFC even more. Includes a wealth of information, including LFC Official Membership for supporters of all ages.

FOREWORD

This is the seventh edition of the Guide, which will again attempt to put last season's campaign into perspective and document the achievements of both the club and its players over the past 100 years or so.

There is a cliché often used in football – a game of two halves – but for Liverpool FC, last season really was a campaign of two halves. There was the tenure of Roy Hodgson and the previous owners, followed by the appointment of Kenny Dalglish and the takeover by the Fenway Sports Group.

In the Guide we will look at the continuing achievements of Pepe Reina and applaud Jamie Carragher, who now finds himself in second place behind Ian Callaghan courtesy of his 666th appearance in the famous shirt. We also look at Kenny Dalglish's record as a manager in his two spells in charge, and compare it with his predecessors. There is a section on Liverpool international players at all age groups, a complete review of the season as well as the usual records section.

It has always been an intention to update records so as to keep our many supporters in touch with the past, as well as the Premier League era. What is always interesting is to place Steven Gerrard and Dirk Kuyt amongst others in the context of players from the past. Once again we reiterate how important it is to have a library to consult rather than the internet, which in many cases are susceptible to errors.

We now look forward to the current campaign and hope that in next year's Guide we will be able to document even more successes. The new owners have inspired us and in one early interview, John W Henry remarked that: "Success is winning championships, it's nothing less than that."

He continued: "When you win a championship – and we will – success isn't measured or accomplished by winning once!" These are words which could well have been the utterances from Bill Shankly, Bob Paisley or Joe Fagan.

Ged Rea & Dave Ball

KEY DATES 2011/12

(Dates are subject to change)

August 2011

13	Barclays Premier League kick-off
23/24	Carling Cup second round
31	Transfer window closes

September 2011

2	Bulgaria v England, Euro 2012 qualifier (Vasil Levski Stadium, Sofia)
	Wales v Montenegro, Euro 2012 qualifier (Cardiff City Stadium, Cardiff)
	Holland v San Marino, Euro 2012 qualifier (Philips Stadion, Eindhoven)
	Republic of Ireland v Slovakia, Euro 2012 qualifier (Aviva Stadium, Dublin)
	Ukraine v Uruguay, international friendly (Metalist Stadium, Kharkiv)
3	Scotland v Czech Republic, Euro 2012 qualifier (Hampden Park, Glasgow)
5	Brazil v Ghana, international friendly (Craven Cottage, London)
6	England v Wales, Euro 2012 qualifier (Wembley Stadium, London)
	Scotland v Lithuania, Euro 2012 qualifier (Hampden Park, Glasgow)
	Finland v Holland, Euro 2012 qualifier (Olympic Stadium, Helsinki)
	Spain v Liechtenstein, Euro 2012 qualifier (Estadio Las Gaunas, Logrono)
	Slovakia v Armenia, Euro 2012 qualifier (Pod Dubnom, Zilina)
20/21	Carling Cup third round

October 2011

7	Montenegro v England, Euro 2012 qualifier (Podgorica City Stadium, Podgorica)
	Wales v Switzerland, Euro 2012 qualifier (Liberty Stadium, Swansea)
	Holland v Moldova, Euro 2012 qualifier (De Kuip, Rotterdam)
	Czech Republic v Spain, Euro 2012 qualifier (Generali Arena, Prague)
	Slovakia v Russia, Euro 2012 qualifier (Pod Dubnom, Zilina)
	Uruguay v Bolivia, World Cup 2014 qualifier (Estadio Centenario, Montevideo)
	Costa Rica v Brazil, international friendly (Estadio Nacional de Costa Rica, San Jose)
8	Liechtenstein v Scotland, Euro 2012 qualifier (Rheinpark Stadium, Vaduz)
11	Spain v Scotland, Euro 2012 qualifier (Estadio Jose Rico Perez, Alicante)
	Bulgaria v Wales, Euro 2012 qualifier (Vasil Levski Stadium, Sofia)
	Sweden v Holland, Euro 2012 qualifier (Rasunda Stadium, Solna)
	Denmark v Portugal, Euro 2012 qualifier (Parken Stadium, Copenhagen)
	Macedonia v Slovakia, Euro 2012 qualifier (Philip II Arena, Skopje)
	Paraguay v Uruguay, World Cup 2014 qualifier (Estadio Defensores del Chaco, Asuncion)
	Mexico v Brazil, international friendly (Estadio Corona, Torreon)
25/26	Carling Cup fourth round

November 2011

11	Holland v Switzerland, international friendly (Amsterdam Arena, Amsterdam)
	Uruguay v Chile, World Cup 2014 qualifier (Estadio Centenario, Montevideo)
	Gabon v Brazil, international friendly (Stade Omar Bongo, Libreville)
11/12	Euro 2012 qualifying play-offs, 1st leg
15	Euro 2012 qualifying play-offs, 2nd leg
	Germany v Holland, international friendly (Imtech Arena, Hamburg)
	Italy v Uruguay, international friendly (TBA)
29/30	Carling Cup quarter-finals

December 2011

2	Euro 2012 draw (Kiev, Ukraine)

KEY DATES 2011/12

(Dates are subject to change)

January 2012

1	Transfer window re-opens
7/8	FA Cup third round
10/11	Carling Cup semi-finals, first leg
21	Africa Cup of Nations begins (Bata, Equatorial Guinea)
24/25	Carling Cup semi-finals, second leg
28/29	FA Cup fourth round
31	Transfer window closes

February 2012

12	Africa Cup of Nations Final (Libreville, Gabon)
25/26	FA Cup fifth round
26	Carling Cup Final (Wembley Stadium, London)
29	Romania v Uruguay, international friendly (Bucharest)

March 2012

17/18	FA Cup quarter-finals
25	International official competition matches
29	International official competition matches

April 2012

14/15	FA Cup semi-finals

May 2012

5	FA Cup Final (Wembley Stadium, London)
9	UEFA Europa League Final (Stadionul National, Bucharest, Romania)
13	Barclays Premier League final day
19	UEFA Champions League Final (Allianz Arena, Munich, Germany)

June 2012

1	International friendlies
3	Uruguay v Venezuela, World Cup 2014 qualifier (Estadio Centenario, Montevideo)
5	International friendlies
8	Euro 2012 begins (National Stadium, Warsaw, Poland)
10	Uruguay v Peru, World Cup 2014 qualifier (Estadio Centenario, Montevideo)

July 2012

1	Euro 2012 Final (Olympic Stadium, Kiev, Ukraine)
25	Olympic football tournament begins (Millennium Stadium, Cardiff, Wales)

THE LIVERPOOL FC MANAGERS

The full record of the club's first-team managers, dates of appointment/departure and respective ages upon appointment, are noted below.

THE COMPLETE LIST 1892-2011

MANAGER	APPOINTED–DEPARTED
Kenny Dalglish	May 2011-
Kenny Dalglish (caretaker)	January 2011-May 2011
Roy Hodgson	July 2010-January 2011
Rafael Benitez	June 2004-June 2010
Gerard Houllier	November 1998-May 2004
Roy Evans (joint manager with Gerard Houllier)	July 1998-November 1998
Roy Evans	January 1994-November 1998
Graeme Souness	April 1991-January 1994
Ronnie Moran (caretaker)	February 1991-April 1991
Kenny Dalglish	May 1985-February 1991
Joe Fagan	July 1983-May 1985
Bob Paisley	July 1974-May 1983
Bill Shankly	December 1959-July 1974
Phil Taylor	May 1956-November 1959
Don Welsh	March 1951-May 1956
George Kay	August 1936-January 1951
George Patterson	March 1928-August 1936
Matt McQueen	February 1923-February 1928
David Ashworth	December 1919-December 1922
Tom Watson	August 1896-May 1915
John McKenna	August 1892-August 1896

OLDEST LIVERPOOL FC MANAGERS

	D.O.B.	DATE APPOINTED	AGE
Roy Hodgson	09/08/1947	01/07/2010	62 years, 326 days
Joe Fagan	12/03/1921	01/07/1983	62 years, 111 days
Kenny Dalglish	04/03/1951	12/05/2011	60 years, 69 days
Matt McQueen	18/05/1863	13/02/1923	59 years, 271 days
Bob Paisley	23/01/1919	26/07/1974	55 years, 184 days
David Ashworth	na/na/1868	17/12/1919	approx. 51 years
Gerard Houllier	03/09/1947	16/07/1998*	50 years, 316 days
Bill Shankly	02/09/1913	01/12/1959	46 years, 90 days
Roy Evans	04/10/1948	31/01/1994	45 years, 119 days
George Kay	21/09/1891	06/08/1936	44 years, 320 days
Rafael Benitez	16/04/1960	16/06/2004	44 years, 61 days
George Patterson	na/na/1887	07/03/1928	approx. 41 years
Don Welsh	25/02/1911	05/03/1951	40 years, 8 days
Phil Taylor	18/09/1917	May 1956	approx. 38 years, 8 months
Graeme Souness	06/05/1953	16/04/1991	37 years, 345 days
Tom Watson	09/04/1859	17/08/1896	37 years, 130 days
John McKenna	03/01/1855	15/03/1892	37 years, 72 days
Kenny Dalglish	04/03/1951	30/05/1985	34 years, 87 days

* date appointed as joint-manager

MANAGER RECORDS

The complete statistical record for every Liverpool boss, in chronological order, up until and including the end of the 2010/11 season. Note Kenny Dalglish's second reign statistics include his stint as caretaker-manager between January and May 2011.

THE COMPLETE LIVERPOOL FC MANAGERS' RECORD

MANAGER	P	W	D	L	F	A	WIN %
John McKenna	105	60	18	27	272	136	57.14
Tom Watson	741	328	141	272	1221	1055	44.26
David Ashworth	139	70	40	29	220	118	50.36
Matt McQueen	229	93	60	76	354	307	40.61
George Patterson	366	137	85	144	665	700	37.43
George Kay	354	140	93	121	545	508	39.55
Don Welsh	232	81	58	93	387	423	34.91
Phil Taylor	150	76	32	42	294	211	50.67
Bill Shankly	783	407	198	178	1307	766	51.98
Bob Paisley	535	308	131	96	955	406	57.57
Joe Fagan	131	71	36	24	225	97	54.20
Kenny Dalglish	307	187	78	42	617	259	60.91
Ronnie Moran (caretaker)	10	4	1	5	20	16	40.00
Graeme Souness	157	66	45	46	248	186	42.04
Roy Evans	226	117	56	53	375	216	51.77
Roy Evans/Gerard Houllier	18	7	6	5	33	20	38.89
Gerard Houllier	307	160	73	74	516	298	52.12
Rafael Benitez	350	197	74	79	585	302	56.29
Roy Hodgson	31	13	8	10	41	33	41.94
Kenny Dalglish	23	11	5	7	36	19	47.83

Bob Paisley, Joe Fagan and one-time caretaker-boss Ronnie Moran on the Reds bench

KENNY DALGLISH'S RECORD

The return of Kenny Dalglish as Liverpool manager for a second spell in 2011 is an ideal opportunity to look back on his first tenure. The King, one of the greatest players in the club's history, took over from the retiring Joe Fagan in May 1985, becoming one of the few managers to become a player/manager. Assisted by Bob Paisley in his first two years in the role, Dalglish made few changes to the squad, with Steve McMahon the only major buy, while players such as Jim Beglin and Steve Nicol became regulars. An impressive run of 11 wins from their final 12 league fixtures secured the First Division title. Needing to win at Chelsea in the final league game of the season to confirm the championship, Kenny scored the only goal to secure a 1-0 win. A week later, the Reds were celebrating their first Double by coming from behind to beat Everton 3-1 in the first all-Merseyside FA Cup final.

Liverpool finished empty handed in the major competitions in 1986/87, only the third time in 15 years this had occurred. Distant runners-up to Everton in the league, the Reds were also runners-up in the League Cup, beaten 2-1 by underdogs Arsenal. There was silverware in the form of the Screen Sports Super Cup, the competition created the previous season for teams who had qualified for European competition denied the opportunity of overseas competitive action due to UEFA's ban on English clubs. Liverpool claimed a 7-2 aggregate success against the Toffees, with the matches held in the autumn of 1986.

But having made some tweaks to his line-up, Dalglish concentrated on his strikeforce. John Aldridge had been signed in February 1987, and in the summer of that year he brought in John Barnes and Peter Beardsley, with Ray Houghton also coming in early in the season. All four players would make an immediate impact. The Reds did not lose until March in the league, equalling Leeds United's 29-match unbeaten run from the start of the campaign. By then they had won 22 and drawn 7, scoring 65 and conceding only 13 in the process. The title was secured with four games to go, with Aldridge (29), Beardsley (18) and Barnes (17) finishing as top goalscorers in all competitions. The only real disappointment being a surprise FA Cup final defeat to Wimbledon, Lawrie Sanchez's header denying the Reds a second Double in three seasons.

The 1988/89 season was overshadowed by the Hillsborough tragedy, with 96 fans losing their lives on the Leepings Lane terrace at the FA Cup semi-final against Nottingham Forest on April 15. On course for a league and cup Double, the side was forced to fit in eight games in the space of 23 days, having been allowed time to postpone games in order to grieve and consider their options. There was speculation that the club would pull out of the FA Cup, but they went ahead, defeating Forest in the re-played semi-final at Old Trafford before landing the trophy by beating Everton 3-2 after extra time at Wembley, a tribute to the fans who had lost their lives. Six days later saw a league title decider against Arsenal. A last-gasp 2-0 defeat at Anfield saw the championship lost, although in light of what had gone before, the defeat paled into insignificance.

DALGLISH AT LIVERPOOL FC – SEASON-BY-SEASON (ALL SEASONS)

SEASON	P	W	D	L	F	A	WIN %
1985/86	63	41	15	7	138	52	65.08
1986/87	57	31	13	13	105	54	54.39
1987/88	50	32	14	4	99	28	64.00
1988/89	53	33	12	8	98	44	62.26
1989/90	50	30	13	7	107	47	60.00
1990/91	34	20	11	3	70	34	58.82
2010/11	23	11	5	7	36	19	47.83
TOTAL	**330**	**198**	**83**	**49**	**653**	**278**	**60.00**

KENNY DALGLISH'S RECORD

The team bounced back for the 1989/90 campaign. The Reds had lost only once in 35 games from New Year's Day to October 1989, and they eventually eased to an 18th championship with Ian Rush, who had returned the previous season, back to his goalscoring best. The end of the season saw Kenny, who retired as a player in May 1990, named Manager of the Year for a third time.

Kenny's sixth season in charge, 1990/91, began in some style. The Reds won 14 and lost only 1 of the first 18 games. Indeed, Liverpool had lost only three games at the turn of the year and were top of the league. Unfortunately, success had bred some criticism in various quarters, be it related to some negative tactical decisions, some questionable buys and fears over an ageing squad. Lurking in the background too was Kenny's health, the increased stresses brought on by Kenny's role in his support for the families of fans who had lost their lives at Hillsborough.

Drawn against Everton in the fifth round of the FA Cup, Liverpool were held to a goalless draw at Anfield. The replay at Goodison Park three days later saw the Reds go ahead four times – and yet they could not secure a passage to the quarter-finals. The 4-4 draw after extra time on February 20 1991 proved to be Dalglish's final game in charge for what would turn out to be a gap of nearly 20 years. The morning after Kenny informed the board of his decision, before facing the world's media at a press conference on Friday February 22. His final words were thus:

"This is the first time since I came to the club that I take the interest of Kenny Dalglish over Liverpool Football Club. This is not a sudden decision. The worst I could have done was not to decide. The main problem is the pressure I put on myself because of my strong desire to succeed. The stress that comes right before and after games has got the better of me. Some might have difficulty understanding my decision but this decision stands. I would be betraying everyone if I wouldn't let them know there is something wrong."

DALGLISH AT LIVERPOOL FC – HONOURS

League championship winner (5):   1978/79, 1979/80, 1981/82, 1982/83, 1983/84.
As player-manager (3):   1985/86, 1987/88, 1989/90.
FA Cup winner as player-manager (2): 1985/86, 1988/89.
League Cup winner (4):   1980/81, 1981/82, 1982/83, 1983/84.
European Cup winner (3):   1977/78, 1980/81, 1983/84.
European Super Cup winner (1):   1977/78.
FA Charity Shield winner (3):   1979, 1980, 1982. Shared (1): 1977.
As player-manager (2):   1988, 1989. Shared (2) 1986, 1990.
Screen Sports Super Cup winner (1):   1985/86.
PFA Player of the Year (1):   1982/83.
FWA Player of the Year (2):   1978/79, 1982/83.
Manager of the Year (3):   1985/86, 1987/88, 1989/90.

DALGLISH AT LIVERPOOL FC – COMPETITION RECORDS

COMPETITION	P	W	D	L	F	A	PTS
League	242	146	59	37	472	204	497
FA Cup	39	23	12	4	79	32	–
League Cup	31	19	6	6	72	29	–
FA Charity Shield	4	2	2	0	5	3	–
Europa League	4	1	2	1	1	1	–
Screen Sport Super Cup	8	6	2	0	19	6	–
Centenary Trophy	2	1	0	1	5	3	–
TOTAL	**330**	**198**	**83**	**49**	**653**	**279**	**–**

KENNY DALGLISH'S RECORD

A statistical breakdown of Kenny's 330 games in charge up to and including the end of 2010/11 season, taking in his two spells as Reds boss, including his months as caretaker-manager in 2011.

KENNY DALGLISH'S CLUB-BY-CLUB RECORD AS LIVERPOOL FC MANAGER

OPPOSITION	P	W	D	L	WIN %
Fulham	4	4	0	0	100
Birmingham City	3	3	0	0	100
Crewe Alexandra	2	2	0	0	100
Middlesbrough	2	2	0	0	100
Oldham Athletic	2	2	0	0	100
Portsmouth	2	2	0	0	100
Sheffield United	2	2	0	0	100
Sunderland	2	2	0	0	100
Walsall	2	2	0	0	100
Brentford	1	1	0	0	100
Carlisle United	1	1	0	0	100
Hull City	1	1	0	0	100
Leeds United	1	1	0	0	100
Wolverhampton W	1	1	0	0	100
Charlton Athletic	8	7	1	0	87.50
Derby County	7	6	1	0	85.71
Oxford United	6	5	1	0	83.33
Millwall	5	4	1	0	80.00
Leicester City	5	4	0	1	80.00
Watford	8	6	1	1	75.00
Chelsea	11	8	3	0	72.73
Coventry City	13	9	2	2	69.23
Manchester City	9	6	2	1	66.67
Brighton & Hove Albion	3	2	1	0	66.67
Stoke City	3	2	1	0	66.67
Wigan Athletic	3	2	1	0	66.67
Ipswich Town	3	2	0	1	66.67
West Bromwich Albion	3	2	0	1	66.67
Southampton	17	11	4	2	64.71
Tottenham Hotspur	14	9	1	4	64.29
Queens Park Rangers	15	9	3	3	60.00
Wimbledon	12	7	3	2	58.33
Nottingham Forest	14	8	4	2	57.14
Everton	23	13	7	3	56.52
Newcastle United	9	5	2	2	55.56
Sheffield Wednesday	10	5	4	1	50.00
West Ham United	10	5	3	2	50.00
Blackburn Rovers	4	2	2	0	50.00
Crystal Palace	4	2	0	2	50.00
Swansea City	2	1	1	0	50.00
Sparta Prague	2	1	1	0	50.00
York City	2	1	1	0	50.00
Luton Town	14	6	5	3	42.86
Arsenal	19	8	5	6	42.10
Norwich City	14	5	7	2	35.71
Aston Villa	12	4	7	1	33.33
Manchester United	17	5	7	5	29.41
Blackpool	1	0	0	1	00.00
Sporting Braga	2	0	1	1	00.00
TOTAL	**330**	**198**	**83**	**49**	**60.00**

Kenny maintained his 100% win record over Fulham (above) and Birmingham in 2010/11

KENNY DALGLISH'S RECORD

The tables below highlight Kenny's transfer dealings during his first stint as manager. His first purchase, Steve McMahon, was signed in September 1985, while the dealings include club record buys for Peter Beardsley and Ian Rush.

LFC TRANSFERS 1985-1991

PLAYER IN	FROM	YEAR	PLAYER OUT	TO	YEAR
Steve McMahon	Aston Villa	1985	Bob Bolder	Sunderland	1985
Mike Hooper	Wrexham	1985	Alan Kennedy	Sunderland	1985
John Durnin	Waterloo Dock	1986	Phil Neal	Bolton	1985
Barry Venison	Sunderland	1986	Sammy Lee	QPR	1986
Steve Staunton	Dundalk	1986	John McGregor	Rangers	1987
Alan Irvine	Falkirk	1986	Ian Rush	Juventus	1987
John Aldridge	Oxford	1987	Alan Irvine	Dundee United	1987
Nigel Spackman	Chelsea	1987	Ken De Mange	Leeds	1987
John Barnes	Watford	1987	Mark Seagraves	Man City	1987
Peter Beardsley	Newcastle	1987	Brian Mooney	Preston	1987
Mike Marsh	Kirkby Town	1987	John Wark	Ipswich	1988
Ray Houghton	Oxford	1987	Paul Walsh	Tottenham	1988
Nick Tanner	Bristol Rovers	1988	Nigel Spackman	QPR	1989
Ian Rush	Juventus	1988	John Durnin	Oxford	1989
David Burrows	West Brom	1988	Kevin MacDonald	Coventry	1989
Barry Jones	Prescot Cables	1989	Jim Beglin	Leeds	1989
Glenn Hysen	Fiorentina	1989	John Aldridge	Real Sociedad	1989
Steve Harkness	Carlisle	1989	Jim Magilton	Oxford	1990
Ronny Rosenthal	Standard Liege	1990	Alex Watson	Bournemouth	1991
Tony Cousins	Dundalk	1990			
Don Hutchison	Hartlepool	1990			
Jimmy Carter	Millwall	1991			
Jamie Redknapp	Bournemouth	1991			
David Speedie	Coventry	1991			

SCOTTISH MANAGERS IN ENGLISH FOOTBALL

This list takes into account every Scottish manager who has taken charge of a club for at least one Premier League game. Caretaker-managers and bosses who have taken charge pre-Premier League era are included. Note that 7 managers – all born in Glasgow – began the 2011/12 campaign in charge of top-flight clubs.

PREMIER LEAGUE CLUBS ONLY (1992-2011)

MANAGER	CLUB	ERA	MANAGER	CLUB	ERA
George Graham	Arsenal	1986-1995	Graeme Souness	Blackburn	2000-2004
Sir Alex Ferguson	Man Utd	1986-	Jim Jeffries	Bradford	2000-2001
Graeme Souness	Liverpool	1991-1994	Gordon Strachan	S'hampton	2001-2004
Ian Porterfield	Chelsea	1991-1993	David Moyes	Everton	2002-
Kenny Dalglish	Blackburn	1991-1995	Eddie Gray	Leeds	2003-2004
John Gorman	Swindon	1993-1994	Graeme Souness	Newcastle	2004-2006
Jimmy Gabriel	Everton	1993-1994	Paul Sturrock	Southampton	2004
George Burley	Ipswich	1994-2002	Roy Aitken	Aston Villa	2006
Kevin MacDonald	Leicester	1994	Alex McLeish	Birmingham	2007-2011
Mark McGhee	Leicester	1994-1995	Archie Knox	Bolton	2007
Stewart Houston	Arsenal	1995, 1996	Owen Coyle	Burnley	2007-2010
Bruce Rioch	Arsenal	1995-1996	Ricky Sbragia	Sunderland	2008-2009
Graeme Souness	Southampton	1996-1997	Paul Lambert	Norwich	2009-
George Graham	Leeds	1996-1998	Owen Coyle	Bolton	2010-
Gordon Strachan	Coventry	1996-2001	Kevin MacDonald	Aston Villa	2010
Kenny Dalglish	Newcastle	1997-1998	Steve Kean	Blackburn	2010-
Walter Smith	Everton	1998-2002	Kenny Dalglish	Liverpool	2011-
George Graham	Tottenham	1998-2001	Alex McLeish	Aston Villa	2011-
Steve Clarke	Newcastle	1999			

MANAGER RECORDS – VARIOUS

Since Liverpool's first foray into Continental competition in 1964, nine men have presided over European campaigns. Roy Hodgson and Kenny Dalglish joined the list in 2010/11, and their respective records, along with the other managers – in success order – are noted here.

BIGGEST WIN RATIO ENJOYED BY LIVERPOOL MANAGERS IN EUROPEAN COMPETITION

MANAGER	P	W	D	L	F	A	WIN %
Joe Fagan	19	14	2	3	34	10	73.7
Bob Paisley	61	39	11	11	140	49	63.9
Roy Hodgson	10	6	4	0	15	4	60.0
Rafael Benitez	85	49	16	20	140	68	57.7
Bill Shankly	65	34	13	18	114	54	52.3
Gerard Houllier	52	26	17	9	78	45	50.0
Roy Evans	16	8	5	3	24	16	50.0
Graeme Souness	12	6	0	6	26	16	50.0
Roy Evans/ Gerard Houllier	4	2	2	0	10	2	50.0
Kenny Dalglish	4	1	2	1	1	1	25.0

The tables below make note of the most successful Liverpool managers in terms of impact made, and win consistency. Other managers, namely Sir Alex Ferguson and Arsene Wenger, have also been used as examples in the race to 100 league wins in the modern era.

FASTEST TO 100 LEAGUE WINS AS LIVERPOOL MANAGER

MANAGER	NUMBER OF GAMES TAKEN	YEAR OF 100TH LEAGUE WIN
Kenny Dalglish	167	1989
Bob Paisley	179	1978
Rafael Benitez	181	2009
Bill Shankly	184	1964
Gerard Houllier	197	2004
Tom Watson	227	1903
George Kay	262	1949
George Patterson	271	1934
CONTEMPORARY COMPARISIONS		
Arsene Wenger	179	2001
Sir Alex Ferguson	231	1992

MANAGERS' RECORD AFTER 250 GAMES IN CHARGE OF LIVERPOOL

MANAGER	SEASON OF 250 GAMES	P	W	D	L	F	A	WIN %
Kenny Dalglish	1989/90	250	152	61	37	493	204	60.8
Rafael Benitez	2008/09	250	145	50	55	410	207	58.0
Bob Paisley	1978/79	250	140	62	48	419	192	56.0
Gerard Houllier	2002/03	250	134	57	59	424	239	53.6
Bill Shankly	1964/65	250	133	54	63	502	307	53.2
Tom Watson	1902/03	250	110	55	85	391	314	44.0
George Kay	1948/49	250	100	63	87	400	376	40.0
George Patterson	1933/34	250	94	58	98	462	486	37.6

MANAGER RECORDS – VARIOUS

Using 150 games as a starting point, the relatives merits of Liverpool managers past and present have been taken into account when ranking the most successful bosses over 150 league games, and 150 top-flight matches.

HIGHEST-RANKED LIVERPOOL MANAGERS - AFTER 150 LEAGUE GAMES
(First 150 league games only - all divisions, listed best to worst)

MANAGER	Pld	W	D	L	F	A	Points
Kenny Dalglish	150	87	39	24	289	123	300
Bob Paisley	150	79	42	29	220	119	279
Gerard Houllier	150	81	35	34	258	142	278
Rafael Benitez	150	81	35	34	230	121	278
Bill Shankly	150	77	33	40	307	195	264
Roy Evans	150	72	39	39	239	148	255
Tom Watson	150	66	29	55	232	192	227
Matt McQueen	150	58	43	49	214	193	217
George Patterson	150	56	39	55	281	276	207
George Kay	150	54	40	56	243	254	202
Don Welsh	150	44	42	64	226	282	174

HIGHEST-RANKED LIVERPOOL MANAGERS - AFTER 150 TOP-FLIGHT LEAGUE GAMES
(First 150 league games in top flight, listed best to worst)

Manager	Played	W	D	L	F	A	Points
Kenny Dalglish	150	87	39	24	289	123	300
Bob Paisley	150	79	42	29	220	119	279
Gerard Houllier	150	81	35	34	258	142	278
Rafael Benitez	150	81	35	34	230	121	278
Roy Evans	150	72	39	39	239	148	255
Bill Shankly	150	75	29	46	279	198	254
Tom Watson	150	66	29	55	232	192	227
Matt McQueen	150	58	43	49	214	193	217
George Patterson	150	56	39	55	281	276	207
George Kay	150	54	40	56	243	254	202
Don Welsh	(NEVER REACHED 150 GAMES IN TOP FLIGHT)						

Top two: Kenny Dalglish and Bob Paisley, the most successful over 150 league games

EX-LIVERPOOL PLAYERS AS MANAGERS

These pages note, in chronological order, the former Liverpool first-team players who have taken charge of current Football League clubs (at the start of 2011/12). The tables take into account the managerial spell, and successes. Excluding Sir Matt Busby at Manchester United, John Toshack is arguably the most successful former Red. As well as achieving domestic success by taking Swansea City from the old Division 4 to the top flight, he achieved league and cup wins with Real Madrid and two successive manager of the year awards in La Liga, as well as Turkish Cup glory with Besiktas. In all he managed 8 overseas clubs, as well as having two spells as Wales boss.

FORMER LIVERPOOL PLAYERS IN LEAGUE MANAGEMENT

MANAGER	CLUB	PERIOD IN CHARGE	HONOURS WON
Alex Raisbeck	Bristol City	1921-1929	3rd Div (South) 1923, 1927
Fred Pagnam	Watford	1926-1929	
Tom Bromilow	Burnley	1932-1935	
Tom Bromilow	Crystal Palace	1935-1936, 1936-1939	
Charlie Hewitt	Millwall	1936-1940, 1948-1956	3rd Div (South) 1938
Tom Bromilow	Leicester City	1939-1945	
Sir Matt Busby	Manchester United	1945-1969, 1970-1971	1st Division 1952, 1956, 1957, 1965, 1967, FA Cup 1948, 1963, European Cup 1968
Gordon Hodgson	Port Vale	1946-1951	
Geoff Twentyman	Hartlepool United	1965	
Les Shannon	Bury	1966-1969	
Les Shannon	Blackpool	1969-1970	
Jimmy Melia	Aldershot	1969-1972	
Gordon Milne	Wigan Athletic	1970-1972	Northern Premier Lge 1972
Jimmy Melia	Crewe Alexandra	1972-1973	
Ron Yeats	Tranmere Rovers	1972-1975	
Gordon Milne	Coventry City	1972-1981	
Ian St John	Portsmouth	1974-1977	
Bobby Campbell	Fulham	1976-1980	
Keith Burkinshaw	Tottenham Hotspur	1976-1984	Promotion to Div 1 1978 FA Cup 1981, 1982, UEFA Cup 1984
Alan A'Court	Stoke City	1978	
John Toshack	Swansea City	1978-1983, 1983-1984	Promotion to Div 3 1978 Promotion to Div 2 1979 Promotion to Div 1 1981 Welsh Cup 1981, 1982, 1983
Emlyn Hughes	Rotherham United	1981-1983	
Larry Lloyd	Wigan Athletic	1981-1983	Promotion to Div 3 1982
Jimmy Melia	Brighton & Hove Albion	1982-1983	
Bobby Campbell	Portsmouth	1982-1984	3rd Division 1983
Gordon Milne	Leicester City	1982-1986	Promotion to Div 1 1983
Larry Lloyd	Notts County	1983-1984	
Phil Neal	Bolton Wanderers	1985-1992	Promotion to Div 3 1988 Sherpa Van Trophy 1989
Jimmy Melia	Stockport County	1986	
Mark Lawrenson	Oxford United	1988	
Keith Burkinshaw	Gillingham	1988-1989	
Bobby Campbell	Chelsea	1988-1991	2nd Division 1989 Zenita Data System Cup 1990
Mark Lawrenson	Peterborough United	1989-1990	
Kenny Dalglish	Blackburn Rovers	1991-1995	1st Div Play-Off 1992 Premier League 1995

EX-LIVERPOOL PLAYERS AS MANAGERS

FORMER LIVERPOOL PLAYERS IN LEAGUE MANAGEMENT

MANAGER	CLUB	PERIOD IN CHARGE	HONOURS WON
Kevin Keegan	Newcastle United	1992-1997, 2008	1st Division 1993
Doug Livermore & Ray Clemence	Tottenham Hotspur	1992-1993	
Ian Ross	Huddersfield Town	1992-1993	
Richard Money	Scunthorpe United	1993-1994	
Keith Burkinshaw	West Bromwich Albion	1993-1994	
Phil Neal	Coventry City	1993-1995	
Ray Clemence	Barnet	1994-1996	
Steve McMahon	Swindon Town	1994-1998	2nd Division 1996
Jimmy Case	Brighton & Hove Albion	1995-1996	
Mick Halsall	Peterborough United	1995-1996	
Ronnie Whelan	Southend United	1995-1997	
Phil Neal	Cardiff City	1996	
Graeme Souness	Southampton	1996-1997	
Jan Molby	Swansea City	1996-1997	
John Aldridge	Tranmere Rovers	1996-2001	
Kenny Dalglish	Newcastle United	1997-1998	
Nigel Spackman	Sheffield United	1997-1998	
Kevin Keegan	Fulham	1998-1999	2nd Division 1999
Paul Jewell	Bradford City	1998-2000	Promotion to Prem Lge 1999
Nigel Clough	Burton Albion	1998-2008	Northern Premier Lge 2002
Paul Jewell	Sheffield Wednesday	2000-2001	
Steve McMahon	Blackpool	2000-2004	3rd Div Play-Off 2001 LDV Vans Trophy 2002, 2004
Graeme Souness	Blackburn Rovers	2000-2004	Promotion to Prem Lge 2001 League Cup 2002
Nigel Spackman	Barnsley	2001	
Mark Wright	Oxford United	2001	
Roy Evans	Swindon Town	2001	
Kevin Keegan	Manchester City	2001-2005	1st Division 2002
Paul Jewell	Wigan Athletic	2001-2007	2nd Division 2003 Promotion to Prem Lge 2005
Jan Molby	Hull City	2002	
Gary McAllister	Coventry City	2002-2003	
Graeme Souness	Newcastle United	2004-2006	
Mark Wright	Peterborough United	2005-2006	
Nigel Spackman	Millwall	2006	
Paul Ince	Macclesfield Town	2006-2007	
Richard Money	Walsall	2006-2008	2nd Division 2007
Jim Magilton	Ipswich Town	2006-2009	
Sammy Lee	Bolton Wanderers	2007	
Paul Jewell	Derby County	2007-2008	
Paul Ince	Milton Keynes Dons	2007-2008, 2009-2010	League 2 2008 Johnstone's Paint Trophy 2008
Paul Ince	Blackburn Rovers	2008	
Gary McAllister	Leeds United	2008	
Jim Magilton	Queens Park Rangers	2009	
John Barnes	Tranmere Rovers	2009	
Gary Ablett	Stockport County	2009-2010	
Nigel Clough	Derby County	2009-	
Paul Jewell	Ipswich Town	2011-	

THE SQUAD 2011/12

LFC stats correct before start of 2011/12 Premier League season

Doni – Squad number 32

Positions	Goalkeeper
Born	Sao Paulo, Brazil
Age (at start of 11/12)	31
Birth date	22/10/1979
Height	6ft 5ins
Other clubs	Botafogo-SP, C'thians, Santos, Cruzeiro, Juventude, Roma
Liverpool debut	–
Liverpool debut	–
Honours	2002 Brazilian Cup, 2003 S. Paulo Champ, 2007, 2008 Italian Cup, 2007 Italian Super Cup
International caps	10
International honours	2007 Copa America

Martin Hansen – Squad number 41

Positions	Goalkeeper
Born	Glostrup, Denmark
Age (at start of 11/12)	21
Birth date	15/06/1990
Height	6ft 2ins
Other clubs	Brondby, Bradford City
Honours	2007 FA Youth Cup
Liverpool debut	–
Liverpool appearances	–
Liverpool goals	–
International caps	0

Brad Jones – Squad number 1

Positions	Goalkeeper
Born	Armadale, Australia
Age (at start of 11/12)	29
Birth date	19/03/1982
Height	6ft 2ins
Other clubs	Middlesbrough, Stockport County, Rotherham United, Blackpool, Sheffield Wednesday, Derby C
Liverpool debut	22/09/10 v Northampton Town
Liverpool appearances	2
International caps	3

Pepe Reina – Squad number 25

Position	Goalkeeper
Born	Madrid, Spain
Age (at start of 11/12)	28
Birth date	31/08/1982
Height	6ft 2ins
Other clubs	Barcelona, Villarreal
Honours	2004, 2005 UEFA Intertoto Cup, 2005 European Super Cup, 2006 FA Cup, 2006 FA Com. Shield
Liverpool debut	13/07/05 v TNS
Liverpool appearances	309
International caps	22
International honours	2008 Euro C'ships, 2010 World Cup

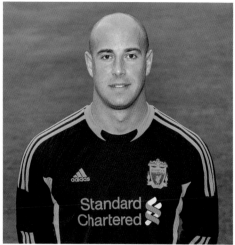

Daniel Agger – Squad number 5

Positions	Left/Central Defence
Born	Hvidovre, Denmark
Age (at start of 11/12)	26
Birth date	12/12/1984
Height	6ft 3ins
Other clubs	Rosenhoj, Brondby
Honours	2005 Danish League and Cup, 2006 FA Com Shield
Liverpool debut	01/02/06 v Birmingham City
Liverpool appearances	124 + 12 as substitute
Liverpool goals	7
International caps	41 (4 goals)

Fabio Aurelio – Squad number 6

Positions	Left Defence/ Midfield
Born	Sao Carlos, Brazil
Age (at start of 11/12)	31
Birth date	24/09/1979
Height	5ft 8ins
Other clubs	Sao Paulo, Valencia
Honours	1998, 2000 Sao Paulo State C'ship, 2002, 2004 Spain League, 2004 Euro. Super Cup, 2006 FA Community Shield
Liverpool debut (first)	13/08/06 v Chelsea
Liverpool appearances	90 + 41 as sub.
Liverpool goals	4

Jamie Carragher – Squad number 23

Positions	Right/Cen. Defence
Born	Bootle, Liverpool
Age (at start of 11/12)	33
Birth date	28/01/1978
Height	6ft 1ins
Honours	2001, 2006 FA Cup, 2001, 2003 Lge Cup, 2001 UEFA Cup, 2001, 2005 Euro Super Cup, 2001, 2006 FA Com Shield, 2005 Champs Lge
Liverpool debut	08/01/97 v Middlesbrough
Liverpool appearances	646 + 22 as sub
Liverpool goals	5
International caps	38 (0 goals)

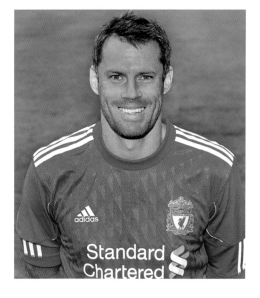

Conor Coady – Squad number 35

Position	Central Defence/Midfield
Born	St Helens
Age (at start of 11/12)	18
Birth date	25/02/1993
Height	6ft 1ins
Other clubs	–
Liverpool debut	–
Liverpool appearances	–
Liverpool goals	–
International caps	0

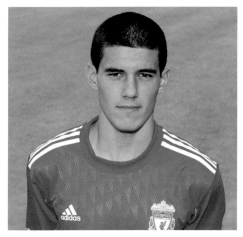

Sebastian Coates – Squad number 16

Position	Central Defence
Born	Montevideo, Uruguay
Age (at start of 11/12)	20
Birth date	07/10/1990
Height	6ft 6ins
Other club	Nacional
Honours	2009, 2011 Uruguayan League
Liverpool debut	–
Liverpool appearances	–
Liverpool goals	–
International caps	5 (0 goals)
International honours	2011 Copa America

Jose Enrique – Squad number 3

Position	Left Defence
Born	Valencia, Spain
Age (at start of 11/12)	25
Birth date	23/01/1986
Height	6ft 0ins
Other clubs	Levante B, Valencia, Celta Vigo, Villarreal, Newcastle United
Honours	2010 Championship
Liverpool debut	–
Liverpool appearances	–
Liverpool goals	–
International caps	0

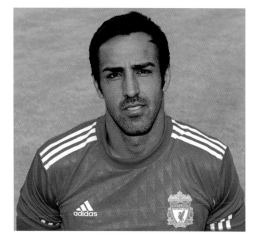

Jon Flanagan – Squad number 38

Position	Right Defence
Born	Liverpool
Age (at start of 11/12)	18
Birth date	01/01/1993
Height	5ft 11ins
Liverpool debut	11/04/11 v Manchester City
Liverpool appearances	7 + 0 as substitute
Liverpool goals	0
International caps	0

Glen Johnson – Squad number 2

Positions	Right/Left Defence
Born	Greenwich, London
Age (at start of 11/12)	26
Birth date	23/08/1984
Height	5ft 11ins
Other clubs	West Ham, Millwall, Chelsea, Portsmouth
Honours	2005 FA Premier League, 2005 League Cup, 2008 FA Cup
Liverpool debut	16/08/09 v Tottenham Hotspur
Liverpool appearances	68 + 2 as substitute
Liverpool goals	5
International caps	34 (1 goal)

Martin Kelly – Squad number 34

Position	Right/Central Defence
Born	Whiston
Age (at start of 11/12)	21
Birth date	27/04/1990
Height	6ft 3ins
Other club	Huddersfield Town
Honours	2008 FA Premier Reserve League
Liverpool debut	09/12/08 v PSV Eindhoven
Liverpool appearances	23 + 4 as substitute
Liverpool goals	0
International caps	0

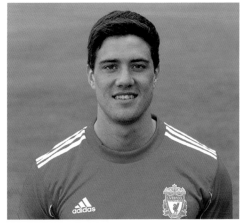

Jack Robinson – Squad number 49

Positions	Left Defence/Midfield
Born	Warrington
Age (at start of 11/12)	17
Birth date	01/09/1993
Height	6ft 1ins
Liverpool debut	09/05/10 v Hull City
Liverpool appearances	1 + 2 as substitute
Liverpool goals	0
International caps	0

Martin Skrtel – Squad number 37

Position	Central Defence
Born	Handlova, Slovakia
Age (at start of 11/12)	26
Birth date	15/12/1984
Height	6ft 3ins
Other clubs	FK AS Trencin, Zenit St. Petersburg
Honours	2007 Russian Premier League
Liverpool debut	21/01/08 v Aston Villa
Liverpool appearances	117 + 11 as substitute
Liverpool goals	3
International caps	47 (5 goals)

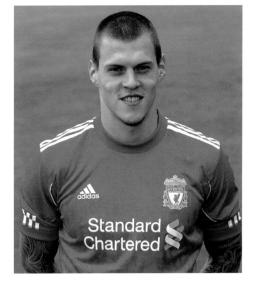

Danny Wilson – Squad number 22

Positions	Central/Left Defence
Born	Edinburgh
Age (at start of 11/12)	19
Birth date	27/12/1991
Height	6ft 1ins
Other club	Rangers
Honours	2009 Scottish Cup, 2010 Scottish Prem. Lge & League Cup
Liverpool debut	22/09/10 v Northampton Town
Liverpool appearances	7 + 1 as substitute
Liverpool goals	0
International caps	4 (1 goal)

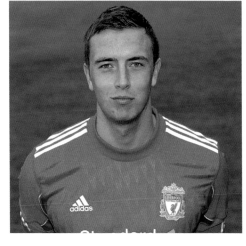

Andre Wisdom – Squad number 47

Positions	Right/Centre Defence or Midfield
Born	Leeds
Age (at start of 11/12)	18
Birth date	09/05/1993
Height	6ft 0ins
Other club	Bradford City
Honours	–
Liverpool debut	–
Liverpool appearances	–
Liverpool goals	–
International caps	0

Charlie Adam - Squad number 26

Position	Central Midfield
Born	Dundee
Age (at start of 11/12)	25
Birth date	10/12/1985
Height	6ft 1ins
Other clubs	Rangers, Ross County, St Mirren, Blackpool
Honours	2005 Scottish Challenge Cup, 2006 Scottish First Division, 2010 Ch'ship Play-Offs
Liverpool debut	–
Liverpool appearances	–
Liverpool goals	–
International caps	12 (0 goals)

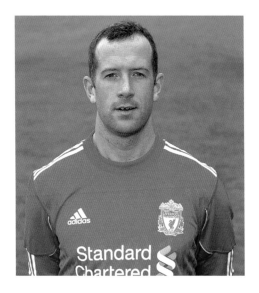

Stewart Downing – Squad number 19

Positions	Left/Right Midfield
Born	Middlesbrough
Age (at start of 11/12)	27
Birth date	22/07/1984
Height	5ft 11ins
Other clubs	Middlesbrough, Sunderland, Aston Villa
Honours	2004 League Cup
Liverpool debut	–
Liverpool appearances	–
Liverpool goals	–
International caps	27 (0 goals)

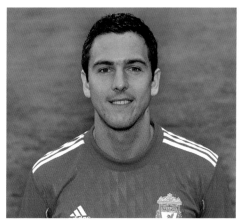

Steven Gerrard MBE – Squad number 8

Positions	Central/Right Midfield or Forward
Born	Whiston
Age (at start of 11/12)	31
Birth date	30/05/1980
Height	6ft 0ins
Honours	2001, 2006 FA Cup, 2001, 2003 Lge Cup, 2001 UEFA Cup, 2001 Euro Super Cup, 2001, 2006 FA Comm Shield, 2005 Champions League
Liverpool debut	29/11/98 v B'burn
Liverpool appearances	510 + 46 as sub.
Liverpool goals	140
International caps	89 (19 goals)

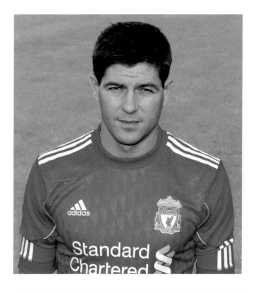

Jordan Henderson – Squad number 14

Position	Central Midfield
Born	Sunderland
Age (at start of 11/12)	21
Birth date	17/06/1990
Height	6ft 0ins
Other clubs	Sunderland, Coventry City
Liverpool debut	–
Liverpool appearances	–
Liverpool goals	–
International caps	1 (0 goals)

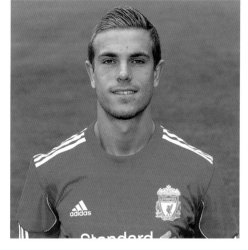

Lucas Leiva – Squad number 21

Position	Central Midfield
Born	Dourados, Brazil
Age (at start of 11/12)	24
Birth date	09/01/1987
Height	5ft 10ins
Other club	Gremio
Honours	2005 Brazilian Serie B, 2006, 2007 Rio Grande do Sul State C'ship, 2008 FA Prem Reserve League
Liverpool debut	28/08/07 v Toulouse
Liverpool appearances	129 + 39 as substitute
Liverpool goals	6
International caps	15 (0 goals)
International honours	2008 Olympics Bronze Medal

Maxi Rodriguez – Squad number 11

Positions	Right/Left Midfield
Born	Rosario, Argentina
Age (at start of 11/12)	30
Birth date	02/01/1981
Height	5ft 11ins
Other clubs	Newell's Old Boys, Real Oviedo, Espanyol, Atletico Madrid
Liverpool debut	16/01/10 v Stoke City
Liverpool appearances	43 + 9 as substitute
Liverpool goals	11
International caps	41 (12 goals)

Jonjo Shelvey – Squad number 33

Position	Central Midfield
Born	Romford
Age (at start of 11/12)	19
Birth date	27/02/1992
Height	6ft 0ins
Other club	Charlton Athletic
Liverpool debut	22/09/10 v Northampton Town
Liverpool appearances	4 + 17 as substitute
Liverpool goals	0
International caps	0

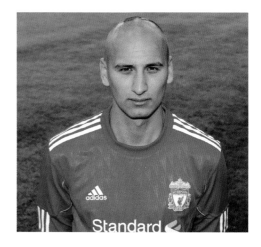

Jay Spearing – Squad number 20

Position	Central Midfield
Born	Wirral
Age (at start of 11/12)	22
Birth date	25/11/1988
Height	5ft 6ins
Other club	Leicester City
Honours	2006, 2007 FA Youth Cup, 2008 FA Premier Reserve League
Liverpool debut	09/12/08 v PSV Eindhoven
Liverpool appearances	19 + 8 as substitute
Liverpool goals	0
International caps	0

Raheem Sterling - Squad number 31

Positions	Right/Left Midfield
Born	Kingston, Jamaica
Age (at start of 11/12)	16
Birth date	08/12/1994
Height	5ft 7ins
Other club	QPR
Liverpool debut	–
Liverpool appearances	–
Liverpool goals	–
International caps	0

Craig Bellamy - Squad number 39

Position	Forward
Born	Cardiff
Age (at start of 11/12)	32
Birth date	13/07/1979
Height	5ft 8ins
Other clubs	Norwich City, Coventry City, Newcastle U, Celtic, Blackburn, West Ham, Man City, Cardiff City
Honours	2005, Scottish Cup, 2006 FA Com. Shield
Liverpool debut (first)	09/08/06 v Maccabi Haifa
Liverpool appearances	33 + 9 as substitute
Liverpool goals	9
International caps	63 (18 goals)

Andy Carroll – Squad number 9

Position	Centre Forward
Born	Gateshead
Age (at start of 11/12)	22
Birth date	06/01/1989
Height	6ft 3ins
Other club	Newcastle United
Honours	2010 Championship
Liverpool debut	06/03/11 v Manchester United
Liverpool appearances	6 + 3 as substitute
Liverpool goals	2
International caps	2 (1 goal)

Jesus Fernandez (Suso) – Squad number 30

Position	Forward
Born	Cadiz, Spain
Age (at start of 11/12)	17
Birth date	19/11/1993
Height	5ft 10ins
Other club	Cadiz
Liverpool debut	–
Liverpool appearances	–
Liverpool goals	–
International caps	0

Dirk Kuyt – Squad number 18

Positions	Right/Centre Midfield or Forward
Born	Katwijk, Holland
Age (at start of 11/12)	31
Birth date	22/07/1980
Height	6ft 0ins
Other clubs	FC Utrecht, Feyenoord
Honours	2003 Dutch Cup
Liverpool debut	26/08/06 v West Ham United
Liverpool appearances	212 + 29 as substitute
Liverpool goals	66
International caps	77 (22 goals)
International honours	2010 World Cup Runner-up

Luis Suarez – Squad number 7

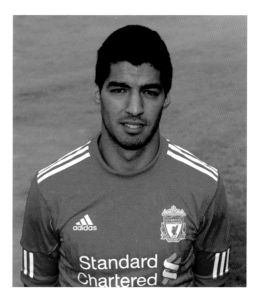

Position	Forward
Born	Salto, Uruguay
Age (at start of 11/12)	24
Birth date	24/01/1987
Height	5ft 11ins
Other clubs	Nacional, Groningen, Ajax
Honours	2006 Uruguayan League, 2010 Dutch Cup, 2011 Dutch League
Liverpool debut	02/02/11 v Stoke City
Liverpool appearances	12 + 1 as substitute
Liverpool goals	4
International caps	48 (21 goals)
International honours	2011 Copa America

Liverpool Under-19s line-up before their opening NextGen Series match against Sporting Lisbon, August 2011 – back row left to right: Sama, Wisdom, Belford, Robinson, McGiveron, Sterling. Front row, left to right: Silva, Shelvey, Fernandez, Coady, Morgan

PLAYERS ON LOAN
2011/12

Alberto Aquilani

Position	Central Midfield
Born	Rome, Italy
Age (at start of 11/12)	26
Liverpool appearances	14 + 14 as substitute
Liverpool goals	2
Loan club	AC Milan
Loan spell	One year

Joe Cole

Position	Midfield/Forward
Born	London
Age (at start of 11/12)	29
Liverpool appearances	19 + 13 as substitute
Liverpool goals	3
Loan club	Lille
Loan spell	One year

Stephen Darby

Position	Right Defence
Born	Liverpool
Age (at start of 11/12)	22
Liverpool appearances	2 + 4 as substitute
Liverpool goals	0
Loan club	Rochdale
Loan spell	One year

Peter Gulacsi

Position	Goalkeeper
Born	Budapest, Hungary
Age (at start of 11/12)	21
Liverpool appearances	0
Liverpool goals	0
Loan club	Hull City
Loan spell	One year

Daniel Pacheco

Position	Forward
Born	Malaga, Spain
Age (at start of 11/12)	20
Liverpool appearances	3 + 11 as substitute
Liverpool goals	0
Loan club	Atletico Madrid
Loan spell	One year

THE MANAGEMENT

Kenny Dalglish – Manager

Appointed	12/05/2011
Born	Glasgow
Birth date	04/03/1951
Other clubs managed	Liverpool, Blackburn Rovers, Newcastle United, Celtic
Honours (as manager & player-manager)	1986, 1988, 1990, 1995 League, 1986, 1989 FA Cup, 1986 (shared), 1988, 1989, 1990 (shared) FA Charity Shield, 1992 Division 2 Play-Off, 2000 Scottish League Cup

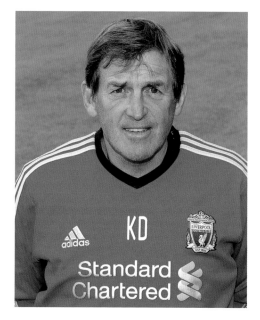

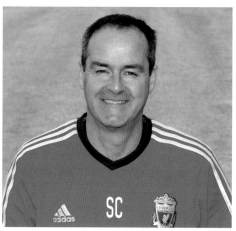

Steve Clarke – Assistant-manager

Appointed	10/01/2011
Born	Saltcoats
Birth date	29/08/1963
Coaching career	Newcastle United, Chelsea, West Ham Utd
Honours (coach)	2005, 2006 League, 2005, 2007 League Cup, 2007 FA Cup
Clubs (player)	St Mirren, Chelsea
Honours (player)	1990 Full Members Cup, 1997 FA Cup, 1998 League Cup, 1998 European Cup-Winners' Cup

Kevin Keen – First-team coach

Appointed	July 2011
Born	Amersham
Birth date	25/02/1967
Coaching career	Macclesfield Town, West Ham United
Clubs (player)	Wycombe Wanderers, West Ham United, Wolves, Stoke City, Macclesfield Town

BACKROOM STAFF
2011/12

John Achterberg – GK Coach

Appointed	June 2009
Born	Utrecht, Holland
Age	40
Birth date	08/07/1971
Other clubs (player)	NAC Breda, Eindhoven, Tranmere Rovers

Dr. Peter Brukner – Head of Sports Med./Sci.

Appointed	July 2010
Born	Australia
Other posts	Melbourne (AFL), Collingwood (AFL), Australia (football, swimming, hockey, athletics)

Rob Price – Senior Physiotherapist

Appointed	September 2005
Born	Oldham
Age	38
Birth date	31/10/1972
Previous role	Football Association

Rodolfo Borrell – Reserves manager

Appointed	May 2011
Born	Spain
Age	40
Birth date	31/07/1971
Other clubs	Barcelona, Iraklis

Goalkeeping coach John Achterberg oversees a drill including Pepe Reina and Brad Jones

SUMMER DIARY 2011

A look back at what went on – and when – during the summer months involving Liverpool FC.

JUNE

1 Reds legend Robbie Fowler confirms he will leave the Australian A-League.

4 Glen Johnson features as England hit back from two-down to draw 2-2 with Switzerland in a Euro 2012 qualifier.

8 The club are forced to cancel their summer trip to South Korea – although they will still play in China and Malaysia.
Luis Suarez and Dirk Kuyt are the goalscorers as Uruguay draw 1-1 with Holland – with the South Americans winning 4-3 on penalties.

9 Pepe Reina undergoes a double hernia operation.

10 Sunderland and England midfielder Jordan Henderson completes his switch.

12 Jordan Henderson plays in England Under-21s' 1-1 draw with their Spanish counterparts in their European U21 Championship opener in Denmark.

15 Henderson plays the full game as England Under-21s are again held, 0-0 by Ukraine.

16 Reserves Deale Chamberlain, Steve Irwin, Alex Cooper and Nikola Saric are released.

17 The Reds will host Sunderland on the first day of the new Premier League season.
It is confirmed that Sotirios Kyrgiakos has earned a new 12-month deal.

19 England Under-21s – for whom Jordan Henderson again starts – go down to a 2-1 defeat to Czech Republic courtesy of two late goals to bow out of the European Championships.
Liverpool prospect Raheem Sterling is on target as England Under-17s begin their World Cup campaign with a 2-0 victory over Rwanda in Mexico. Academy team-mates Brad Smith, Matty Regan and Adam Morgan also make appearances.

22 Adam Morgan is on the scoresheet as England Under-17s draw 2-2 with Canada in their latest World Cup group match.

23 Luis Suarez has a hand in one of the goals as Uruguay win their final Copa America warm-up 3-0 against Estonia.

26 Brad Smith plays the full game whilst Jack Dunn comes on as a second-half sub as England Under-17s go through to the World Cup second round courtesy of a 2-0 defeat of Uruguay.

30 Sammy Lee leaves the club, having been on the coaching staff since May 2008.
Raheem Sterling is on target as England reach the last eight of the Under-17s World Cup by defeating Argentina 4-2 on penalties, after the match had finished 1-1.

JULY

4 Former West Ham midfielder Kevin Keen joins the club as the Reds' first-team coach.
England Under-17s – including Raheem Sterling and Brad Smith – bow out of the World Cup at the quarter-final stage as Germany win 3-2.

5 Former favourite Dietmar Hamann lands his first managerial post, taking over at newly-relegated Conference side Stockport County.

6 England full-back Glen Johnson signs a new contract with the club.

7 Reserve defender Stephen Darby joins Rochdale on loan for the 2011/12 season.

8 Scotland international midfielder Charlie Adam completes his move from Blackpool.
Young defenders Jon Flanagan and Andre Wisdom agree new deals.
The Reds are set to return to Istanbul later in the month, having agreed to face Galatasaray in a pre-season friendly.

11 Robbie Fowler completes a surprise move to Thailand to play for Muang Thong United.

13 Paul Konchesky completes his move to Championship side Leicester City.
Youngster Conor Coady is on target while Charlie Adam makes his debut as the Reds begin their pre-season programme with a 4-3 victory over Guangdong Sunray Cave.

14 Lucas Leiva plays the full 90 minutes as Brazil reach the last eight of the Copa America with a 4-2 victory over Ecuador.

SUMMER DIARY 2011

A look back at what went on – and when – during the summer months involving Liverpool FC.

JULY

15 England winger Stewart Downing finalises his switch from Aston Villa.

16 Brazilian goalkeeper Doni joins the club from Roma on a two-year deal.
Charlie Adam is on target from the penalty spot in a 6-3 success over a Malaysia XI.
Luis Suarez's Uruguay reach the last four of the Copa America after a 5-4 penalty shootout triumph over hosts Argentina after the match had finished 1-1.

18 Gerardo Bruna joins Blackpool on a two-year deal.

19 Luis Suarez hits both goals to send Uruguay through to the Copa America final at the expense of Peru.
Reserve defender Chris Mavinga returns to France, joining Rennes.

23 Hull City – who include newly loaned out Liverpool goalkeeper Peter Gulacsi in their side – defeat the Reds 3-0 in a pre-season friendly.

24 There's another goal for Luis Suarez as his opener sets Uruguay on the way to Copa America success courtesy of a 3-0 victory over Paraguay.

27 Goalkeeper Martin Hansen joins Bradford City on a month's loan.

28 Liverpool's return to Istanbul ends in defeat, as Galatasaray prevail 3-0 in a friendly.

AUGUST

1 Andy Carroll and Daniel Agger (2) are on target in a 3-3 friendly draw at Valerenga.

4 A niggling calf injury appears likely to keep Martin Skrtel out for the start of the season.

5 Milan Jovanovic completes a move back to Belgium with Anderlecht.
Thomas Ince joins Blackpool on a two-year contract.

6 Goals from Andy Carroll and Dirk Kuyt earn a 2-0 victory over Valencia in the club's final pre-season friendly of the summer.

10 Alberto Aquilani and Charlie Adam are the main names to contribute in the night's friendly internationals. Aquilani hits the winner for Italy in a 2-1 victory over world champions Spain, whilst Adam's free-kick, which is deflected in for an own goal, sets Scotland on the way to a 2-1 success against Denmark.

11 Newcastle United left-back Jose Enrique completes his move to the club.

13 Luis Suarez scores the Premier League's first goal of the new season – having also missed a penalty – but the Reds are pegged back to draw 1-1 against Sunderland.

15 Defender Daniel Ayala completes his move to Premier League newcomers Norwich City.
Daniel Pacheco's Spain are knocked out of the Under-20s World Cup in Colombia, going out 4-2 on penalties to Brazil after a 2-2 draw in their quarter-final clash.

19 Nabil El Zhar is released by the club, with a move to Spanish side Levante likely.

20 An Aaron Ramsey own goal and Luis Suarez earn an impressive 2-0 victory at Arsenal.
Former Reds Champions League winner Harry Kewell joins Melbourne Victory.

22 Greek defender Sotirios Kyrgiakos pens a two-year deal with German side Wolfsburg.

24 Daniel Pacheco agrees a one-season loan back in his homeland with Atletico Madrid.
Kenny Dalglish celebrates his 200th victory as Liverpool manager as the Reds progress to the third round of the Carling Cup courtesy of a 3-1 success at Exeter City. Luis Suarez is again among the goals – netting his third in three games.

25 Midfielder Alberto Aquilani returns to Italy, joining AC Milan on loan.

27 Defender Emiliano Insua agrees to join Portuguese side Sporting Lisbon.
The Reds face a trip to Brighton in the third round of the Carling Cup.
Jordan Henderson and Charlie Adam net their first goals for the club as the Reds go top by defeating Bolton Wanderers 3-1 at Anfield.

30 Uruguay defender Sebastian Coates completes his move from Nacional.

31 Comings and goings on transfer deadline day see Wales striker Craig Bellamy return to the club, while American youngster Villyan Bijev completes a deal before being loaned out to Fortuna Dusseldorf. Joe Cole (Lille), David Ngog (Bolton) and Christian Poulsen (Evian) move on – the former on loan – while Philipp Degen is released.

FIRST-TEAM FIXTURE LIST 2011/12

August 2011

13	Sunderland	(H)	–	1–1
20	Arsenal	(A)	–	2–0
24	Exeter City (CARLING CUP 2)	(A)	–	3-1
27	Bolton Wanderers	(H)	–	3-1

September 2011

10	Stoke City	(A)	–	3pm
18	Tottenham Hotspur	(A)	–	1.30pm
21	Brighton & Hove Albion (CC3)	(A)	–	7.45pm
24	Wolverhampton Wanderers	(H)	–	3pm

October 2011

1	Everton	(A)	–	12.45pm
15	Manchester United	(H)	–	12.45pm
22	Norwich City	(H)	–	5.30pm
25/26	CARLING CUP 4			
29	West Bromwich Albion	(A)	–	5.30pm

November 2011

5	Swansea City	(H)	–	3pm
20	Chelsea	(A)	–	4pm
27	Manchester City	(H)	–	4pm
29/30	CARLING CUP QUARTER-FINALS			

December 2011

3	Fulham	(A)	–	3pm
10	Queens Park Rangers	(H)	–	3pm
17	Aston Villa	(A)	–	3pm
20	Wigan Athletic	(A)	–	7.45pm
26	Blackburn Rovers	(H)	–	3pm
31	Newcastle United	(H)	–	12.45pm

January 2012

2	Manchester City	(A)	–	3pm
7/8	FA CUP THIRD ROUND			
10/11	CARLING CUP SEMI-FINALS, FIRST LEG			

FIRST-TEAM FIXTURE LIST 2011/12

January 2012

14	Stoke City	(H)	–	3pm
21	Bolton Wanderers	(A)	–	3pm
24/25	CARLING CUP SEMI-FINALS, SECOND LEG			
28/29	FA CUP FOURTH ROUND			
31	Wolverhampton Wanderers	(A)	–	7.45pm

February 2012

4	Tottenham Hotspur	(H)	–	3pm
11	Manchester United	(A)	–	3pm
18/19	FA CUP FIFTH ROUND			
25	Everton	(H)	–	3pm
26	CARLING CUP FINAL			

March 2012

3	Arsenal	(H)	–	3pm
10	Sunderland	(A)	–	3pm
17	Queens Park Rangers	(A)	–	3pm
17/18	FA CUP QUARTER-FINALS			
24	Wigan Athletic	(H)	–	3pm
31	Newcastle United	(A)	–	3pm

April 2012

7	Aston Villa	(H)	–	3pm
9	Blackburn Rovers	(A)	–	3pm
14	Fulham	(H)	–	12.45pm
14/15	FA CUP SEMI-FINALS			
21	West Bromwich Albion	(H)	–	3pm
28	Norwich City	(A)	–	3pm

May 2012

5	Chelsea	(H)	–	3pm
5	FA CUP FINAL			
9	UEFA EUROPA LEAGUE FINAL			
13	Swansea City	(A)	–	3pm
19	UEFA CHAMPIONS LEAGUE FINAL			

Please note all fixtures, kick-off times and dates are subject to change

FA PREMIER RESERVE LEAGUE NORTHERN SECTION & NEXTGEN SERIES GROUP FIXTURES 2011/12

AUGUST

17 Sporting Lisbon (NGS)   (H)
31 Swansea City   (A)

SEPTEMBER

07 Molde (NGS)   (A) – 6pm KO
14 Wolfsburg (NGS)   (H)
21 Wolfsburg (NGS)   (A) – TBC KO
29 Molde (NGS)   (H)

OCTOBER

18 Newcastle United   (A)
25 Chelsea   (H) – 2pm KO

NOVEMBER

01 Bolton Wanderers   (H) – 2pm KO
07 Blackburn Rovers   (A)
15 Sporting Lisbon (NGS)   (A) – TBC KO
22 Sunderland   (H) – 2pm KO
29 Wolverhampton Wanderers   (A)

DECEMBER

06 Wigan Athletic   (H) – 2pm KO
15 Manchester United   (A)

DECEMBER

20 Fulham   (A)

JANUARY

10 Bolton Wanderers   (A)
16 Manchester United   (H) – 2pm KO
24 Blackburn Rovers   (H) – 2pm KO

FEBRUARY

07 Norwich City   (H) – 2pm KO
14 Sunderland   (A)
21 Everton   (H) – 2pm KO
28 Wigan Athletic   (A) – 2pm KO

MARCH

06 Everton   (A)
13 Newcastle United   (H) – 2pm KO
20 Arsenal   (H) – 2pm KO

APRIL

02 Aston Villa   (A)
10 West Bromwich Albion   (H) – 2pm KO

All fixtures 7pm unless stated,
subject to change.

Reserves boss Rodolfo Borrell

FA PREMIER ACADEMY LEAGUE
FIXTURES 2011/12

AUGUST

20	Cardiff City	(H)
27	Portsmouth	(A)

SEPTEMBER

03	Derby County	(H) – 12pm KO
10	Leeds United	(A) – 11.30am KO
17	Barnsley	(H) – 11.30am KO
24	Wolves	(A) – 11.30am KO

OCTOBER

01	Blackburn Rovers	(H)
08	Everton	(A)
14	Manchester United	(H) – 12pm KO
29	West Bromwich Albion	(A) – 11.30am KO

NOVEMBER

05	Crewe Alexandra	(A)
12	Bolton Wanderers	(H)
19	Manchester City	(A)

DECEMBER

03	Stoke City	(H)
10	Manchester United	(A)
17	West Bromwich Albion	(H)

JANUARY

07	Crewe Alexandra	(H)
14	Bolton Wanderers	(A)
21	Manchester City	(H)
28	Stoke City	(A)

FEBRUARY

11	Wolves	(H)
18	Blackburn Rovers	(A)
25	Everton	(H)

MARCH

03	Middlesbrough	(A) – 12pm KO
10	Sheffield Wednesday	(H) – 12pm KO
17	Sunderland	(A) – 1pm KO

MARCH

31	Huddersfield Town	(H)

APRIL

21	Newcastle United	(A)

FA YOUTH CUP DATES

R3	To be played by December 17
R4	To be played by January 21
R5	To be played by February 11
R6	To be played by February 25
SF1	To be played by March 17
SF2	To be played by March 31
F1	TBC
F2	TBC

All fixtures 11am unless stated,
subject to change.
End-of-season play-off dates TBC.

**Adam Hajdu – Looking to make
a big impact in 2011/12**

KENNY
DALGLISH
IS
COOLER
THAN THE
FONZ

THE 2010/11 SEASON

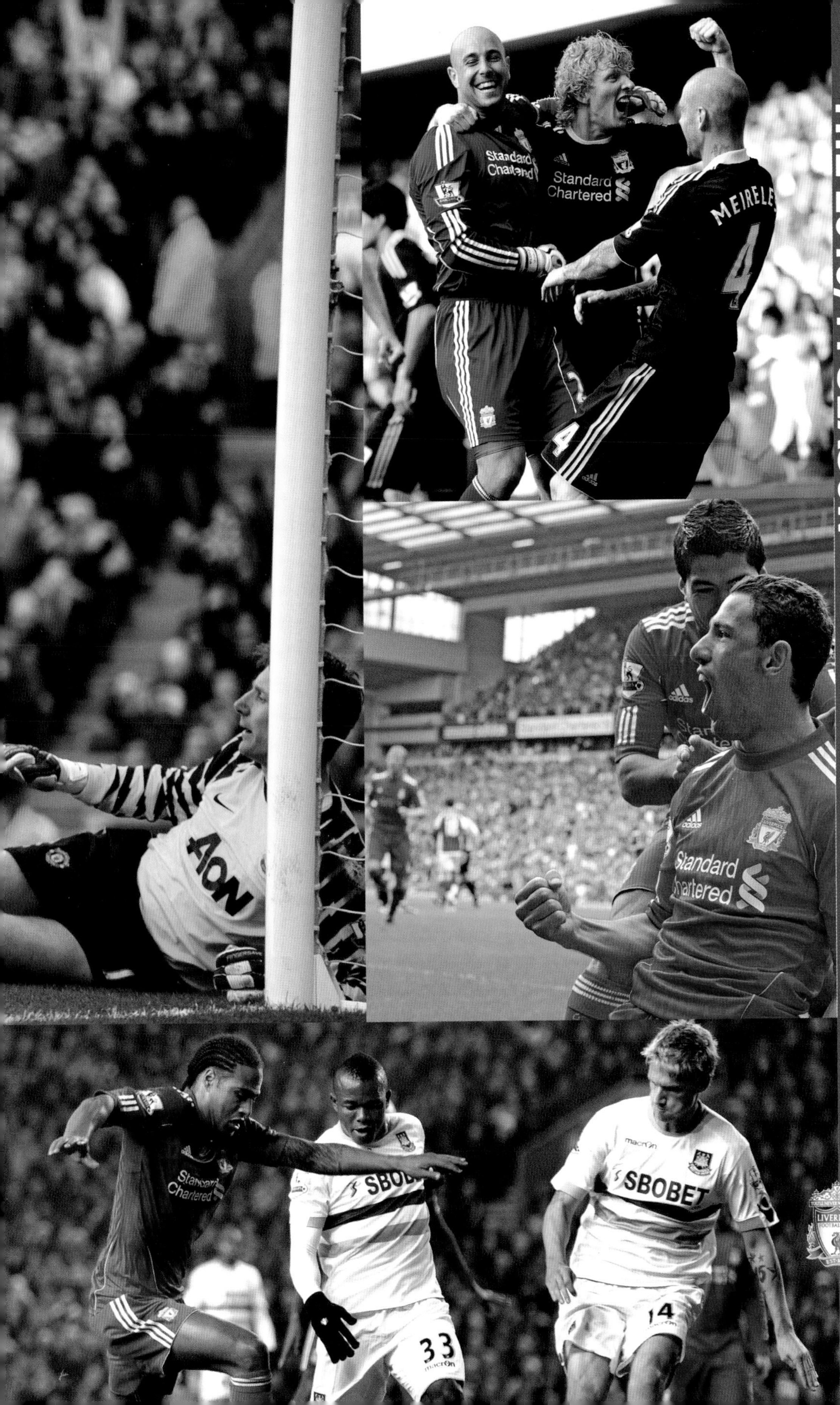

LOOKING BACK

July

1   Roy Hodgson is appointed Liverpool's new boss, signing a three-year contract.

2   Yossi Benayoun completes his move to Chelsea.

9   Forward Milan Jovanovic completes his Bosman free transfer move.

11   Pepe Reina and Fernando Torres taste World Cup success as Spain defeat Holland 1-0.

14   Francisco Duran and goalkeeper Nikolay Mihaylov are released.

19   England international Joe Cole agrees to join the club on a four-year contract.

20   Scottish Young Player of the Year Danny Wilson becomes Roy Hodgson's third major signing, the defender moving from SPL champions Rangers.

24   Albert Riera completes his move to Greek champions Olympiakos.

29   David Ngog scores twice in the Europa League as Roy Hodgson wins his first competitive game in charge, Liverpool earning a 2-0 win at FK Rabotnicki.

31   Fabio Aurelio re-signs for the club on a two-year deal.

August

1   Joe Cole appears in the 1-0 friendly defeat to Borussia Moenchengladbach in Germany.

2   It's revealed that ex-defender and reserve coach Gary Ablett is battling blood cancer.

5   Joe Cole impresses on his full debut in the 2-0 home victory over FK Rabotnicki.

9   Philipp Degen joins German Bundesliga side VfB Stuttgart on a season-long loan deal.

11   Captain Steven Gerrard scores both goals as England come from behind to defeat Hungary 2-1 at Wembley Stadium.

12   Denmark international midfielder Christian Poulson signs from Juventus.

15   A late Pepe Reina own goal denies 10-man Liverpool a winning start to the season, a game in which Joe Cole is sent off on his league debut.

17   Australian goalkeeper Brad Jones completes his move from Middlesbrough.

18   Martin Skrtel pens a two-year contract extension.

19   Christian Poulson makes his debut in the 1-0 Europa League win over Trabzonspor.

21   Alberto Aquilani returns to his homeland, signing a year's loan with Juventus.

23   The Reds suffer a first league defeat of the season, 3-0 at Manchester City.

26   Reserve striker Krisztian Nemeth joins Olympiakos.
    Progress to the Europa League groups is confirmed after a 2-1 victory at Trabzonspor.

27   Napoli, Steaua Bucharest and FC Utrecht are drawn in Liverpool's Europa group.

28   Liverpool complete the signing of Portugal midfielder Raul Meireles, a replacement for Barcelona-bound Javier Mascherano.

29   Fernando Torres fires the only goal in victory over West Brom – his 50th at Anfield.

31   Transfer deadline day ends with Paul Konchesky joining from Fulham – Lauri Dalla Valle and Alex Kacaniklic heading in the other direction. Youngsters Suso and Adam Hajdu are also signed, from FC Cadiz and MTK respectively while Emiliano Insua, Damien Plessis, Nabil El Zhar and Vincent Weijl also make moves to overseas clubs.

Quotes of the month:

"When you speak about Liverpool you are speaking about one of the biggest clubs in the world – maybe for me, the biggest."

Milan Jovanovic

"I want to be at the start of something fresh and new. It's something I'm very excited about. It's a new chapter. We've got the new manager, new backroom staff and I'm a small part of it. I want to help this team and help us to achieve something."

Joe Cole

"It was special being out on the pitch hearing the Kop singing 'You'll Never Walk Alone. I was sat in the stand for the Arsenal game and it was great to see, but to be out on the pitch was fantastic."

Christian Poulsen

JULY/AUGUST

THE GAMES

29	Rabotnicki	A	2-0	Ngog 17, 59
5	Rabotnicki	H	2-0	Ngog 22, Gerrard 40 (pen)
15	Arsenal	H	1-1	Ngog 46
19	Trabzonspor	H	1-0	Babel 45
23	Manchester City	A	0-3	
26	Trabzonspor	A	2-1	Kacar 83 (o.g.), Kuyt 88
29	West Bromwich Albion	H	1-0	Torres 65

WHERE THEY STOOD

10	Sunderland
11	Tottenham Hotspur
12	Blackpool
13	**Liverpool**
14	Fulham
15	Blackburn Rovers
16	West Bromwich Albion

THE BOSS:

'It was impossible to turn down. It's going to be the highlight of my career. I feel very pleased and proud.'

LOOKING BACK

September

3   Steven Gerrard captains England to a 4-0 victory over Bulgaria in their opening Euro
         2012 qualifier. Amongst the Reds' other international contingent, Fernando Torres
         scores twice in Spain's 4-0 win in Liechtenstein, Dirk Kuyt nets from the spot in
         Holland's 5-0 stroll in San Marino while Raul Meireles is on target as Portugal are held
         4-4 by Cyprus.

4   Nearly 35,000 turn out for Jamie Carragher's testimonial, who see a Liverpool XI defeat
         an Everton XI 4-1 – with Carra scoring at both ends.

7   Steven Gerrard and Glen Johnson play the full 90 minutes in England's impressive 3-1
         win in Switzerland.
         Martin Skrtel, Daniel Agger and Christian Poulsen also enjoy qualifying wins with their
         countries.

8   It is confirmed that Dirk Kuyt will ruled out for a month with a shoulder injury picked up
         on international duty.

10   Gerard Houllier is appointed as Aston Villa's new manager.
         Daniel Ayala joins Hull City on an emergency loan.

12   The Reds are held to a goalless draw at Birmingham.

16   Joe Cole scores Liverpool's quickest goal in European competition as a much-changed
         side defeat Steaua Bucherest 4-1 in the first Europa League group phase clash.

19   Steven Gerrard scores twice as the Reds hit back from two-down – but Manchester
         United's Dimitar Berbatov nets the winner to complete his hat-trick at Old Trafford.

20   Daniel Ayala's loan spell with Hull City is extended until the end of the year.

22   Milan Jovanovic nets his first for the club – but a weakened side bow out of the League
         Cup 4-2 on penalties to Northampton Town, the game having finished 2-2 after extra
         time at Anfield.

25   Steven Gerrard's header rescues a point in a 2-2 draw with Sunderland at Anfield.

30   Liverpool come away from FC Utrecht with a 0-0 draw in the Europa League.

Quotes of the month:

"You tend to associate players these days moving around a lot but Carra is, in many ways, a one-off
and nobody deserves to celebrate their career more. He has put so much effort in to his career,
has shown so much desire and sweated blood for the club. He's been a big influence on me ever
since I arrived at Melwood on day one. We come from similar backgrounds, so it was easy bouncing
ideas off each other and I've got nothing but the utmost respect for him as a player and person."

Steven Gerrard on Jamie Carragher

"With the help of God and Jesus Christ we'll defeat Liverpool. A draw isn't a bad result either."

Steaua Bucharest owner Gigi Becali

"We have to get used to the new players and then the system. Of course our target is to be up there
but we have to be realistic. We will find out at the end of the season what we can achieve. Maybe it
will take a while and we all have to be patient. April and May is the time to talk about targets."

Pepe Reina

"Judge us in May. We have had a tough start with the fixture list and with Fernando not being match
fit, and also the change of personnel with the change of manager. We will pick up, I am convinced."

Joe Cole post-Manchester United

"Catastrophe. I am so disappointed. What can I say? It was a very difficult night for me, for all the
players and the team. Of course we feel sorry for the fans."

Milan Jovanovic, post-Northampton Town

SEPTEMBER

THE GAMES

12	Birmingham City	A	0-0	
16	**Steaua Bucharest**	H	**4-1**	Cole 1, Ngog 55 (pen), 90, Lucas 81
19	Manchester United	A	2-3	Gerrard 64 (pen), 70
22	**Northampton Town**	H	**2-2 aet**	Jovanovic 9, Ngog 116
	* Northampton Town win 4-2 on penalties			
25	Sunderland	H	2-2	Kuyt 5, Gerrard 64
30	**FC Utrecht**	A	0-0	

WHERE THEY STOOD

14	Stoke City
15	Blackpool
16	**Liverpool**
17	Wolverhampton Wanderers
18	Wigan Athletic
19	West Ham United
20	Everton

THE BOSS:

'We'd like to have been near the top of the table...we'd have been happy as sand-boys...you don't always get what you want.'

LOOKING BACK

October

3 The Reds suffer a shock 2-1 home defeat at the hands of Blackpool, with Fernando Torres coming off early with a groin injury.

4 Joe Cole is recalled to the England squad for the upcoming Euro 2012 qualifier against Montenegro.

5 Chairman Martin Broughton agrees the sale of the club to New England Sports Ventures, owners of the Boston Red Sox baseball franchise.

8 Raul Meireles' Portugal enjoy a 3-1 victory over Denmark, for whom Christian Poulsen starts. Dirk Kuyt and Lucas Leiva also enjoy wins for their respective countries.

11 Lucas Leiva impresses again for his country, as Brazil defeat Ukraine 2-0 at Derby County's Pride Park.

12 There is mixed news from the latest round of midweek internationals as Dirk Kuyt, Daniel Agger and Glen Johnson pick up injuries. Raul Meireles scores for Portugal while Steven Gerrard plays as England are held 0-0 by Montenegro.

15 The club's sale to John Henry's NESV is finally given the green light after a protracted takeover saga.
Jamie Carragher pens a new two-year contract extension.

17 Liverpool's new owners see the Reds go down 2-0 in the Merseyside derby at Goodison.

19 Christian Purslow stands down as managing director – although will remain as a non-executive director and advisor to the club's new owners.

21 A weakened side earn a 0-0 draw at Napoli in the Europa League.

24 Fernando Torres hits the winner as Liverpool secure a first win in eight, a 2-1 victory over Blackburn Rovers at Anfield.

31 A late Maxi Rodriguez strike earns a hard-fought 1-0 win at Bolton.

Quotes of the month:

"To be applauded off at what is almost the home of football is so special. That is what I dreamed of. When the fans were singing You'll Never Walk Alone – it's my dad's favourite song but he's no longer with me – I was singing myself and it was a bit emotional. These supporters have seen some of the best football ever, which started when Mr Shankly had his dream. In my era, there was no better football club in the world."

Blackpool manager Ian Holloway

"The situation is not dire. The league table is separated by five points from third-bottom to fourth, so there's a long way to go. Stay patient, the team has quality in it. Give Roy a bit of time and by Christmas see where we are and everyone will be happier."

Danny Murphy

"It's hard to imagine doing anything else like playing, coaching, managing or scouting for another team. I've been with Liverpool ever since I was a young boy so not being part of this club would be difficult. When I say life I mean it. I want to stay here. When I say that, it's not talk, I really mean it."

Jamie Carragher

"They seem genuine and they seem like they are doing it through passion. Clubs are going to be made to work from their revenues rather than just throwing money at it. That can only be good for the game, and with the solid base a club like Liverpool has got, we can put ourselves back on top."

Joe Cole on the Liverpool takeover

"I am enjoying playing for the manager. He has everything to succeed at Liverpool. He is also a nice man because he always talks to us, he likes to know about our wellbeing and asks us about our family. Every day we are working hard in training and we all want to do well for the manager."

Raul Meireles

OCTOBER

THE GAMES

3	Blackpool	H	1-2	Kyrgiakos 53
17	Everton	A	0-2	
21	**Napoli**	**A**	**0-0**	
24	Blackburn Rovers	H	2-1	Kyrgiakos 48, Torres 53
31	Bolton Wanderers	A	1-0	Rodriguez 86

WHERE THEY STOOD

9	Fulham
10	Bolton Wanderers
11	Sunderland
12	**Liverpool**
13	Aston Villa
14	Birmingham City
15	Stoke City

THE BOSS:

'We got behind them down the flanks, and Jamie Carragher was bombing down there like Carlos Alberto.'

LOOKING BACK

November

1 Joe Cole faces a spell on the sidelines with a hamstring problem picked up at Bolton.

2 Youngsters Stephen Darby and Thomas Ince join League One Notts County for a two-month loan spell.

3 The Reds appoint former Tottenham sporting director Damien Comolli to oversee transfers and scouting.

4 Steven Gerrard hits a hat-trick as Liverpool come from behind to defeat Napoli 3-1 in the Europa League.

6 Tom Werner is confirmed as the club's new chairman.

7 A superb Fernando Torres double downs leaders Chelsea 2-0 at Anfield.

9 Defender Danny Wilson earns his first call-up for Scotland.

10 An early Fernando Torres goal is cancelled out in the second half as Liverpool four-match winning run comes to an end at Wigan courtesy of a 1-1 draw.

11 Martin Kelly is named in the England U21s' squad to face Germany.

13 Two second-half goals condemn the Reds to defeat at Stoke City.

14 Steven Gerrard is included by England for the midweek friendly against France, while Fernando Torres will join up with Spain despite an ankle problem.

16 Danny Wilson scores on his international debut in Scotland's 3-0 friendly win over the Faroe Islands.

17 An injury to Steven Gerrard tops off a miserable night for England, fortunate to only go down 2-1 to France at Wembley.

20 Glen Johnson opens the scoring against one of his former clubs as Liverpool ease to a 3-0 home victory over West Ham.

22 Spanish prospect Suso pens his first professional contract.

23 A Far East tour is confirmed for summer 2011.

28 Jamie Carragher's 450th Premier League game for the Reds ends in heartbreak – a dislocated shoulder and injury-time Aaron Lennon goal contributing to a cruel 2-1 loss. A trip to Manchester United awaits after the draw is made for the FA Cup third round.

Quotes of the month:

"I feel very good about it. It is something the owners were very keen to put in place. The days of the dictator-type English manager have long since passed when everything went through one man."

Roy Hodgson on Damien Comolli

"He was outstanding. In the second half his entry was a catalyst. It galvanised the crowd and the team. I'm delighted we got a reward for it but we do owe a big debt of gratitude to him. It was a real leader's performance. That is certainly appreciated by me and my staff as well as the crowd."

Roy Hodgson on Napoli hat-trick hero Steven Gerrard

"He's dangerous for every set play, every corner and free-kick. He's No.1 in the air at our club and maybe in the Premier League. He's showed he's a good player and that he could score goals for Liverpool. I've been a bit unlucky but I'll try to improve and try to be more dangerous."

Martin Skrtel on Sotirios Kyrgiakos

"We want to get young English or British kids. That's important if we want to keep an identity to get those kids into the club. Spotting a fantastic player is not that difficult, convincing them to come, that comes back to competition and that can be more difficult. We will have to be very good at it."

Damien Comolli

"They are getting down to it in a professional way. I have been impressed. It's what I expected. They are taking their time, doing it carefully, thinking, not being rushed. They're the right people."

Departing chairman Martin Broughton on New England Sports Ventures' Tom Werner

NOVEMBER

THE GAMES

4	**Napoli**	H	3-1	Gerrard 75, 88 (pen), 89
7	Chelsea	H	2-0	Torres 11, 44
10	Wigan Athletic	A	1-1	Torres 7
13	Stoke City	A	0-2	
20	West Ham United	H	3-0	Johnson 18, Kuyt 27 (pen), Rodriguez 38
28	Tottenham Hotspur	A	1-2	Skrtel 42

WHERE THEY STOOD

7	Sunderland
8	Stoke City
9	Newcastle United
10	**Liverpool**
11	Blackpool
12	West Bromwich Albion
13	Blackburn Rovers

THE BOSS:

'Jamie is a major, major figure at the club...if anyone deserves the accolades it's him.'

LOOKING BACK

December

2   A 1-1 draw at Steaua Bucharest earns the Reds a place in the last 32 of the Europa League.

3   Martin Kelly and Daniel Pacheco pen contract extensions with the club.

6   Early goals from David Ngog and Ryan Babel set the Reds on their way to a 3-0 win over Aston Villa at a freezing Anfield. The clean sheet is also Pepe Reina's 100th in the league for the club, reaching the landmark faster than any other Liverpool goalkeeper.

10   Goalkeeper Charles Itandje is released by the club.

11   Dirk Kuyt is on target but the Reds' away woes continue, as Alan Pardew's first game in charge of Newcastle ends in a 3-1 win for the home side.

13   Liverpool's owners appear on LFC TV for the first time, vowing to help improve the club on and off the pitch.

15   The Reds' final Europa League group match, against Utrecht, ends in a 0-0 draw at Anfield.

17   Sparta Prague are next up in the Europa League last 32 phase.

18   Overnight snow and icy conditions mean the home clash with Fulham is called off.

21   Young prospects Kristoffer Peterson and Youse Mersin, both 16, join the club's Academy.

26   The clash at Blackpool is called off due to a frozen pitch – a second successive postponement for the Reds.

27   Daniel Ayala returns from his loan spell at Hull having picked up an injury.

28   Brad Jones is named in Australia's squad for the upcoming Asian Cup.

29   Tributes are paid to former full-back Avi Cohen, who passes away at the age of 54 having been critically injured in a motorbike accident.
       The Reds go down to a shock 1-0 home defeat to Wolves.

Quotes of the month:

"They've done great, and it's credit to the manager as well for putting them in. Even one of the qualifying rounds – Trabzonspor was a tough place to go. To come through was great. It's been great experience for them and it bodes well. It's been great for the club to see local lads coming through, so you have to give a pat on the back and also to the manager for giving them a chance."

Jamie Carragher on Roy Hodgson's decision to give youth a chance

"Everyone at the club, but in particular the senior players and his England colleagues here, have done a great job. The coaching staff have tried to encourage him, saying 'don't worry Joe it will come right'. I know that he's desperate to show what he can do."

Roy Hodgson on Joe Cole

"I'm looking forward to going back. It was fairytale stuff the two years I had there. It will be special to go back. I think it raised a few eyebrows when my name was mentioned going there - a 35-year-old baldy Scotsman. It was arriving at the right place at the right time when I went to Liverpool. To say after one season you pick up five trophies I would have laughed in their face."

Gary McAllister

"A record is nice to achieve but it is down to the enormous team-mates I've had. I am pleased but at the same time thankful to them."

Pepe Reina, goalkeeping record-breaker

"Steven helps all players, and it is harder to find leaders in the world of football today. Today it is not so easy to pick out the leaders. We are lucky to have one or two but what you are fighting for as a coach is to get more leaders in your team."

Roy Hodgson on Steven Gerrard

DECEMBER

THE GAMES

2	**Steaua Bucharest**	A	1-1	Jovanovic 19
6	Aston Villa	H	3-0	Ngog 14, Babel 16, Rodriguez 55
11	Newcastle United	A	1-3	Kuyt 49
15	**FC Utrecht**	**H**	0-0	
29	Wolverhampton W.	H	0-1	

WHERE THEY STOOD

9	Blackburn Rovers
10	Stoke City
11	Everton
12	**Liverpool**
13	Newcastle United
14	West Bromwich Albion
15	Aston Villa

THE BOSS:

'I'm expecting to see the team climb the table. I don't have any fears or concerns.'

LOOKING BACK

January

1 A last-gasp Joe Cole goal – his first in the league for Liverpool – earns a much-needed 2-1 victory over Bolton.

5 Steven Gerrard scores – and misses a penalty – in a defeat at Blackburn Rovers.

7 Roy Hodgson leaves the club by mutual consent.

8 Kenny Dalglish is confirmed as Liverpool caretaker-manager.

9 An early Ryan Giggs penalty and a Steven Gerrard red card contribute to a third-round FA Cup exit at Manchester United.

10 Steve Clarke joins the backroom staff as first-team coach, with Mike Kelly leaving.

12 An early Fernando Torres strike proves a false dawn as the Reds lose at Blackpool.

13 Reserve striker Nathan Eccleston completes a loan move to Charlton Athletic until the end of the season.

16 Dirk Kuyt's second-half penalty ensures a share of the spoils in the Merseyside derby, after Everton had hit back from a half-time deficit to lead 2-1.

19 Conor Coady and Suso are promoted to Melwood to train with the first team.

21 Stephen Darby returns to Notts County on loan until the end of the season.

22 Fernando Torres' double and a stunner from Raul Meireles gives Kenny Dalglish his first win in his second spell as boss, courtesy of a 3-0 victory at Wolves.

25 Liverpool agree a fee with Hoffenheim for the sale of Ryan Babel – the Dutchman completing his move to Germany the following day.

26 The Reds claim a hard-fought 1-0 home victory over Fulham to move up to seventh.

29 Reserve midfielder Victor Palsson signs for Hibernian.

31 A busy transfer deadline day sees Newcastle striker Andy Carroll sign for the club for a record fee, while Luis Suarez also completes a move from Ajax and Coventry youngster Conor Thomas in a loan deal. Fernando Torres leaves for Chelsea for a British record fee while Paul Konchesky leaves on loan, signing for Nottingham Forest.

Quotes of the month:

"Steven is a class player and everyone knows what he brings to this team. The likes of him and Carragher are the mainstays of this team and indeed the football club."

Sammy Lee

"Being asked to manage Liverpool was a great privilege. Any manager would be honoured to manage a club with such an incredible history, such embedded tradition and such an amazing set of fans. Liverpool is one of the great clubs in world football. The club has some great, world-class players, with whom it has been a pleasure to work and I wish the entire squad well."

Roy Hodgson

"I'm going to do the best I can to try to help the club, but everybody has to pull in the same direction. There's no point not being a unified unit. If we pull in different directions we won't get anywhere. We won't always be successful...we have to say `Let's just start walking before we run'."

Kenny Dalglish

"His nickname, the King, says it all really. It's time to regroup and for us all to be pulling in the right direction because this season certainly hasn't been good enough."

Steven Gerrard

"He understand's the club's philosophy and that is a relentless kind of attack. Bill Shankly understood that you cannot be satisfied with a draw. We have to start winning consistently. I'm optimistic we're going to do that in the short run and Kenny is the right man for the job right now."

Chairman Tom Werner on Kenny Dalglish's appointment

JANUARY

THE GAMES

1	Bolton Wanderers	H	2-1	Torres 49, Cole 90
5	Blackburn Rovers	A	1-3	Gerrard 81
9	**Manchester United**	**A**	**0-1**	
12	Blackpool	A	1-2	Torres 3
16	Everton	H	2-2	Meireles 29, Kuyt 68 (pen)
22	Wolverhampton W.	A	3-0	Torres 36, 90, Meireles 50
26	Fulham	H	1-0	Pantsil 52 (o.g.)

WHERE THEY STOOD

4	Chelsea
5	Tottenham Hotspur
6	Sunderland
7	**Liverpool**
8	Blackburn Rovers
9	Newcastle United
10	Stoke City

KING KENNY:

'I'm going to do the best I can to try to help the club, but everybody has to pull in the same direction.'

LOOKING BACK

February

2 Luis Suarez marks his Liverpool debut with a goal as Stoke City are defeated 2-0.

6 Raul Meireles nets the only goal as the Reds earn an impressive 1-0 win at Chelsea.

9 Daniel Agger is on target for Denmark – but England, who included Glen Johnson, run out 2-1 victors in an international friendly. In other friendly games, Dirk Kuyt scores a penalty in Holland's 3-1 win over Austria.

11 Jonjo Shelvey could be ruled out for the rest of the season with a knee injury.

12 Lucas makes his 100th league appearance for the Reds in a 1-1 draw with Wigan.

16 Forward Raheem Sterling, a five-goal scorer in the 9-0 FA Youth Cup victory over Southend United, is included in the first-team squad for the Europa League trip to Sparta Prague.

17 Kenny Dalglish's first European game in charge of the club ends in a 0-0 draw in the Czech Republic.

24 A late Dirk Kuyt goal sees the Reds through in the Europa League, following a 1-0 home victory over Anfield in what was an unusual 6pm kick-off.

27 Liverpool suffer a European hangover as West Ham secure a 3-1 victory to end the Reds' eight-match unbeaten run.

28 Reserve winger David Amoo joins Hull City on loan until the end of the season.

Quotes of the month:

"Goals have always been in my game so I'm very confident I can score for Liverpool. The number nine is a big number and the one I wanted. To get it at Liverpool is a great feeling. I want to go out there and play the football that has brought me here. I'll bring as much as I can to the team – I'll score goals, create chances, hold up the ball and just try my best. They have spent a lot of money on getting me here and I just want to repay them for what they have spent. I'll do my best and think I can do it. I want to win trophies with this club and help push us forward."

Andy Carroll

"I want to show the fans how hard I am ready to work. I want to put a lot of effort in to show my capabilities. My ambitions are to do my very best for Liverpool, to try to learn more about English football and become a champion. Liverpool is a very famous club – the most famous in England – and I watched Liverpool and English football as a boy. It's a dream to be able to play here."

Luis Suarez

"It is a dream debut. Anyone would say it is a dream debut. Just to be on the field for a few minutes and to manage to score in front of the Kop, it's what dreams are made of."

Luis Suarez

"I know he has wanted to be in this position. The philosophy didn't seem to suit the club and we knew we had to make a change. We knew we wanted to move to a more positive pass-and-move philosophy. I can't imagine how anyone can be more beloved, not just for what he accomplished on the field but off the field through some difficult times for the club and supporters."

John W Henry on Kenny Dalglish

"It's like getting a new player in because after he did his shoulder he was a long time out. It's great credit to Carra's level of fitness, especially at his age. It was very important for us to have him in defence to talk and encourage and push people into positions. He's a fantastic asset to this club."

Kenny Dalglish hails the returning Jamie Carragher v Chelsea

"Dalglish's presence and who he is has galvanised the whole club – players and supporters. I don't need to tell you what he means to the club and the fans."

Jamie Carragher

FEBRUARY

THE GAMES

2	Stoke City	H	2-0	Meireles 47, Suarez 79
6	Chelsea	A	1-0	Meireles 69
12	Wigan Athletic	H	1-1	Meireles 24
17	**Sparta Prague**	**A**	**0-0**	
24	**Sparta Prague**	**H**	**1-0**	Kuyt 86
27	West Ham United	A	1-3	Johnson 84

WHERE THEY STOOD

3	Manchester City
4	Tottenham Hotspur
5	Chelsea
6	**Liverpool**
7	Bolton Wanderers
8	Sunderland
9	Newcastle United

KING KENNY:

'Liverpool is a fantastic institution and everybody that is here has to show respect to that.'

LOOKING BACK

March

2   Martin Kelly is ruled out for a month with a hamstring injury.

6   Dirk Kuyt's hat-trick gives the Reds a memorable 3-1 victory over Manchester United, a game in which Andy Carroll comes on to make his Liverpool debut.

8   A hamstring injury for Fabio Aurelio adds to the Reds' injury woes.

10   An early Alan penalty sees the Reds go down 1-0 to Braga in the Europa League – although Andy Carroll impresses after coming off the bench in the second half.

11   Steven Gerrard faces a month out with a groin problem.

12   It is confirmed that reserve-team manager John McMahon has left the club, with Academy technical director Pep Segura taking charge for the rest of the season.

13   Manchester United end the Under-18s' FA Youth Cup dreams, winning 3-2 at Anfield in the last eight.

17   A 0-0 draw at home to Braga sees the Reds bow out of Europe.

20   Luis Suarez is amongst the goals as Sunderland are defeated 2-0.

21   Glen Johnson and Andy Carroll are named in the England squad for games against Wales and Ghana.

22   Commercial director Ian Ayre is confirmed as the club's new Managing Director, while Damien Comolli is made Director of Football.

24   Daniel Pacheco joins Championship promotion-chasers Norwich City on loan until the end of the season.

25   Goalkeeper Brad Jones agrees to link up with Derby County in a loan deal.
Dirk Kuyt is on target in Holland's 4-0 Euro 2012 qualifying win in Hungary.

26   Glen Johnson is influential in England's 2-0 victory against Wales.

29   Andy Carroll is on target in England's 1-1 friendly draw with Ghana while Dirk Kuyt is again on target for his country in a thrilling 5-3 win in the return Euro 2012 qualifier at home to Hungary.

30   Lucas Leiva pens a new contract with the club.

Quotes of the month:

"This game is probably the best atmosphere you can experience in a football match in any stadium in the world. Especially when it's at Anfield."

Pepe Reina on Liverpool v Manchester United

"He works tirelessly for the cause and any reward he gets he works really hard for. If someone has been generous to him and laid something on for him a yard in front of goal then good luck to him, he deserves it. For us it is a huge win and the lads deserve great credit for the way they played."

Kenny Dalglish, post-Manchester United

"You always dream about a hat-trick and to make a hat-trick against United is the best feeling ever. We can compete against the best. We showed it against Chelsea and we showed it against United."

Dirk Kuyt, post-Manchester United

"Suarez has only played a few games but we know he will be a top player. Training and playing with him he has been strong and technically good. Liverpool are in a better position having two top forwards instead of one. I enjoyed playing behind Fernando but if you said I could have Fernando on form or Andy Carroll and Luis Suarez on form, I would take the two over one."

Steven Gerrard

"It would be fantastic to play for Liverpool in the Champions League again and I don't see why we can't. We have a squad that is united in its will and desire to return this club to where it belongs."

Lucas Leiva

MARCH

THE GAMES

6	Manchester United	H	3-1	Kuyt 34, 39, 65
10	**Braga**	A	0-1	
17	**Braga**	H	0-0	
20	Sunderland	A	2-0	Kuyt 33 (pen), Suarez 77

WHERE THEY STOOD

3	Chelsea
4	Manchester City
5	Tottenham Hotspur
6	**Liverpool**
7	Bolton Wanderers
8	Everton
9	Sunderland

KING KENNY:

'That would be the highest point for the fans...to be part of it was an absolute pleasure.'

LOOKING BACK

April

2 Two Chris Brunt penalties, the second two minutes from time, prove decisive as the injury-hit Reds go down 2-1 at West Brom.

6 Daniel Agger is ruled out for the rest of the season due to the knee injury picked up against West Brom, while Glen Johnson could also be absent for the final games due to hamstring problem picked up in the same game.

7 The club confirm a pre-season Far East tour for July, which will include games in China, Malaysia and South Korea.

Basketball star LeBron James acquires a minority stake in the Reds as part of a deal with the club's owners.

8 Steven Gerrard will miss the rest of the season after suffering a setback in his recovery from a groin injury.

9 Liverpool confirm a pre-season game against Valerenga, on August 1.

10 Andy Carroll scores the first two goals of his Reds career as an impressive Liverpool ease to a 3-0 victory over Manchester City.

16 Dirk Kuyt pens a new contract.

17 A Dirk Kuyt penalty 10 minutes into injury time earns a 1-1 draw at Arsenal, just minutes after the Gunners had seemingly secured a victory with a Robin van Persie spot-kick.

21 Raul Meireles is voted the PFA Fans' Player of the Year.

22 A new £25m a year record kit deal is announced with Warrior Sports, a subsidiary of New Balance.

23 Maxi Rodriguez fires a hat-trick as the Reds ease to a 5-0 victory over relegation-threatened Birmingham City.

Quotes of the month:

"At this particular moment in time, I'm as good a player as Steven!"

Kenny Dalglish trumpets his own on-field worth in the wake of Steven Gerrard's injury news

"Steven is the best, full stop. He has been fantastic and often puts his club, and country, before himself and he has played when maybe he shouldn't have. The work he has put in to get himself fit has been incredible. He has put his body through the mincer to play and deserves a bit of luck over injuries. Hopefully the break to rest his groin injury will see him return as strong as ever."

Kenny Dalglish on Steven Gerrard

"There will be a feel-good factor going into the summer and the start of next season. As players we have to look after ourselves and do our own job but we are like supporters as well, we love to see top players coming to the club and hopefully that will be the case. Everyone is delighted with the business we did in January and hopefully similar things will happen in the summer."

Jamie Carragher

"He never knew he was playing until about quarter to six – we wouldn't have had enough tickets to go round if we had told him he was playing! He did fantastic. He just went out and played. He took one down on his chest early doors and passed it away, and I think that settled him down. He did not look fazed in any way and it's a fantastic credit to him that he did as well as he did. It's a reflection of the good work that has been done at the Academy in the last year and a half."

Kenny Dalglish on debutant Jon Flanagan

"Carra has been a fantastic servant. He's filled in loyally and comfortably in many positions and he's someone who has been very pleased to be associated with Liverpool – and we're pleased to be associated with him. The most important thing is his ability and his desire and commitment."

Kenny Dalglish on Jamie Carragher

APRIL

THE GAMES

2	West Bromwich Albion	A	1-2	Skrtel 50
11	Manchester City	H	3-0	Carroll 13, 35, Kuyt 34
17	Arsenal	A	1-1	Kuyt 90 (pen)
23	Birmingham City	H	5-0	Rodriguez 7, 66, 73, Kuyt 23, Cole 86

WHERE THEY STOOD

3	Arsenal
4	Manchester City
5	Tottenham Hotspur
6	**Liverpool**
7	Everton
8	Bolton Wanderers
9	Fulham

KING KENNY:

'We are still the best club in English football, if not world football.'

LOOKING BACK

May

1   A 3-0 victory over Newcastle moves the Reds up to fifth, with Maxi Rodriguez again amongst the scorers.

2   Former favourite Sami Hyypia confirms he will retire at the end of the season, and will join the coaching staff at Bayer Leverkusen.

6   Jay Spearing pens a contract extension after impressing since becoming a regular under Kenny Dalglish.

9   The Reds run riot at Fulham, claiming a 5-2 victory with Maxi Rodriguez again hitting a hat-trick to take his run to 7 in 3 games, while Dirk Kuyt is on target for a fifth successive match. The game is also notable for Jamie Carragher playing his 666th game for the club, moving up to second on the Reds' all-time appearance list.

11   Jay Spearing is named in a provisional 40-man England Under-21s squad for the summer European Championships.

12   Kenny Dalglish agrees a three-year contract to become the club's full-time manager for the second time, with Steve Clarke confirmed as his assistant.

15   Liverpool's hopes of fifth place are hit as fellow Europa League hopefuls Tottenham win 2-0 at Anfield.

20   Lucas Leiva is named in Brazil's squad for friendlies against Holland and Romania.

21   Istanbul hero Jerzy Dudek confirms his retirement after featuring for Real Madrid in their last game of the season.

22   A 1-0 defeat at Aston Villa on the final days means no European football for the Reds next season – although Martin Skrtel's 90-minute involvement means the defender is one of only two outfield players to play every minute of his side's 2010/11 Premier League games.

26   Pepe Reina is included in Spain's end-of-season friendlies against USA and Venezuela.

29   Luis Suarez plays in Uruguay's 2-1 friendly defeat to Germany.

Quotes of the month:

"It's difficult to put your finger on what he's done. He's Kenny Dalglish – he's a legend as a player and a manager. His record speaks for itself – four championships. There aren't many managers who can say that. He's had a massive impact on the club and we're just enjoying it."

Jamie Carragher

"It is a great accolade for him to be the second in the table for most appearances as a Liverpool player. He has been here a while and hopefully he will be here for a lot longer. Cally is iconic here not just because of the number of games he played but for the service he gave to the club and the success he brought. He was there at the start of the foundations, he was in there with Shanks."

Kenny Dalglish on Jamie Carragher

"It's fantastic for Pepe. It's great for him to make 150 consecutive appearances. He's our goalkeeper and it's important we have that continuity. The quality of his performances have been fantastic. I'm sure it's a milestone that he will think about very fondly. He's a huge influence on us. Not only does he stop goals – he creates them as well. It's great for us to have him between the sticks, and for me – if he's not the best – then I would like to see the one that is better than him."

Kenny Dalglish on Pepe Reina

"It was obvious that the atmosphere had been transformed. No-one else could have produced such a response. We have seen first-hand his love for the club, and his determination to produce a winning side again. He has a unique relationship with our supporters and embodies everything that is special about the Liverpool way of doing things."

John W Henry following Kenny Dalglish's full-time appointment

MAY

THE GAMES

1	Newcastle United	H	3-0	Rodriguez 10, Kuyt 59 (pen), Suarez 65
9	Fulham	A	5-2	Rodriguez 1, 7, 70, Kuyt 16, Suarez 75
15	Tottenham Hotspur	H	0-2	
22	Aston Villa	A	0-1	

WHERE THEY FINISHED

3	Manchester City
4	Arsenal
5	Tottenham Hotspur
6	**Liverpool**
7	Everton
8	Fulham
9	Aston Villa

KING KENNY:

'This is a unique club and I am delighted to have the opportunity to help build something special here again.'

2010/11

Player columns (left to right):

1	Brad Jones
2	Glen Johnson
3	Paul Konchesky
4	Raul Meireles
5	Daniel Agger
6	Fabio Aurelio
7	Luis Suarez
8	Steven Gerrard
9	Andy Carroll
10	Joe Cole
12	Daniel Pacheco
14	Milan Jovanovic
16	Sotirios Kyrgiakos
17	Maxi Rodriguez
18	Dirk Kuyt
21	Lucas Leiva

	DATE	OPPONENTS		RES	ATT
Aug	Thu 29 July	Rabotnicki (E Lge 3rd qual 1st leg)	A	2-0	22,000
	Thu 05 Aug	Rabotnicki (E Lge 3rd qual 2nd leg)	H	2-0	31,202
	Sun 15 Aug	Arsenal	H	1-1	44,722
	Thu 19 Aug	Trabzonspor (E Lge play-off 1st leg)	H	1-0	40,941
	Mon 23 Aug	Manchester City	A	0-3	47,087
	Thu 26 Aug	Trabzonspor (E Lge play-off 2nd leg)	A	2-1*	21,065
Sep	Sun 29 Aug	West Bromwich Albion	H	1-0	41,994
	Sun 12 Sep	Birmingham City	A	0-0	27,333
	Thu 16 Sep	Steaua Bucharest (EL match 1)	H	4-1	25,605
	Sun 19 Sep	Manchester United	A	2-3	75,213
	Wed 22 Sep	Northampton Town (Carling Cup 3rd)	H	2-2**	22,577
	Sat 25 Sep	Sunderland	H	2-2	43,626
Oct	Thu 30 Sep	Utrecht (Europa League match 2)	A	0-0	23,662
	Sun 03 Oct	Blackpool	H	1-2	43,156
	Sun 17 Oct	Everton	A	0-2	39,673
	Thu 21 Oct	Napoli (Europa League match 3)	A	0-0	55,489
	Sun 24 Oct	Blackburn Rovers	H	2-1	43,328
	Sun 31 Oct	Bolton Wanderers	A	1-0	25,171
Nov	Thu 04 Nov	Napoli (E League match 4)	H	3-1	33,895
	Sun 07 Nov	Chelsea	H	2-0	44,238
	Wed 10 Nov	Wigan Athletic	A	1-1	16,754
	Sat 13 Nov	Stoke City	A	0-2	27,286
	Sat 20 Nov	West Ham United	H	3-0	43,024
	Sun 28 Nov	Tottenham Hotspur	A	1-2	35,962
Dec	Thu 02 Dec	Steaua Bucharest (E Lge match 5)	A	1-1	20,000
	Mon 06 Dec	Aston Villa	H	3-0	39,079
	Sat 11 Dec	Newcastle United	A	1-3	50,137
	Wed 15 Dec	Utrecht (E League match 6)	H	0-0	37,800
Jan	Wed 29 Dec	Wolverhampton Wanderers	H	0-1	41,614
	Sat 01 Jan	Bolton Wanderers	H	2-1	35,400
	Wed 05 Jan	Blackburn Rovers	A	1-3	24,522
	Sun 09 Jan	Manchester Utd (FA Cup 3rd)	A	0-1	74,727
	Wed 12 Jan	Blackpool	A	1-2	16,089
	Sun 16 Jan	Everton	H	2-2	44,795
	Sat 22 Jan	Wolverhampton Wanderers	A	3-0	28,869
Feb	Wed 26 Jan	Fulham	H	1-0^	40,466
	Wed 02 Feb	Stoke City	H	2-0	40,254
	Sun 06 Feb	Chelsea	A	1-0	41,829
	Sat 12 Feb	Wigan Athletic	H	1-1	44,609
	Thu 17 Feb	Sparta Prague (EL last 32 1st leg)	A	0-0	17,564
	Thu 24 Feb	Sparta Prague (EL last 32 2nd leg)	H	1-0	42,949
Mar	Sun 27 Feb	West Ham United	A	1-3	34,941
	Sun 06 Mar	Manchester United	H	3-1	44,753
	Thu 10 Mar	SC Braga (EL last 16 1st leg)	A	0-1	12,991
	Thu 17 Mar	SC Braga (EL last 16 2nd leg)	H	0-0	37,494
Apr	Sun 20 Mar	Sunderland	A	2-0	47,207
	Sat 02 Apr	West Bromwich Albion	A	1-2	26,196
	Mon 11 Apr	Manchester City	H	3-0	44,776
	Sun 17 Apr	Arsenal	A	1-1	60,029
May	Sat 23 Apr	Birmingham City	H	5-0	44,734
	Sun 01 May	Newcastle United	H	3-0	44,923
	Mon 09 May	Fulham	A	5-2	25,693
	Sun 15 May	Tottenham Hotspur	H	0-2	44,893
	Sun 22 May	Aston Villa	A	0-1	42,785

• Liverpool's score is always shown first

* Own Goal v Trabzonspor (Kacar)
** aet, lost 4-2 on penalties
^ Own Goal v Fulham (Pantsil)

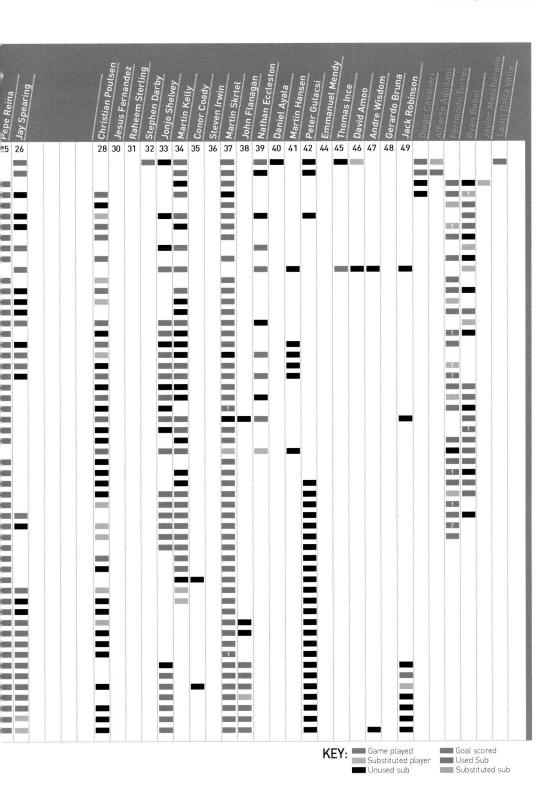

KEY:
- Game played
- Substituted player
- Unused sub
- Goal scored
- Used Sub
- Substituted sub

SIX OF THE BEST

Maxi goal machine

Although Maxi Rodriguez has been a regular fixture in and around the first team, nobody could have predicted the Argentine's late season run of seven goals in three games – including magnificent hat-tricks against Birmingham City (below) and Fulham.

Reds give Chelsea the Blues

Deserving 2-0 victors at Anfield earlier in the campaign, Liverpool travelled to Stamford Bridge in February with few fancying them to spoil Fernando Torres' Chelsea debut. But Raul Meireles' second-half goal ensured a deserved success.

4

Dirk 3 United 1

Or the 'seven-yard hat-trick' as it will become known, as the Dutch forward showed his close-range predatory instincts to see off Sir Alex Ferguson's side at Anfield back in March.

3

Cally...then Carra

Having enjoyed a deserved testimonial against Everton in September 2010, Jamie Carragher climbed up to second in the club's all-time appearances list – behind Ian Callaghan – when making his 663rd first-team appearance at Fulham in May.

2

Super Suarez

Although Andy Carroll's signing gained more of the headlines, the January purchase of Luis Suarez proved key in the Reds' improved form in the second half of the season. Amongst his highlights was this stunning match-clincher at Sunderland.

The return of the King

Following Roy Hodgson's departure, the supporters' chants were answered when a legend returned to steady the ship and help reignite the club. Kenny Dalglish stepped up to take charge of the first team in January, landing the job on a permanent basis in May.

PLAYER STATISTICS 2010/2011

PLAYER	PLAYED	SUBBED	SUB UNUSED	MINS PLAYED	GOALS
Cavalieri	2	0	2	180	0
Johnson	35	1	2	3068	2
Konchesky	18	5	1	1496	0
Meireles	40+1	19	1	3232	5
Aquilani	1+1	1	0	111	0
Agger	17+4	5	1	1546	0
Aurelio	13+8	5	5	1065	0
Suarez	12+1	3	1	1102	4
Gerrard	22+2	1	0	2008	8
Carroll	6+3	4	0	570	2
Torres	24+2	6	1	2107	9
Cole	19+13	9	6	1722	3
Pacheco	3+4	2	11	341	0
Jovanovic	13+5	8	13	1083	2
Kyrgiakos	20+8	2	20	2099	2
Rodriquez	29+6	17	12	2459	10
Kuyt	39+2	8	0	3468	15
Babel	7+10	4	8	708	2
Mascherano	1	1	0	78	0
Lucas	43+4	3	3	3883	1
Wilson	7+1	0	15	726	0
Carragher	37+1	3	2	3299	0
Ngog	18+20	10	11	1938	8
Reina	50	0	0	4500	0
Spearing	16+4	2	11	1425	0
Poulsen	18+3	8	21	1469	0
Darby	0+1	0	0	18	0
Shelvey	4+17	0	8	735	0
Kelly	22+1	2	13	1925	0
Coady	0	0	2	0	0
Skrtel	46+3	1	3	4108	2
Dalla Valle	0+1	0	0	7	0
Flanagan	7	1	3	621	0
Eccleston	1+6	1	4	141	0
Ayala	0	0	1	0	0
Hansen	0	0	6	0	0
Gulacsi	0	0	27	0	0
Ince	0+1	0	1	15	0
Amoo	1	1	1	83	0
Wisdom	0	0	2	0	0
Robinson	1+1	1	7	147	0

FINAL LEAGUE TABLE 2010/11

	Team	Pd	HOME					AWAY					Pts	GD
			W	D	L	F	A	W	D	L	F	A		
1	Man Utd	38	18	1	0	49	12	5	10	4	29	25	80	+41
2	Chelsea	38	14	3	2	39	13	7	5	7	30	20	71	+36
3	Man City	38	13	4	2	34	12	8	4	7	26	21	71	+27
4	Arsenal	38	11	4	4	33	15	8	7	4	39	28	68	+29
5	Tottenham	38	9	9	1	30	19	7	5	7	25	27	62	+9
6	**Liverpool**	**38**	**12**	**4**	**3**	**37**	**14**	**5**	**3**	**11**	**22**	**30**	**58**	**+15**
7	Everton	38	9	7	3	31	23	4	8	7	20	22	54	+6
8	Fulham	38	8	7	4	30	23	3	9	7	19	20	49	+6
9	Aston Villa	38	8	7	4	26	19	4	5	10	22	40	48	-11
10	Sunderland	38	7	5	7	25	27	5	6	8	20	29	47	-11
11	West Brom	38	8	6	5	30	30	4	5	10	26	41	47	-15
12	Newcastle	38	6	8	5	41	27	5	5	9	15	30	46	-1
13	Stoke City	38	10	4	5	31	18	3	3	13	15	30	46	-2
14	Bolton	38	10	5	4	34	24	2	5	12	18	32	46	-4
15	Blackburn	38	7	7	5	22	16	4	3	12	24	43	43	-13
16	Wigan	38	5	8	6	22	34	4	7	8	18	27	42	-21
17	Wolves	38	8	4	7	30	30	3	3	13	16	36	40	-20
18	Birmingham	38	6	8	5	19	22	2	7	10	18	36	39	-21
19	Blackpool	38	5	5	9	30	37	5	4	10	25	41	39	-23
20	West Ham	38	5	5	9	24	31	2	7	10	19	39	33	-27

Pepe Reina (above, most minutes) and Dirk Kuyt (below, top scorer) in 2010/11

APPEARANCES & GOALS FOR LIVERPOOL

AT END OF 2010/11 – SORTED BY SQUAD NUMBER ORDER (AT START OF 2011/12)

PLAYER	LGE GMS	LGE GLS	FA GMS	FA GLS	L. CUP GMS	L. CUP GLS	EURO GMS	EURO GLS	OTHER GMS	OTHER GLS	LFC GMS	LFC GLS
Jones	0	0	0	0	1	0	1	0	0	0	2	0
Johnson	53	5	0	0	1	0	16	0	0	0	70	5
Aquilani	18	1	2	0	1	0	7	1	0	0	28	2
Agger	93	3	4	0	5	2	33	2	1	0	136	7
Aurelio	85	3	5	0	5	0	35	1	1	0	131	4
Suarez	13	4	0	0	0	0	0	0	0	0	13	4
Gerrard	387	84	29	10	20	7	116	38	4	1	556	140
Carroll	7	2	0	0	0	0	2	0	0	0	9	2
Cole	20	2	0	0	0	0	12	1	0	0	32	3
Pacheco	5	0	0	0	1	0	8	0	0	0	14	0
Rodriguez	45	11	1	0	0	0	6	0	0	0	52	11
Kuyt	174	49	10	2	3	0	54	15	0	0	241	66
Lucas	111	1	9	1	6	1	42	3	0	0	168	6
Wilson	2	0	0	0	1	0	5	0	0	0	8	0
Carragher	463	4	34	0	28	0	139	1	4	0	668	5
Reina	220	0	9	0	1	0	76	0	3	0	309	0
Spearing	14	0	0	0	3	0	10	0	0	0	27	0
Darby	1	0	1	0	1	0	3	0	0	0	6	0
Shelvey	15	0	1	0	1	0	4	0	0	0	21	0
Kelly	12	0	1	0	1	0	13	0	0	0	27	0
Skrtel	92	3	6	0	2	0	28	0	0	0	128	3
Flanagan	7	0	0	0	0	0	0	0	0	0	7	0
Eccleston	2	0	0	0	2	0	5	0	0	0	9	0
Amoo	0	0	0	0	0	0	1	0	0	0	1	0
Robinson	3	0	0	0	0	0	0	0	0	0	3	0

LFC MAGAZINE AWARDS
2010/11

Player of the season: Luis Suarez

Steven Gerrard received LFC Magazine most man-of-the-match votes, eight compared to Lucas and Luis Suarez's five apiece, but it was the Uruguayan who made such a big imact in the second half of the season with his goals and creativity.

Young player of the season: Martin Kelly

With honourable mention to midfielder Jay Spearing, Kelly impressed on the right-hand side of defence, starting Kenny Dalglish's first 11 games as caretaker-boss before injury ended his campaign.

Goal of the season: Dirk Kuyt (first goal) v Manchester United

Although the eventual finish was a simple tap-in, it was the approach work from Luis Suarez, beating three defenders before squaring for the Dutch forward, which earned the LFC Magazine writers' vote.

RESERVES 2010/11

SEASON REVIEW

The reserves endured an inconsistent campaign, despite finishing third in their mini regional league. The chopping and changing in team selection could be attributed to some of the poor results as 51 players were used in the league plus the additional four games in the Liverpool and Lanashire Senior Cup competitions. However, there was progression to the first team for a number of reserve players, including Jon Flanagan. Jack Robinson, who made his first-team debut at the age of 16 at the end of 2009/10, also made his second XI bow.

RES. LGE & CUP APPS. & GOALS 2010/11

	Appearances	Goals
Krisztian Adorjan	1	0
David Amoo	12	4
Fabio Aurelio	1	0
Ryan Babel	1	0
Jason Banton	2	0
Tyrell Belford	1	0
Dean Bouzanis	2	0
Gerardo Bruna	11	4
Deale Chamberlain	2	0
Conor Coady	3	0
Joe Cole	2	0
Alex Cooper	8	0
Stephen Darby	9	0
Nathan Eccleston	8	4
Jon Flanagan	12	0
Peter Gulacsi	3	0
Adam Hajdu	1	0
Martin Hansen	12	0
Thomas Ince	17	2
Steven Irwin	19	0
Brad Jones	3	0
Tom King	2	0
Nicolaj Kohlert	3	0
Chris Mavinga	4	0
Emmanuel Mendy	15	0
Matty McGiveron	2	0
Emmanuel Mendy	14	1
Adam Morgan	1	1
Henoc John Mukendi	1	0
David Ngog	2	0
Michael Ngoo	4	0
Daniel Pacheco	10	3
Victor Palsson	5	0
Christian Poulsen	1	0
Patrick Poor	1	0
Matt Regan	4	0
Michael Roberts	14	0
Jack Robinson	11	0
Craig Roddan	1	0
Stephen Sama	3	0

RES. LGE & CUP APPS. & GOALS 2010/11

	Appearances	Goals
Nikola Saric	10	2
Jonjo Shelvey	5	1
Toni Silva	8	2
Jakub Sokolik	4	0
Jay Spearing	5	0
Jamie Stephens	1	0
Suso	19	3
Conor Thomas	8	0
Tom Walsh	2	0
Danny Wilson	7	1
Andre Wisdom	11	0

RESERVES LEAGUE RESULTS 2010/11

			Result
01.09.10	Wigan Athletic	H	0-0
07.09.10	Newcastle United	A	2-2
14.09.10	Wolverhampton W.	H	2-0
27.09.10	Chelsea	A	1-3
05.10.10	West Ham United	H	0-1
19.10.10	Blackburn Rovers	A	3-3
02.11.10	Sunderland	A	2-1
16.11.10	Blackpool	H	1-1
23.11.10	Everton	A	1-1
11.01.11	Sunderland	H	2-1
28.02.11	Blackburn Rovers	H	2-0
03.03.11	Blackpool	A	1-1
08.03.11	West Bromwich Alb,	H	1-1
16.03.11	Arsenal	A	1-2
24.03.11	Everton	H	2-2
04.04.11	Aston Villa	A	1-3
12.04.11	Bolton Wanderers	H	1-0
18.04.11	Manchester City	A	0-1
05.05.11	Manchester United	H	2-2

RESERVES LEAGUE NORTH GROUP B TABLE 2010/11

		Pld	W	D	L	F	A	Pts
1	Blackburn	19	7	5	7	39	38	26
2	Sunderland	19	6	6	7	29	27	24
3	**Liverpool**	**19**	**5**	**8**	**6**	**25**	**26**	**23**
4	Everton	19	4	3	12	23	34	15
5	Blackpool	19	4	2	13	23	49	14

RESERVES/ACADEMY CUP RESULTS 2010/11

LIVERPOOL IN THE LIVERPOOL SENIOR CUP 2010/11

Quarter-final

1st February 2011
Prescot Cables 1-2 Liverpool   (Valerie Park)

Liverpool goalscorers: Bruna (11, pen), Ince (23)

Team: Bouzanis, Flanagan, Cooper, Roberts, Sokolik, Regan, Ince, Kohlert (Walsh), Saric, Bruna, Banton.

Semi-final

20th May 2011
Liverpool 1-4 Everton   (Liverpool Academy)

Liverpool goalscorer: Amoo (18)

Team: Chamberlain, Darby, Irwin, Roberts, Wilson, Mendy, Amoo, Kohlert (Sokolik), Eccleston, Suso, Ince.

LIVERPOOL IN THE LANCASHIRE SENIOR CUP 2010/11

Quarter-final

19th January 2011
Manchester City 0-1 Liverpool   (Hyde Park)

Liverpool goalscorer: Bruna (33)

Team: Gulacsi, Flanagan, Robinson, Darby, Wilson (Mendy), Roberts, Pacheco, Bruna, Ince, Cole (Amoo 46, Banton 78), Saric.

Semi-final

30th March 2011
Preston North End 1-1 Liverpool   (Deepdale)
Preston North End win 5-4 on penalties

Liverpool goalscorer: Silva (19)

Team: Hansen, Flanagan, Cooper, Mendy, McGiveron, Thomas, Suso, Roberts, Silva, Irwin, Hajdu (Mukendi).

LIVERPOOL IN THE FA YOUTH CUP 2010/11

Round 3

15th December 2010
Notts County 0-4 Liverpool   (Meadow Lane)

Liverpool goalscorers: Adorjan (9), Ngoo (47, s/h), Stirling (67)

Team: Belford, Flanagan, Robinson, Sama, McGiveron, Coady, Roddan (Aylmer), Suso, Sterling (Morgan), Ngoo, Adorjan (Silva).

Round 4

8th January 2011
Liverpool 3-1 Crystal Palace (aet)   (Anfield)

Liverpool goalscorers: Emilsson (54, 103), Coady (118, pen)

Team: Belford, Flanagan, Robinson, Sama, McGiveron, Coady, Sterling, Roddan, Morgan (Emilsson), Adorjan (Silva), Suso.

Round 5

14th February 2011
Liverpool 9-0 Southend United   (Anfield)

Liverpool goalscorers: Sterling (18, 21, 35, 56, 85), Coady (24), Sama (37), Morgan (45), Silva (90)

Team: Belford, Flanagan, Robinson, Sama, McGiveron, Coady, Sterling, Roddan, Morgan (Sumner), Adorjan (Silva), Suso (Banton).

Quarter-final

13th March 2011
Liverpool 2-3 Manchester United   (Anfield)

Liverpool goalscorers: Morgan (35, 53)

Team: Belford, Flanagan, Sama, Wisdom, Smith, Coady, Roddan (McGiveron), Sterling, Suso (Ngoo), Adorjan, Morgan (Silva).

THE ACADEMY 2010/11

SEASON REVIEW

The Under-18s were pipped to the league title, with a 2-2 draw on the final day condemning the young Reds to runners-up in Group C. The disappointment was more stark considering the side averaged towards three goals a game, the total of 73 by far the best in the division. Adam Morgan, one of six Liverpool players in England Under-17s World Cup squad in 2011, finished with a better than goal-a-game average (the statistics include FA Youth Cup matches), while Matty McGiveron, Jamie Stephens and Matt Regan were among players who stepped up to the reserves in 2010/11.

U18s APPEARANCES & GOALS 2010/11

	Appearances	Goals
Krisztian Adorjan	27	9
Peter Aylmer	4	0
Jason Banton	3	0
Tyrell Belford	18	0
Karl Clair	2	0
Conor Coady	28	9
Alex Cooper	1	0
Jack Dunn	2	0
Kristjan Gauti Emilsson	7	3
Jon Flanagan	7	0
Adam Hajdu	3	0
Lewis Hatch	2	0
Thomas Ince	1	0
Tom King	2	0
Matty McGiveron	29	0
Adam Morgan	20	21
Henoc John Mukendi	9	2
Michael Ngoo	21	15

U18s APPEARANCES & GOALS 2010/11

	Appearances	Goals
Kristoffer Peterson	1	0
Patrick Poor	12	0
Joe Rafferty	11	0
Matt Regan	11	2
Michael Roberts	6	0
Jack Robinson	3	0
Chris Roddan	29	1
Stephen Sama	32	2
Toni Silva	29	10
Brad Smith	23	1
Jamie Stephens	14	0
Raheem Sterling	24	13
Josh Sumner	8	0
Suso	5	0
Conor Thomas	1	0
Tom Walsh	13	1
Andre Wisdom	3	0

U18s LEAGUE & YOUTH CUP RESULTS 10/11

			Result
21.08.10	Aston Villa	A	2-2
28.08.10	Bristol City	H	3-0
04.09.10	Sunderland	A	2-2
11.09.10	Derby County	H	3-2
18.09.10	Leeds United	A	2-0
25.09.10	Stoke City	A	0-1
02.10.10	Crewe Alexandra	H	4-2
09.10.10	Blackburn Rovers	A	2-3
16.10.10	West Bromwich Albion	H	2-4
06.11.10	Bolton Wanderers	A	6-0
13.11.10	Everton	H	1-1
20.11.10	Manchester City	A	2-2
15.12.10	Notts County (FAYC3)	A	4-0
08.01.11	Crystal Palace (FAYC4)	H	3-1
15.01.11	Bolton Wanderers	H	3-1
05.02.11	Manchester City	H	2-1
14.02.11	Southend Utd (FAYC5)	H	9-0
19.02.11	Stoke City	H	4-1
23.02.11	Huddersfield Town	H	4-1
26.02.11	Crewe Alexandra	A	2-1
05.03.11	Blackburn Rovers	H	5-1
13.03.11	Man Utd (FAYC6)	H	2-3
19.03.11	Newcastle United	A	2-1
26.03.11	Nottingham Forest	H	2-4

U18s LEAGUE & YOUTH CUP RESULTS 10/11

			Result
04.04.11	Manchester United	A	2-1
09.04.11	Sheffield Wednesday	H	3-0
16.04.11	Manchester United	H	6-0
20.04.11	West Bromwich Albion	A	2-0
26.04.11	Everton	A	0-4
30.04.11	Sheffield United	A	1-1
03.05.11	Wolverhampton Wan.	A	4-0
06.05.11	Wolverhampton Wan.	H	2-2

FA PREMIER ACADEMY 2010/11 GROUP C

	P	W	D	L	F	A	Pts
1 Everton	28	17	7	4	55	30	58
2 Liverpool	28	17	6	5	73	38	57
3 Man City	28	14	10	4	50	41	52
4 Bolton W.	28	14	4	10	43	39	46
5 Man Utd	28	13	5	10	63	50	44
6 West Brom	28	11	8	9	60	55	41
7 Wolves	28	11	5	12	51	50	38
8 Blackburn	28	10	6	12	56	55	36
9 Crewe Alex.	28	11	3	14	62	67	36
10 Stoke City	28	5	3	20	27	58	18

LIVERPOOL LADIES 2011

SEASON REVIEW

Robbie Johnson's side were one of eight teams who began the inaugural Super League season. The league, which is also due to operate on a closed basis in 2012 before it is ingratiated into the pyramid system, received national publicity for the launch. The Reds' first league game ended with a dramatic 3-3 draw with Everton, and by then the team had reached the FA Cup semi-final, with Ruesha Littlejohn's hat-trick against Charlton a highlight of the run. Unfortunately, the Reds suffered a 3-0 defeat to Bristol Academy at Southport FC.

With England competing at the World Cup in Germany, in which they reached the quarter-finals, the mid-season break saw the side without a league win. It wasn't until the third-to-last game that the drought was broken, with Chloe Jones netting the winner at Chelsea. The side will be aiming to improve in 2012, with the season due to start in March/April. Most home games are played at Skelmersdale United FC, and for more on the team, log on to **www.liverpoolladiesfc.co.uk**

2011 STATISTICS

LADIES LEAGUE & CUP RESULTS 2011

			Result
13.03.11	Charlton Athletic (FAC)	H	5-0
27.03.11	Doncaster RB (FAC)	H	3-0
14.04.11	Everton	H	3-3
17.04.11	Bristol Academy (FAC)	H	0-3
20.04.11	Birmingham City	H	0-4
23.04.11	Bristol Academy	A	1-1
01.05.11	Chelsea	H	1-2
04.05.11	Doncaster Rovers Belles	A	0-1
08.05.11	Lincoln	H	0-1
12.05.11	Birmingham City	A	0-0
24.07.11	Arsenal	A	0-3
27.07.11	Everton	A	0-1
31.07.11	Bristol Academy	H	0-2
03.08.11	Doncaster Rovers Belles	H	1-1
07.08.11	Chelsea	A	1-0
14.08.11	Lincoln	A	2-4
28.08.11	Arsenal	H	1-3
04.09.11	Arsenal (CC)	H	0-4

FA WOMEN'S SUPER LEAGUE 2011

	P	W	D	L	F	A	Pts
1 Arsenal	14	10	2	2	29	9	32
2 Birmingham	14	8	5	1	29	13	29
3 Everton	14	7	4	3	19	13	25
4 Lincoln	14	6	3	5	18	16	21
5 Bristol	14	4	4	6	14	20	16
6 Chelsea	14	4	3	7	14	19	15
7 Doncaster	14	2	3	9	9	26	9
8 Liverpool	**14**	**1**	**4**	**9**	**10**	**26**	**7**

LADIES LEAGUE APPS & GOALS 2011

	Appearances	Goals
Elizabeth Bailey	3	0
Carmel Bennett	5	0
Katie Brusell	15	2
Samantha Chappell	15	0
Caroline Charlton	4	0
Michelle Evans	14	1
Cheryl Foster	14	1
Danielle Gibbons	10	0
Nicki Harding	12	2
Chloe Jones	8	1
Emma Jones	3	0
Kelly Jones	15	1
Vicky Jones	15	0
Suzanne Lappin	9	0
Ruesha Littlejohn	11	1
Natalie Sage	1	0
Lynda Shepherd	14	0
Jo Traynor	1	0
Nicola Twohig	14	1
Gemma Watson	10	0
Andrea Worrall	6	0

Liverpool Ladies' skipper Vicky Jones

FK RABOTNICKI   0
LIVERPOOL FC   2

UEFA Europa League
Third qualifying round, first leg
Skopje City Stadium, Skopje
Thursday July 29, 2010.
Attendance: 23,000

Goals: Ngog (17, 59)
Bookings: None
Referee: Antonio Damato (Italy)
Possession: FK Rabotnicki **43%**, Liverpool **57%**
Shots on (off) target: FK Rabotnicki **4 (3)**,
Liverpool **3 (4)**

Team line-ups

FK Rabotnicki (4-4-2):

Da Silva   Dos Santos

Filho   Todorovski   Gligorov   Tunevski

Sekulovski   Belica   Lopes   Dimovski

Bogatinov

Subs: Adem (Sekulovski) 43, Mojsov (Filho) 57,
Petkovski (Tuneski) 77
Subs not used: Kandikijan, Roberto Carlos,
Marcio, Sinkovic

Liverpool (4-4-1-1):

Ngog

Aquilani

Jovanovic   Lucas   Spearing   Amoo

Agger   Skrtel   Kyrgiakos   Kelly

Cavalieri

Subs: Darby (Agger) 72, Eccleston (Amoo) 83,
Dalla Valle (Aquilani) 83
Subs not used: Gulacsi, Ayala, Shelvey, Ince

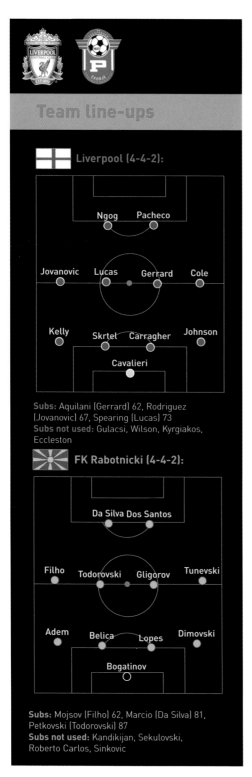

Team line-ups

Liverpool (4-4-2):

Ngog   Pacheco

Jovanovic   Lucas   Gerrard   Cole

Kelly   Skrtel   Carragher   Johnson

Cavalieri

Subs: Aquilani (Gerrard) 62, Rodriguez
(Jovanovic) 67, Spearing (Lucas) 73
Subs not used: Gulacsi, Wilson, Kyrgiakos,
Eccleston

FK Rabotnicki (4-4-2):

Da Silva Dos Santos

Filho   Todorovski   Gligorov   Tunevski

Adem   Belica   Lopes   Dimovski

Bogatinov

Subs: Mojsov (Filho) 62, Marcio (Da Silva) 81,
Petkovski (Todorovski) 87
Subs not used: Kandikijan, Sekulovski,
Roberto Carlos, Sinkovic

LIVERPOOL FC   2
FK RABOTNICKI   0

UEFA Europa League
Third qualifying round, second leg
Anfield, Liverpool
Thursday August 5, 2010.
Attendance: 31,202

Goals: Ngog (22), Gerrard (40, pen)
Bookings: Filho, Mojsov (Rabotnicki Skopje)
Referee: Peter Sippel (Germany)
Possession: Liverpool 66%, FK Rabotnicki 34%
Shots on (off) target: Liverpool 13 (10),
FK Rabotnicki 2 (5)

Team line-ups

Liverpool (4-4-1-1):

Babel

Cole

Jovanovic   Poulsen   Lucas   Rodriguez

Aurelio   Kyrgiakos   Carragher   Kelly

Reina

Subs: Torres (Babel) 46, Ngog (Rodriguez) 73
Subs not used: Cavalieri, Skrtel, Wilson,
Spearing, Pacheco

Trabzonspor (4-4-2):

Gutierrez   Bulut

Colman   Inan   Yilmaz   Balci

Gulselam   Cale   Korkmaz   Glowacki

Kivrak

Subs: Alanzinho (Yilmaz) 56,
Kacar (Colman) 77, Yattara (Bulut) 86
Subs not used: Zengin, Atas, Badur, Jaja

LIVERPOOL FC   1
TRABZONSPOR   0

UEFA Europa League
Play-off, first leg
Anfield, Liverpool
Thursday August 19, 2010.
Attendance: 40,941

Goal: Babel (45)
Bookings: Cale, Gulselam, Korkmaz, Balci
(Trabzonspor)
Referee: Thomas Einwaller (Austria)
Possession: Liverpool 53%, Trabzonspor 47%
Shots on (off) target: Liverpool 8 (6),
Trabzonspor 4 (5)

Team line-ups

Trabzonspor (4-2-1):

Gutierrez Yattara

Colman Inan Yilmaz Balci

Gulselam Cale Korkmaz Kacar

Kivrak

Subs: Alanzinho (Yattara) 46, Atas (Gulselam) 65, Jaja (Cale) 86
Subs not used: Zengin, Baytar, Badur, Oztorun

Liverpool (4-4-2):

Ngog Kuyt

Cole Poulsen Lucas Johnson

Aurelio Kyrgiakos Carragher Kelly

Reina

Subs: Pacheco (Aurelio) 77, Babel (Ngog) 86, Skrtel (Kuyt) 90
Subs not used: Gulacsi, Spearing, Shelvey, Eccleston

TRABZONSPOR 1
LIVERPOOL FC 2

UEFA Europa League
Play-off, second leg
Huseyin Avni Aker Stadium, Trabzon
Thursday August 26, 2010.
Attendance: 21,065

Goals: Gutierrez (4), Kacar (83, o.g.), Kuyt (88)
Bookings: Gulselam, Yilmaz, Korkmaz (Trabzonspor)
Referee: Ivan Bebek (Croatia)
Possession: Trabzonspor 52%, Liverpool 48%
Shots on (off) target: Trabzonspor 5 (3), Liverpool 4 (6)

LIVERPOOL FC 4
STEAUA BUCHAREST 1

Team line-ups

Liverpool (4-2-3-1)

Ngog

Babel   Cole   Rodriguez

Spearing ● Meireles

Konchesky   Kelly
Agger   Kyrgiakos

Reina

Subs: Lucas (Babel) 78, Pacheco (Rodriguez) 85, Eccleston (Cole) 88
Subs not used: Jones, Johnson, Carragher, Shelvey

Steaua Bucharest (4-4-1-1)

Kapetanos

Stancu

Tanase   Bicfalvi   Angelov   Radut

Latovlevici   Emeghara
      Alves   Abrudan

Tatarusanu

Subs: Nicolita (Emeghara) 20, Bonfim (Angelov) 52, Surdu (Radut) 73
Subs not used: Lungu, Gardos, Gomes, Apostol

UEFA Europa League
Group K game 1
Anfield, Liverpool
Thursday September 16, 2010.
Attendance: 25,605

Goals: Cole (1), Tanase (13), Ngog (56 pen, 90) Lucas (81)
Bookings: Rodriguez (Liverpool), Abrudan, Eder, Kapetanos (Steaua Bucharest)
Referee: Cesar Muniz Fernandez (Spain)
Possession: Liverpool 52%, Steaua Bucharest 48%
Shots on (off) target: Liverpool 11 (5), Steaua Bucharest 3 (1)

Team line-ups

Steaua Bucharest (4-4-2):

Surdu Stancu

Tanase Bicfalvi Ricardo Nicolita

Latovlevici Geraldo Gardos Bonfim

Tatarusanu

Subs: Angelov (Bicfalvi) 46, Szekely (Surdu) 80
Subs not used: Lungu, Emeghara, Abrudan, Martinovic, Matei

Liverpool (4-2-3-1):

Babel

Jovanovic Cole Pacheco

Poulsen Shelvey

Aurelio Wilson Kyrgiakos Kelly

Reina

Subs: Ngog (Cole) 75, Eccleston (Jovanovic) 78, Lucas (Pacheco) 89
Subs not used: Jones, Skrtel, Flanagan, Robinson

STEAUA BUCHAREST 1
LIVERPOOL FC   1

UEFA Europa League
Group K game 5
Steaua Stadium, Bucharest
Thursday December 2, 2010.
Attendance: 20,000

Goals: Jovanovic (19), Eder (61)
Bookings: Eder, Nicolita, Surdu (Steaua Bucharest)
Referee: Bulent Yildirim (Turkey)
Possession: Steaua Bucharest 60%, Liverpool 40%
Shots on (off) target: Steaua Bucharest 3 (7), Liverpool 1 (2)

Team line-ups

FC Utrecht (4-3-3)

Mulenga
Van Wolfswinkel
Duplan

Mertens
Lensky
Silberbauer

Nesu
Cornelisse
Wuytens
Schut

Vorm

Subs: Maguire (Duplan) 69, Nijholt (Lensky) 82.
Subs not used: Sinouh, Keller, Vorstermams,
Van Der Maarel, Demouge

Liverpool (4-4-1-1)

Torres
Kuyt

Cole
Lucas
Poulsen
Meireles

Kelly
Skrtel
Carragher
Johnson

Reina

Sub: Rodriguez (Cole) 81
Subs not used: Jones, Kyrgiakos, Spearing,
Jovanovic, Babel, Ngog

FC UTRECHT   0
LIVERPOOL FC   0

UEFA Europa League
Group K game 2
Stadion Galgenwaard, Utrecht
Thursday September 30, 2010.
Attendance: 23,662

Bookings: Kelly, Meireles, Lucas (Liverpool)
Referee: Duarte Gomes (Portugal)
Possession: FC Utrecht 58%, Liverpool 42%
Shots on (off) target: FC Utrecht 3 (7),
Liverpool 5 (5)

LIVERPOOL FC 0
FC UTRECHT 0

UEFA Europa League
Group K game 6
Anfield, Liverpool
Wednesday December 15, 2010.
Attendance: 37,800

Booking: Eccleston (Liverpool)
Referee: Kristinn Jakobsson (Iceland)
Possession: Liverpool 44%, FC Utrecht 56%
Shots on (off) target: Liverpool 6 (3),
FC Utrecht 4 (3),

Team line-ups

Liverpool (4-4-2):

Eccleston Babel

Jovanovic Poulsen Shelvey Cole

Aurelio Wilson Skrtel Kelly

Jones

Subs: Kyrgiakos (Skrtel) 46, Pacheco
(Eccleston) 56, Kuyt (Jovanovic) 73
Subs not used: Hansen, Johnson, Meireles,
Torres

FC Utrecht (4-4-1-1):

Van Wolfswinkel

Maguire

Mertens Nijholt Silberbauer Duplan

Nesu Wuytens Keller Cornelisse

Vorm

Subs: De Kogel (Van Wolfswinkel) 45, Oar
(Duplan) 71, Adam Sarota (Maguire) 84
Subs not used: Cummings, Vorstermams, Van
der Maarel

Team line-ups

Napoli (3-4-2-1)

Cavani

Lavezzi   Hamsik

Gargano   Pazienza

Dossena   Maggio

Aronica   Cannavaro   Campagnaro

De Sanctis

Subs: Zuniga (Maggio) 75, Yebda (Gargano) 83, Sosa (Hamsik) 85
Subs not used: Iezzo, Grava, Cribari, Dumitru

Liverpool (4-2-3-1)

Ngog

Jovanovic   Shelvey   Babel

Poulsen   Spearing

Konchesky   Skrtel   Carragher   Kelly

Reina

Subs: Kyrgiakos (Carragher) 46, Aurelio (Konchesky) 65, Cole (Babel) 77
Subs not used: Jones, Wilson, Rodriguez, Eccleston

NAPOLI   0
LIVERPOOL FC   0

UEFA Europa League
Group K game 3
Stadio San Paolo, Naples
Thursday October 21, 2010.
Attendance: 55,489

Bookings: Pazienza (Napoli), Skrtel (Liverpool)
Referee: Thomas Kinhofer (Germany)
Possession: Napoli 51%, Liverpool 49%
Shots on (off) target: Napoli 3 (4),
Liverpool 5 (1)

LIVERPOOL FC 3
NAPOLI 1

UEFA Europa League
Group K game 4
Anfield, Liverpool
Thursday November 4, 2010.
Attendance: 33,895

Goals: Lavezzi (28), Gerrard (75, 88 pen, 89)
Bookings: Johnson, Kyrgiakos (Liverpool), De Sanctis, Dossena, Campagnaro, Cavani (Napoli)
Referee: Fredy Fautrel (France)
Possession: Liverpool 52%, Napoli 48%
Shots on (off) target: Liverpool 7 (8), Napoli 3 (4)

Team line-ups

Liverpool (4-2-3-1)

Ngog
Jovanovic Spearing Meireles
Poulsen Shelvey
Konchesky Kyrgiakos Carragher Johnson
Reina

Subs: Gerrard (Jovanovic) 46, Eccleston (Poulsen) 65, Lucas (Ngog) 82
Subs not used: Hansen, Wilson, Kelly, Skrtel

Napoli (3-4-2-1)

Cavani
Lavezzi Hamsik
Dossena Gargano Pazienza Maggio
Aronica Cannavaro Campagnaro
De Sanctis

Sub: Yebda (Hamsik) 84
Subs not used: Gianello, Grava, Santacroce, Zuniga, Sosa, Dumitru

Team line-ups

Sparta Prague (4-4-1-1)

Leonard Kweuke

Abena

Kadlec   Matejovsky   Vacek   Keric

Pamic   Brabec   Repka   Kusnir

Blazek

Subs: Sionko (Keric) 73, Zeman (Kadlec) 89, Pekhart (Matejovsky) 90
Subs not used: Zitka, Bondoa, Husek, Podany

Liverpool (4-2-3-1)

Ngog

Rodriguez   Meireles   Kuyt

Aurelio   Lucas

Wilson   Kyrgiakos   Carragher   Johnson

Reina

Subs: Cole (Aurelio) 38, Skrtel (Ngog) 84
Subs not used: Gulacsi, Kelly, Coady, Jovanovic, Pacheco

SPARTA PRAGUE   0
LIVERPOOL FC   0

UEFA Europa League
Round of 32, 1st Leg
Generali Arena, Prague
Thursday February 17, 2011.
Attendance: 17,564

Bookings: Repka (Sparta Prague), Ngog, Cole (Liverpool)
Referee: Florian Meyer (Germany)
Possession: Sparta Prague 50%, Liverpool 50%
Shots on (off) target: Sparta Prague 4 (9), Liverpool 0 (3)

Team line-ups

Liverpool (4-2-3-1)

Ngog

Cole   Meireles   Kuyt

Lucas   Poulsen

Wilson   Agger   Kyrgiakos   Kelly

Reina

Subs: Carragher (Kelly) 46, Spearing (Poulsen) 65, Skrtel (Agger) 85
Subs not used: Gulacsi, Rodriguez, Jovanovic, Pacheco

Sparta Prague (4-4-1-1)

Leonard Kweuke

Kadlec

Abena   Matejovsky   Vacek   Sionko

Pamic   Brabec   Repka   Kusnir

Blazek

Subs: Podany (Sionko) 73, Pekhart (Abena) 78, Keric (Pamic) 90
Subs not used: Zitka, Kladrubsky, Husek, Zeman

LIVERPOOL FC   1
SPARTA PRAGUE   0

UEFA Europa League
Round of 32, 2nd Leg
Anfield, Liverpool
Thursday February 24, 2011.
Attendance: 42,949

Goal: Kuyt (86)
Bookings: Kelly, Poulsen, Carragher, Lucas (Liverpool), Pamic, Matejovsky, Leonard Kweuke (Sparta Prague)
Referee: Milorad Mazic (Serbia)
Possession: Liverpool 48%, Sparta Prague 52%
Shots on (off) target: Liverpool 10 (11), Sparta Prague 4 (5)

Team line-ups

Braga (4-2-3-1)

Lima

Cesar   Mossoro   Alan

Viana   Salino

Silvio   Rodriguez   Kaka   Garcia

Artur

Subs: Paulao (Mossoro) 69, Meyong (Lima) 77,
Barbosa (Cesar) 90
Subs not used: Cristiano, Dani, Anibal,
Peterson

Liverpool (4-2-3-1)

Kuyt

Cole   Meireles   Spearing

Lucas   Poulsen

Johnson   Kyrgiakos   Skrtel   Carragher

Reina

Sub: Carroll (Poulsen) 57
Subs not used: Gulacsi, Wilson, Flanagan,
Rodriguez, Pacheco, Ngog

BRAGA   1
LIVERPOOL FC   0

**UEFA Europa League
Round of 16, 1st Leg
Estadio Municipal, Braga**
Thursday March 10, 2011.
Attendance: 12,991

Goal: Alan (18, pen)
Bookings: Kaka (Braga), Poulsen (Liverpool)
Referee: Serge Gumienny (Belgium)
Possession: Braga 50%, Liverpool 50%
Shots on (off) target: Braga 2 (3),
Liverpool 4 (2)

LIVERPOOL FC   0
BRAGA   0

Team line-ups

Liverpool (4-4-2)

Carroll   Kuyt

Cole   Rodriguez
    Lucas   Meireles

Wilson   Skrtel Carragher   Johnson

Reina

Subs: Ngog (Cole) 75, Spearing (Rodriguez) 76,
Subs not used: Gulacsi, Kyrgiakos, Flanagan,
Poulsen, Pacheco

Braga (4-5-1)

Lima

Alan
Cesar   Viana   Salino   Vandinho

Silvio   Rodriguez   Paulao   Garcia

Artur

Subs: Kaka (Vandinho) 73, Meyong (Lima) 84,
Mossoro (Salino) 89
Subs not used: Cristiano, Dani, Peterson,
Barbosa

**UEFA Europa League
Round of 16, 2nd Leg
Anfield, Liverpool**
Thursday March 17, 2011.
Attendance: 37,494

Bookings: Carroll, Skrtel, Meireles (Liverpool),
Paulao, Vandinho (Braga)
Referee: Gianluca Rocchi (Italy)
Possession: Liverpool 67%, Braga 33%
Shots on (off) target: Liverpool 5 (8),
Braga 4 (5)

EUROPEAN/WORLD ROLL OF HONOUR

EUROPEAN CHAMPIONS CUP/UEFA CHAMPIONS LEAGUE

WINNERS
1976/1977, 1977/1978, 1980/1981, 1983/1984, 2004/2005

RUNNERS-UP
1984/1985, 2006/2007

SEMI-FINALISTS
1964/1965, 2007/2008

INTER-CITIES FAIRS CUP/UEFA CUP/UEFA EUROPA LEAGUE

WINNERS
1972/1973, 1975/1976, 2000/2001

SEMI-FINALISTS
1970/1971, 2009/2010

EUROPEAN CUP-WINNERS' CUP/UEFA CUP-WINNERS' CUP

RUNNERS-UP
1965/1966

SEMI-FINALISTS
1996/1997

EUROPEAN SUPER CUP/UEFA SUPER CUP

WINNERS
1977, 2001, 2005

RUNNERS-UP
1978, 1985

INTERCONTINENTAL CUP/FIFA CLUB WORLD CUP

RUNNERS-UP
1981, 1984, 2005

LIVERPOOL FC RESULTS IN EUROPEAN COMPETITION

Season	Round	Venue	Opponents	Opponent Country	Score	Scorers	Att
1964/65	**EUROPEAN CHAMPIONS CUP**			**(WINNERS – INTER MILAN)**			
17th Aug	1 Leg 1	(a)	Reykjavik	Ice	5-0	Wallace 2, Hunt 2, Chisnall	10,000
14th Sept	1 Leg 2	(h)	Reykjavik	"	6-1	Byrne, St John 2, Hunt, Graham, Stevenson	32,957
25th Nov	2 Leg 1	(h)	Anderlecht	Bel	3-0	St John, Hunt, Yeats	44,516
16th Dec	2 Leg 2	(a)	Anderlecht	"	1-0	Hunt	60,000
10th Feb	3 Leg 1	(a)	FC Cologne	W.Ger	0-0		40,000
17th Mar	3 Leg 2	(h)	FC Cologne	"	0-0		48,432
24th Mar	Replay	Rotterdam	FC Cologne	"	2-2	St John, Hunt	45,000
			(Liverpool won on toss of a coin)				
4th May	SF Leg 1	(h)	Inter Milan	Ita	3-1	Hunt, Callaghan, St John	54,082
12th May	SF Leg 1	(a)	Inter Milan	"	0-3		90,000
1965/66	**EUROPEAN CUP-WINNERS' CUP**			**(WINNERS – BORUSSIA DORTMUND)**			
29th Sept	Pr Leg 1	(a)	Juventus	Ita	0-1		12,000
13th Oct	Pr Leg 2	(h)	Juventus	"	2-0	Lawler, Strong	51,055
1st Dec	1 Leg 1	(h)	Standard Liege	Bel	3-1	Lawler 2, Thompson	46,112
15th Dec	1 Leg 2	(a)	Standard Liege	"	2-1	Hunt, St John	35,000
1st Mar	2 Leg 1	(a)	Honved	Hun	0-0		20,000
8th Mar	2 Leg 2	(h)	Honved	"	2-0	Lawler, St John	54,631
14th Apr	SF Leg 1	(a)	Celtic	Sco	0-1		80,000
19th Apr	SF Leg 2	(h)	Celtic	"	2-0	Smith, Strong	54,208
5th May	Final	Glasgow	B. Dortmund	W.Ger	1-2 aet	Hunt	41,657
1966/67	**EUROPEAN CHAMPIONS CUP**			**(WINNERS – CELTIC)**			
28th Sept	Pr Leg 1	(h)	Petrolul Ploesti	Rom	2-0	St John, Callaghan	44,463
12th Oct	Pr Leg 2	(a)	Petrolul Ploesti	"	1-3	Hunt	20,000
19th Oct	Replay	Brussels	Petrolul Ploesti	"	2-0	St John, Thompson	15,000
7th Dec	1 Leg 1	(a)	Ajax Amsterdam	Hol	1-5	Lawler	65,000
14th Dec	1 Leg 2	(h)	Ajax Amsterdam	"	2-2	Hunt 2	53,846
1967/68	**INTER-CITIES FAIRS CUP**			**(WINNERS – LEEDS UNITED)**			
19th Sept	1 Leg 1	(a)	Malmo	Swe	2-0	Hateley 2	14,314
4th Oct	1 Leg 2	(h)	Malmo	"	2-1	Yeats, Hunt	39,795
7th Nov	2 Leg 1	(h)	TSV Munich 1860	W.Ger	8-0	St John, Hateley, Smith (pen) Hunt 2, Thompson, Callaghan 2	44,812
14th Nov	2 Leg 2	(a)	TSV Munich 1860	"	1-2	Callaghan	10,000
28th Nov	3 Leg 1	(a)	Ferencvaros	Hun	0-1		30,000
9th Jan	3 Leg 2	(h)	Ferencvaros	"	0-1		46,892
1968/69	**INTER-CITIES FAIRS CUP**			**(WINNERS – NEWCASTLE UNITED)**			
18th Sept	1 Leg 1	(a)	Athletic Bilbao	Spa	1-2	Hunt	35,000
2nd Oct	1 Leg 2	(h)	Athletic Bilbao	"	2-1 aet	Lawler, Hughes	49,567
			(Liverpool lost on toss of coin)				
1969/70	**INTER-CITIES FAIRS CUP**			**(WINNERS – ARSENAL)**			
16th Sept	1 Leg 1	(h)	Dundalk	Rep. Ire	10-0	Evans 2, Lawler, Smith 2, Graham 2, Lindsay, Thompson, Callaghan	32,562
30th Sept	1 Leg 2	(a)	Dundalk	"	4-0	Thompson 2, Graham, Callaghan	6,000
12th Nov	2 Leg 1	(a)	Vitoria Setubal	Por	0-1		16,000
26th Nov	2 Leg 2	(h)	Vitoria Setubal	"	3-2	Smith (pen), Evans, Hunt	41,633

LIVERPOOL FC RESULTS IN EUROPEAN COMPETITION

Season	Round	Venue	Opponents	Opponent Country	Score	Scorers	Att
1970/71	INTER-CITIES FAIRS CUP			(WINNERS – LEEDS UNITED)			
15th Sept	1 Leg 1	(h)	Ferencvaros	Hun	1-0	Graham	37,531
29th Sept	1 Leg 2	(a)	Ferencvaros	"	1-1	Hughes	25,000
21st Oct	2 Leg 1	(h)	D. Bucharest	Rom	3-0	Lindsay, Lawler, Hughes	36,525
4th Nov	2 Leg 2	(a)	D. Bucharest	"	1-1	Boersma	45,000
9th Dec	3 Leg 1	(a)	Hibernian	Sco	1-0	Toshack	30,296
22nd Dec	3 Leg 2	(h)	Hibernian	"	2-0	Heighway, Boersma	37,815
10th Mar	4 Leg 1	(h)	Bayern Munich	W.Ger	3-0	Evans 3	45,616
24th Mar	4 Leg 2	(a)	Bayern Munich	"	1-1	Ross	23,000
14th Apr	SF Leg 1	(h)	Leeds United	Eng	0-1		52,577
28th Apr	SF Leg 2	(a)	Leeds United	"	0-0		40,462
1971/72	EUROPEAN CUP-WINNERS' CUP			(WINNERS – RANGERS)			
15th Sept	1 Leg 1	(a)	Servette Geneva	Swi	1-2	Lawler	16,000
29th Sept	1 Leg 2	(h)	Servette Geneva	"	2-0	Hughes, Heighway	38,591
20th Oct	2 Leg 1	(h)	Bayern Munich	W.Ger	0-0		42,949
3rd Nov	2 Leg 2	(a)	Bayern Munich	"	1-3	Evans	40,000
1972/73	UEFA CUP			(WINNERS – LIVERPOOL)			
12th Sept	1 Leg 1	(h)	E. Frankfurt	W.Ger	2-0	Keegan, Hughes	33,380
26th Sept	1 Leg 2	(a)	E. Frankfurt	"	0-0		20,000
24th Oct	2 Leg 1	(h)	AEK Athens	Gre	3-0	Boersma, Cormack, Smith (pen)	31,906
7th Nov	2 Leg 2	(a)	AEK Athens	"	3-1	Hughes 2, Boersma	25,000
29th Nov	3 Leg 1	(a)	Dynamo Berlin	E.Ger	0-0		19,000
13th Dec	3 Leg 2	(h)	Dynamo Berlin	"	3-1	Boersma, Heighway, Toshack	34,140
7th Mar	4 Leg 1	(h)	Dynamo Dresden	E.Ger	2-0	Hall, Boersma	33,270
21st Mar	4 Leg 2	(a)	Dynamo Dresden	"	1-0	Keegan	35,000
10th Apr	SF Leg 1	(h)	Tottenham H.	Eng	1-0	Lindsay	42,174
25th Apr	SF Leg 2	(a)	Tottenham H.	"	1-2	Heighway	46,919
10th May	F Leg 1	(h)	B. Moench'bach	W.Ger	3-0	Keegan 2, Lloyd	41,169
23rd May	F Leg 2	(a)	B. Moench'bach	"	0-2		35,000
1973/74	EUROPEAN CHAMPIONS CUP			(WINNERS – BAYERN MUNICH)			
19th Sept	1 Leg 1	(a)	Jeunesse D'Esch	Lux	1-1	Hall	5,000
3rd Oct	1 Leg 2	(h)	Jeunesse D'Esch	"	2-0	Mond o.g., Toshack	28,714
24th Oct	2 Leg 1	(a)	R.S. Belgrade	Yug	1-2	Lawler	40,000
6th Nov	2 Leg 2	(h)	R.S. Belgrade"		1-2	Lawler	41,774
1974/75	EUROPEAN CUP-WINNERS' CUP			(WINNERS – DYNAMO KIEV)			
17th Sept	1 Leg 1	(h)	Stromsgodset	Nor	11-0	Lindsay (pen), Boersma 2, Thompson 2, Heighway, Cormack, Hughes, Smith Callaghan, Kennedy	24,743
1st Oct	1 Leg 2	(a)	Stromsgodset	"	1-0	Kennedy	17,000
23rd Oct	2 Leg 1	(h)	Ferencvaros	Hun	1-1	Keegan	35,027
5th Nov	2 Leg 2	(a)	Ferencvaros	"	0-0		30,000
1975/76	UEFA CUP			(WINNERS – LIVERPOOL)			
17th Sept	1 Leg 1	(a)	Hibernian	Sco	0-1		19,219
30th Sept	1 Leg 2	(h)	Hibernian	"	3-1	Toshack 3	29,963
22nd Oct	2 Leg 1	(a)	Real Sociedad	Spa	3-1	Heighway, Callaghan, Thompson	20,000
4th Nov	2 Leg 2	(h)	Real Sociedad	"	6-0	Toshack, Kennedy 2, Fairclough Heighway, Neal	23,796

LIVERPOOL FC RESULTS IN EUROPEAN COMPETITION

Season	Round	Venue	Opponents	Opponent Country	Score	Scorers	Att
1975/76	UEFA CUP (cont)			(WINNERS – LIVERPOOL)			
26th Nov	3 Leg 1	(a)	Slask Wroclaw	Pol	2-1	Kennedy, Toshack	46,000
10th Dec	3 Leg 2	(h)	Slask Wroclaw	"	3-0	Case 3	17,886
3rd Mar	4 Leg 1	(a)	Dynamo Dresden	E.Ger	0-0		33,000
17th Mar	4 Leg 2	(h)	Dynamo Dresden	"	2-1	Case, Keegan	39,300
30th Mar	SF Leg 1	(a)	Barcelona	Spa	1-0	Toshack	70,000
14th Apr	SF Leg 2	(h)	Barcelona	"	1-1	Thompson	55,104
28th Apr	F Leg 1	(h)	FC Bruges	Bel	3-2	Kennedy, Case, Keegan (pen)	49,981
19th May	F Leg 2	(a)	FC Bruges	"	1-1	Keegan	33,000
1976/77	EUROPEAN CHAMPIONS CUP			(WINNERS – LIVERPOOL)			
14th Sept	1 Leg 1	(h)	Crusaders	N.Ire	2-0	Neal (pen), Toshack	22,442
28th Sept	1 Leg 2	(a)	Crusaders	"	5-0	Keegan, Johnson 2, McDermott Heighway	10,500
20th Oct	2 Leg 1	(a)	Trabzonspor	Tur	0-1		25,000
3rd Nov	2 Leg 2	(h)	Trabzonspor	"	3-0	Heighway, Johnson, Keegan	42,275
2nd Mar	3 Leg 1	(a)	St Etienne	Fra	0-1		38,000
16th Mar	3 Leg 2	(h)	St Etienne	"	3-1	Keegan, Kennedy, Fairclough	55,043
6th Apr	SF Leg 1	(a)	FC Zurich	Swi	3-1	Neal 2 (1 pen), Heighway	30,500
20th Apr	SF Leg 2	(h)	FC Zurich	"	3-0	Case 2, Keegan	50,611
25th May	Final	Rome	B. Moench'bach	W.Ger	3-1	McDermott, Smith, Neal (pen)	52,078
1977/78	EUROPEAN CHAMPIONS CUP			(WINNERS – LIVERPOOL)			
19th Oct	2 Leg 1	(h)	Dynamo Dresden	E.Ger	5-1	Hansen, Case 2, Neal (pen) Kennedy	39,835
2nd Nov	2 Leg 2	(a)	Dynamo Dresden	"	1-2	Heighway	33,000
1st Mar	3 Leg 1	(a)	Benfica	Por	2-1	Case, Hughes	70,000
15th Mar	3 Leg 2	(h)	Benfica	"	4-1	Callaghan, Dalglish, McDermott, Neal	48,364
29th Mar	SF Leg 1	(a)	B. Moench'bach	W.Ger	1-2	Johnson	66,000
12th Apr	SF Leg 2	(h)	B. Moench'bach	"	3-0	Kennedy, Dalglish, Case	51,500
10th May	Final	Wembley	FC Bruges	Bel	1-0	Dalglish	92,000
1977/78	EUROPEAN SUPER CUP			(WINNERS – LIVERPOOL)			
22nd Nov	Leg 1	(a)	SV Hamburg	W.Ger	1-1	Fairclough	16,000
6th Dec	Leg 2	(h)	SV Hamburg	"	6-0	Thompson, McDermott 3 Fairclough, Dalglish	34,931
1978/79	EUROPEAN CHAMPIONS CUP			(WINNERS – NOTTINGHAM FOREST)			
13th Sept	1 Leg 1	(a)	Nottingham Forest	Eng	0-2		38,316
27th Sept	1 Leg 2	(h)	Nottingham Forest	"	0-0		51,679
1978/79	EUROPEAN SUPER CUP			(WINNERS – ANDERLECHT)			
4th Dec	1 Leg 1	(a)	Anderlecht	Bel	1-3	Case	35,000
19th Dec	1 Leg 2	(h)	Anderlecht	"	2-1	Hughes, Fairclough	23,598

LIVERPOOL FC RESULTS IN EUROPEAN COMPETITION

Season	Round	Venue	Opponents	Opponent Country	Score	Scorers	Att
1979/80	**EUROPEAN CHAMPIONS CUP**			**(WINNERS – NOTTINGHAM FOREST)**			
19th Sept	1 Leg 1	(h)	Dynamo Tblisi	Rus	2-1	Johnson, Case	35,270
3rd Oct	1 Leg 2	(a)	Dynamo Tblisi	"	0-3		80,000
1980/81	**EUROPEAN CHAMPIONS CUP**			**(WINNERS – LIVERPOOL)**			
17th Sept	1 Leg 1	(a)	Oulu Palloseura	Fin	1-1	McDermott	14,000
1st Oct	1 Leg 2	(h)	Oulu Palloseura	"	10-1	Souness 3 (1pen), McDermott 3, Lee, R.Kennedy, Fairclough 2	21,013
22nd Oct	2 Leg 1	(a)	Aberdeen	Sco	1-0	McDermott	24,000
5th Nov	2 Leg 2	(h)	Aberdeen	"	4-0	Miller o.g., Neal, Dalglish, Hansen	36,182
4th Mar	3 Leg 1	(h)	CSKA Sofia	Bul	5-1	Souness 3, Lee, McDermott	37,255
18th Mar	3 Leg 2	(a)	CSKA Sofia	"	1-0	Johnson	65,000
8th Apr	SF Leg 1	(h)	Bayern Munich	W.Ger	0-0		44,543
22nd Apr	SF Leg 2	(a)	Bayern Munich	"	1-1	R.Kennedy	77,600
27th May	Final	Paris	Real Madrid	Spa	1-0	A.Kennedy	48,360
1981/82	**EUROPEAN CHAMPIONS CUP**			**(WINNERS – ASTON VILLA)**			
16th Sept	1 Leg 1	(a)	Oulu Palloseura	Fin	1-0	Dalglish	8,400
30th Sept	1 Leg 2	(h)	Oulu Palloseura	"	7-0	Dalglish, McDermott 2, R.Kennedy, Johnson, Rush, Lawrenson	20,789
21st Oct	2 Leg 1	(a)	AZ '67 Alkmaar	Hol	2-2	Johnson, Lee	15,000
4th Nov	2 Leg 2	(h)	AZ '67 Alkmaar	"	3-2	McDermott (pen), Rush, Hansen	29,703
3rd Mar	3 Leg 1	(h)	CSKA Sofia	Bul	1-0	Whelan	27,388
17th Mar	3 Leg 2	(a)	CSKA Sofia	"	0-2 aet		60,000
1982/83	**EUROPEAN CHAMPIONS CUP**			**(WINNERS – HAMBURG)**			
14th Sept	1 Leg 1	(a)	Dundalk	Rep. Ire	4-1	Whelan 2, Rush, Hodgson	16,500
28th Sept	1 Leg 2	(h)	Dundalk	"	1-0	Whelan	12,021
19th Oct	2 Leg 1	(a)	HJK Helsinki	Fin	0-1		5,722
2nd Nov	2 Leg 2	(h)	HJK Helsinki	"	5-0	Dalglish, Johnson, Neal, A.Kennedy 2	16,434
2nd Mar	3 Leg 1	(a)	Widzew Lodz	Pol	0-2		45,531
16th Mar	3 Leg 2	(h)	Widzew Lodz	"	3-2	Neal (pen), Rush, Hodgson	44,494
1983/84	**EUROPEAN CHAMPIONS CUP**			**(WINNERS – LIVERPOOL)**			
14th Sept	1 Leg 1	(a)	BK Odense	Den	1-0	Dalglish	30,000
28th Sept	1 Leg 2	(h)	BK Odense	"	5-0	Robinson 2, Dalglish 2, Clausen o.g.	14,985
19th Oct	2 Leg 1	(h)	Athletic Bilbao	Spa	0-0		33,063
2nd Nov	2 Leg 2	(a)	Athletic Bilbao	"	1-0	Rush	47,500
7th Mar	3 Leg 1	(h)	Benfica	Por	1-0	Rush	39,096
21st Mar	3 Leg 2	(a)	Benfica	"	4-1	Whelan 2, Johnston, Rush	70,000
11th Apr	SF Leg 1	(h)	D. Bucharest	Rom	1-0	Lee	36,941
25th Apr	SF Leg 2	(a)	D. Bucharest	"	2-1	Rush 2	60,000
30th May	Final	Rome	AS Roma	Ita	1-1 aet	Neal	69,693
			(Liverpool won 4-2 on penalties)				

LIVERPOOL FC RESULTS IN EUROPEAN COMPETITION

Season	Round	Venue	Opponents	Opponent Country	Score	Scorers	Att
1984/85	**EUROPEAN CHAMPIONS CUP**			**(WINNERS – JUVENTUS)**			
19th Sept	1 Leg 1	(a)	Lech Poznan	Pol	1-0	Wark	35,000
3rd Oct	1 Leg 2	(h)	Lech Poznan	"	4-0	Wark 3, Walsh	22,143
24th Oct	2 Leg 1	(h)	Benfica	Por	3-1	Rush 3	27,733
7th Nov	2 Leg 2	(a)	Benfica	"	0-1		50,000
6th Mar	3 Leg 1	(a)	Austria Vienna	Aut	1-1	Nicol	21,000
20th Mar	3 Leg 2	(h)	Austria Vienna	"	4-1	Walsh 2, Nicol, Obermayer o.g.	32,761
10th Apr	SF Leg 1	(h)	Panathinaikos	Gre	4-0	Wark, Rush 2, Beglin	39,488
24th Apr	SF Leg 2	(a)	Panathinaikos	"	1-0	Lawrenson	60,000
29th May	Final	Brussels	Juventus	Ita	0-1		60,000
1984/85	**EUROPEAN SUPER CUP**			**(WINNERS – JUVENTUS)**			
16th Jan		(a)	Juventus	Ita	0-2		60,000
1991/92	**UEFA CUP**			**(WINNERS – AJAX)**			
18th Sept	1 Leg 1	(h)	Kuusysi Lahti	Fin	6-1	Saunders 4, Houghton 2	17,131
2nd Oct	1 Leg 2	(a)	Kuusysi Lahti	"	0-1		8,435
23rd Oct	2 Leg 1	(a)	Auxerre	Fra	0-2		16,500
6th Nov	2 Leg 2	(h)	Auxerre	"	3-0	Molby (pen), Marsh, Walters	23,094
27th Nov	3 Leg 1	(a)	Swarovski Tirol	Aut	2-0	Saunders 2	12,500
11th Dec	3 Leg 2	(h)	Swarovski Tirol	"	4-0	Saunders 3, Venison	16,007
4th Mar	4 Leg 1	(a)	Genoa	Ita	0-2		40,000
18th Mar	4 Leg 2	(h)	Genoa	"	1-2	Rush	38,840
1992/93	**EUROPEAN CUP-WINNERS' CUP**			**(WINNERS – PARMA)**			
16th Sept	1 Leg 1	(h)	Apollon Limassol	Cyp	6-1	Stewart 2, Rush 4	12,769
29th Sept	1 Leg 2	(a)	Apollon Limassol	"	2-1	Rush, Hutchison	8,000
22nd Oct	2 Leg 1	(a)	Spartak Moscow	Rus	2-4	Wright, McManaman	60,000
4th Nov	2 Leg 2	(h)	Spartak Moscow	"	0-2		37,993
1995/96	**UEFA CUP**			**(WINNERS – BAYERN MUNICH)**			
12th Sept	1 Leg 1	(a)	S. Vladikavkaz	Rus	2-1	McManaman, Redknapp	43,000
26th Sept	1 Leg 2	(h)	S. Vladikavkaz	"	0-0		35,042
17th Oct	2 Leg 1	(a)	Brondby	Den	0-0		37,648
31st Oct	2 Leg 2	(h)	Brondby	"	0-1		35,878
1996/97	**UEFA CUP-WINNERS' CUP**			**(WINNERS – FC BARCELONA)**			
12th Sept	1 Leg 1	(a)	MyPa 47	Fin	1-0	Bjornebye	5,500
26th Sept	1 Leg 2	(h)	MyPa 47	"	3-1	Berger, Collymore, Barnes	39,013
17th Oct	2 Leg 1	(a)	Sion	Swi	2-1	Fowler, Barnes	16,500
31st Oct	2 Leg 2	(h)	Sion	"	6-3	McManaman, Bjornebye Barnes, Fowler 2, Berger	38,514
6th Mar	3 Leg 1	(a)	Brann Bergen	Nor	1-1	Fowler	12,700
20th Mar	3 Leg 2	(h)	Brann Bergen	"	3-0	Fowler 2 (1 pen), Collymore	40,326
10th Apr	SF Leg 1	(a)	Paris St Germain	Fra	0-3		35,142
24th Apr	SF Leg 2	(h)	Paris St Germain	"	2-0	Fowler, Wright	38,984

LIVERPOOL FC RESULTS IN EUROPEAN COMPETITION

Season	Round	Venue	Opponents	Opponent Country	Score	Scorers	Att
1997/98	**UEFA CUP**			**(WINNERS – INTER MILAN)**			
16th Sept	1 Leg 1	(a)	Celtic	Sco	2-2	Owen, McManaman	48,526
30th Sept	1 Leg 2	(h)	Celtic	"	0-0		38,205
21st Oct	2 Leg 1	(a)	RC Strasbourg	Fra	0-3		18,813
4th Nov	2 Leg 2	(h)	RC Strasbourg	"	2-0	Fowler (pen), Riedle	32,426
1998/99	**UEFA CUP**			**(WINNERS – PARMA)**			
15th Sept	1 Leg 1	(a)	FC Kosice	Slovakia	3-0	Berger, Riedle, Owen	4,500
29th Sept	1 Leg 2	(h)	FC Kosice	"	5-0	Redknapp 2, Ince, Fowler 2	23,792
20th Oct	2 Leg 1	(h)	Valencia	Spa	0-0		36,004
3rd Nov	2 Leg 2	(a)	Valencia	"	2-2	McManaman, Berger	49,000
24th Nov	3 Leg 1	(a)	Celta Vigo	Spa	1-3	Owen	32,000
8th Dec	3 Leg 2	(h)	Celta Vigo	"	0-1		30,289
2000/01	**UEFA CUP**			**(WINNERS – LIVERPOOL)**			
14th Sept	1 Leg 1	(a)	Rapid Bucharest	Rom	1-0	Barmby	12,000
28th Sept	1 Leg 2	(h)	Rapid Bucharest	"	0-0		37,954
26th Oct	2 Leg 1	(a)	Slovan Liberec	Cz Rep	1-0	Heskey	29,662
9th Nov	2 Leg 2	(a)	Slovan Liberec	"	3-2	Barmby, Heskey, Owen	6,808
23rd Nov	3 Leg 1	(a)	Olympiakos	Gre	2-2	Barmby, Gerrard	43,855
7th Dec	3 Leg 2	(h)	Olympiakos	"	2-0	Heskey, Barmby	35,484
15th Feb	4 Leg 1	(a)	AS Roma	Ita	2-0	Owen 2	59,718
22nd Feb	4 Leg 2	(h)	AS Roma	"	0-1		43,688
8th Mar	5 Leg 1	(a)	FC Porto	Por	0-0		21,150
15th Mar	5 Leg 2	(h)	FC Porto	"	2-0	Murphy, Owen	40,502
5th Apr	SF Leg 1	(a)	Barcelona	Spa	0-0		90,000
19th Apr	SF Leg 2	(h)	Barcelona	"	1-0	McAllister	44,203
16th May	Final	Dortmund	Alaves	Spa	5-4 aet	Babbel, Gerrard, McAllister (pen), Fowler, Geli o.g.	65,000

(Liverpool won on golden goal)

Season	Round	Venue	Opponents	Opponent Country	Score	Scorers	Att
2001/02	**UEFA CHAMPIONS LEAGUE**			**(WINNERS – REAL MADRID)**			
8th Aug	Q. Leg 1	(a)	FC Haka	Fin	5-0	Heskey, Owen 3, Hyypia	33,217
21st Aug	Q. Leg 2	(h)	FC Haka	"	4-1	Fowler, Redknapp, Heskey, Wilson o.g.	31,602
			First Group Stage				
11th Sept	Group B	(h)	Boavista	Por	1-1	Owen	30,015
19th Sept	Group B	(a)	B. Dortmund	Ger	0-0		50,000
26th Sept	Group B	(h)	Dynamo Kiev	Ukr	1-0	Litmanen	33,513
16th Oct	Group B	(a)	Dynamo Kiev	"	2-1	Murphy, Gerrard	55,000
24th Oct	Group B	(a)	Boavista	Por	1-1	Murphy	6,000
30th Oct	Group B	(h)	B. Dortmund	Ger	2-0	Smicer, Wright	41,507
			Second Group Stage				
20th Nov	Group B	(h)	Barcelona	Spa	1-3	Owen	41,521
5th Dec	Group B	(a)	AS Roma	Ita	0-0		57,819
20th Feb	Group B	(h)	Galatasaray	Tur	0-0		41,605
26th Feb	Group B	(a)	Galatasaray	"	1-1	Heskey	22,100
13th Mar	Group B	(a)	Barcelona	Spa	0-0		75,362
19th Mar	Group B	(h)	AS Roma	Ita	2-0	Litmanen (pen), Heskey	41,794
3rd Apr	QF Leg 1	(h)	B. Leverkusen	Ger	1-0	Hyypia	42,454
9th Apr	QF Leg 2	(a)	B. Leverkusen	"	2-4	Xavier, Litmanen	22,500

LIVERPOOL FC RESULTS IN EUROPEAN COMPETITION

Season	Round	Venue	Opponents	Opponent Country	Score	Scorers	Att
2001/02	**EUROPEAN SUPER CUP**			**(WINNERS – LIVERPOOL)**			
24th Aug		Monaco	Bayern Munich	Ger	3-2	Riise, Heskey, Owen	15,000
2002/03	**UEFA CHAMPIONS LEAGUE**			**(WINNERS – AC MILAN)**			
			First Group Stage				
17th Sept	Group B (a)		Valencia	Spa	0-2		43,000
25th Sept	Group B (h)		FC Basel	Swi	1-1	Baros	37,634
2nd Oct	Group B (h)		Spartak Moscow	Rus	5-0	Heskey 2, Cheyrou, Hyypia, Diao	40,812
22nd Oct	Group B (a)		Spartak Moscow	"	3-1	Owen 3	15,000
30th Oct	Group B (h)		Valencia	Spa	0-1		41,831
12th Nov	Group B (a)		FC Basel	Swi	3-3	Murphy, Smicer, Owen	35,000
2002/03	**UEFA CUP**			**(WINNERS – FC PORTO)**			
28th Nov	3 Leg 1 (a)		Vitesse Arnhem	Hol	1-0	Owen	28,000
12th Dec	3 Leg 2 (h)		Vitesse Arnhem	"	1-0	Owen	23,576
20th Feb	4 Leg 1 (a)		Auxerre	Fra	1-0	Hyypia	20,452
27th Feb	4 Leg 2 (h)		Auxerre	"	2-0	Owen, Murphy	34,252
13th Mar	5 Leg 1 (a)		Celtic	Sco	1-1	Heskey	59,759
20th Mar	5 Leg 2 (h)		Celtic	"	0-2		44,238
2003/04	**UEFA CUP**			**(WINNERS – VALENCIA)**			
24th Sept	1 Leg 1 (a)		Olimpija Ljubljana	Slovenia	1-1	Owen	10,000
15th Oct	1 Leg 2 (h)		Olimpija Ljubljana	"	3-0	LeTallec, Heskey, Kewell	42,880
6th Nov	2 Leg 1 (a)		Steaua Bucharest	Rom	1-1	Traore	25,000
27th Nov	2 Leg 2 (h)		Steaua Bucharest	"	1-0	Kewell	42,837
26th Feb	3 Leg 1 (h)		Levski Sofia	Bul	2-0	Gerrard, Kewell	39,149
3rd Mar	3 Leg 2 (a)		Levski Sofia	"	4-2	Gerrard, Owen, Hamann, Hyypia	40,281
11th Mar	4 Leg 1 (h)		O. Marseille	Fra	1-1	Baros	41,270
25th Mar	4 Leg 2 (a)		O. Marseille	"	1-2	Heskey	50,000
2004/05	**UEFA CHAMPIONS LEAGUE**			**(WINNERS – LIVERPOOL)**			
10th Aug	Q. Leg 1 (a)		AK Graz	Aut	2-0	Gerrard 2	15,000
24th Aug	Q. Leg 2 (h)		AK Graz	"	0-1		42,950
			Group Stage				
15th Sept	Group A (h)		AS Monaco	Fra	2-0	Cisse, Baros	33,517
28th Sept	Group A (a)		Olympiakos	Gre	0-1		33,000
19th Oct	Group A (h)		D. La Coruna	Spa	0-0		40,236
3rd Nov	Group A (a)		D. La Coruna	"	1-0	Andrade o.g.	32,000
23rd Nov	Group A (a)		AS Monaco	Fra	0-1		15,000
8th Dec	Group A (h)		Olympiakos	Gre	3-1	Sinama-Pongolle, Mellor, Gerrard	42,045
22nd Feb	L. 16 L1 (h)		B. Leverkusen	Ger	3-1	Garcia, Riise, Hamann	40,942
9th Mar	L. 16 L2 (a)		B. Leverkusen	"	3-1	Garcia 2, Baros	23,000
5th Apr	QF Leg 1 (h)		Juventus	Ita	2-1	Hyypia, Garcia	41,216
13th Apr	QF Leg 2 (a)		Juventus	"	0-0		55,464
27th Apr	SF Leg 1 (a)		Chelsea	Eng	0-0		40,497
3rd May	SF Leg 2 (h)		Chelsea	"	1-0	Garcia	42,529
25th May	Final	Istanbul	AC Milan	Ita	3-3 aet	Gerrard, Smicer, Alonso	65,000
			(Liverpool won 3-2 on penalties)				

LIVERPOOL FC RESULTS IN EUROPEAN COMPETITION

Season	Round	Venue	Opponents	Opponent Country	Score	Scorers	Att
2005/06	**UEFA CHAMPIONS LEAGUE**			**(WINNERS – FC BARCELONA)**			
13th July	Q.1 Leg 1	(h)	TNS	Wal	3-0	Gerrard 3	44,760
19th July	Q.1 Leg 2	(a)	TNS	"	3-0	Cisse, Gerrard 2	8,009
26th July	Q.2 Leg 1	(a)	FBK Kaunas	Lith	3-1	Cisse, Carragher, Gerrard (pen)	8,300
2nd Aug	Q.2 Leg 2	(h)	FBK Kaunas	"	2-0	Gerrard, Cisse	43,717
10th Aug	Q.3 Leg 1	(a)	CSKA Sofia	Bul	3-1	Cisse, Morientes 2	16,512
23rd Aug	Q.3 Leg 2	(h)	CSKA Sofia	"	0-1		42,175
			Group Stage				
13th Sept	Group G	(a)	Real Betis	Spa	2-1	Sinama-Pongolle, Garcia	45,000
28th Sept	Group G	(h)	Chelsea	Eng	0-0		42,743
19th Oct	Group G	(a)	Anderlecht	Bel	1-0	Cisse	25,000
1st Nov	Group G	(h)	Anderlecht	Bel	3-0	Morientes, Garcia, Cisse	42,607
23rd Nov	Group G	(h)	Real Betis	Spa	0-0		42,077
6th Dec	Group G	(a)	Chelsea	Eng	0-0		41,598
21st Feb	L. 16 L1	(a)	Benfica	Por	0-1		65,000
8th Mar	L. 16 L2	(h)	Benfica	Por	0-2		42,745
2005/06	**UEFA SUPER CUP**			**(WINNERS – LIVERPOOL)**			
26th Aug		Monaco	CSKA Moscow	Rus	3-1 aet	Cisse 2, Garcia	18,000
2006/07	**UEFA CHAMPIONS LEAGUE**			**(WINNERS – AC MILAN)**			
9th Aug	Q.3 Leg 1	(h)	Maccabi Haifa	Isr	2-1	Bellamy, Gonzalez	40,058
22nd Aug	Q.3 Leg 2	(a)	Maccabi Haifa	"	1-1	Crouch	12,500
			Group Stage				
12th Sept	Group C	(a)	PSV Eindhoven	Hol	0-0		35,000
27th Sept	Group C	(h)	Galatasaray	Tur	3-2	Crouch 2, Garcia	41,976
18th Oct	Group C	(a)	Bordeaux	Fra	1-0	Crouch	33,000
31st Oct	Group C	(h)	Bordeaux	Fra	3-0	Garcia 2, Gerrard	41,978
22nd Nov	Group C	(h)	PSV Eindhoven	Hol	2-0	Gerrard, Crouch	41,948
5th Dec	Group C	(a)	Galatasaray	Tur	2-3	Fowler 2	23,000
21st Feb	L. 16 L1	(a)	Barcelona	Spa	2-1	Bellamy, Riise	88,000
6th Mar	L. 16 L2	(h)	Barcelona	Spa	0-1		42,579
3rd Apr	QF L1	(a)	PSV Eindhoven	Hol	3-0	Gerrard, Riise, Crouch	36,500
11th Apr	QF L2	(h)	PSV Eindhoven	Hol	1-0	Crouch	41,447
25th Apr	SF L1	(a)	Chelsea	Eng	0-1		39,483
1st May	SF L2	(h)	Chelsea	Eng aet	1-0	Agger	42,554
			(Liverpool won 4-1 on penalties)				
23rd May	Final	Athens	AC Milan	Ita	1-2	Kuyt	74,000
2007/08	**UEFA CHAMPIONS LEAGUE**			**(WINNERS – MANCHESTER UNITED)**			
15th Aug	Q. Leg 1	(a)	Toulouse	Fra	1-0	Voronin	30,380
28th Aug	Q. Leg 2	(h)	Toulouse	"	4-0	Crouch, Hyypia, Kuyt 2	43,118
			Group Stage				
18th Sept	Group A	(a)	FC Porto	Por	1-1	Kuyt	41,208
3rd Oct	Group A	(h)	Marseille	Fra	0-1		41,355
24th Oct	Group A	(a)	Besiktas	Tur	1-2	Gerrard	32,500
6th Nov	Group A	(h)	Besiktas	"	8-0	Crouch 2, Benayoun 3, Gerrard, Babel 2	41,143

LIVERPOOL FC RESULTS IN EUROPEAN COMPETITION

Season	Round	Venue	Opponents	Opponent Country	Score	Scorers	Att
2007/08 UEFA CHAMPIONS LEAGUE (cont) (WINNERS – MANCHESTER UNITED)							
28th Nov	Group A (h)		FC Porto	Por	4-1	Torres 2, Gerrard (pen), Crouch	41,095
11th Dec	Group A (a)		Marseille	Fra	4-0	Gerrard, Torres, Kuyt, Babel	53,000
19th Feb	L. 16 L1 (h)		Inter Milan	Ita	2-0	Kuyt, Gerrard	41,999
11th Mar	L. 16 L2 (a)		Inter Milan	"	1-0	Torres	80,000
2nd Apr	QF Leg 1 (a)		Arsenal	Eng	1-1	Kuyt	60,041
8th Apr	QF Leg 2 (h)		Arsenal	"	4-2	Hyypia, Torres, Gerrard (pen), Babel	41,985
22nd Apr	SF Leg 1 (h)		Chelsea	Eng	1-1	Kuyt	42,180
30th Apr	SF Leg 2 (a)		Chelsea	"	2-3 aet	Torres, Babel	38,900
2008/09 UEFA CHAMPIONS LEAGUE (WINNERS – FC BARCELONA)							
13th Aug	Q.3 Leg 1 (a)		Standard Liege	Bel	0-0		25,000
27th Aug	Q.3 Leg 2 (h)		Standard Liege	"	1-0 aet	Kuyt	43,889
42,175			Group Stage				
16th Sept	Group D (a)		Marseille	Fra	2-1	Gerrard 2 (1 pen)	45,000
1st Oct	Group D (h)		PSV Eindhoven	Hol	3-1	Kuyt, Keane, Gerrard	41,097
22nd Oct	Group D (a)		Atletico Madrid	Spa	1-1	Keane	48,769
4th Nov	Group D (h)		Atletico Madrid	Spa	1-1	Gerrard (pen)	42,010
26th Nov	Group D (h)		Marseille	Fra	1-0	Gerrard	40,024
9th Dec	Group D (a)		PSV Eindhoven	Hol	3-1	Babel, Riera, Ngog	35,000
25th Feb	L. 16 L1 (a)		Real Madrid	Spa	1-0	Benayoun	85,000
10th Mar	L. 16 L2 (h)		Real Madrid	"	4-0	Torres, Gerrard 2 (1 pen) Dossena	42,550
8th Apr	QF Leg 1 (h)		Chelsea	Eng	1-3	Torres	42,543
14th Apr	QF Leg 2 (a)		Chelsea	"	4-4	Aurelio, Alonso (pen), Lucas, Kuyt	38,286
2009/10 UEFA CHAMPIONS LEAGUE (WINNERS – INTER MILAN)							
			Group Stage				
16th Sept	Group E (h)		Debreceni VSC	Hun	1-0	Kuyt	41,591
29th Sept	Group E (a)		Fiorentina	Ita	0-2		33,426
20th Oct	Group E (h)		Lyon	Fra	1-2	Benayoun	41,562
4th Nov	Group E (a)		Lyon	Fra	1-1	Babel	39,180
24th Nov	Group E (a)		Debreceni VSC	Hun	1-0	Ngog	41,500
9th Dec	Group E (h)		Fiorentina	Ita	1-2	Benayoun	40,863
2009/10 UEFA EUROPA LEAGUE (WINNERS – ATLETICO MADRID)							
18th Feb	R. 32 L1 (h)		Unirea Urziceni	Rom	1-0	Ngog	40,450
25th Feb	R. 32 L2 (a)		Unirea Urziceni	"	3-1	Mascherano, Babel, Gerrard	25,000
11th Mar	R. 16 L1 (a)		Lille	Fra	0-1		18,000
18th Mar	R. 16 L2 (h)		Lille	"	3-0	Gerrard (pen), Torres 2	38,139
1st Apr	QF Leg 1 (a)		Benfica	Por	1-2	Agger	62,629
8th Apr	QF Leg 2 (h)		Benfica	"	4-1	Kuyt, Lucas, Torres 2	42,377
22nd Apr	SF Leg 1 (a)		Atletico Madrid	Spa	0-1		50,000
29th Apr	SF Leg 2 (h)		Atletico Madrid	"	2-1 aet	Aquilani, Benayoun	42,040

LIVERPOOL FC RESULTS IN EUROPEAN COMPETITION

Season	Round	Venue	Opponents	Opponent Country	Score	Scorers	Att
2010/11	UEFA EUROPA LEAGUE			(WINNERS – FC PORTO)			
29th July	Q.3 Leg 1	(a)	FK Rabotnicki	Mace	2-0	Ngog 2	23,000
5th Aug	Q.3 Leg 2	(h)	FK Rabotnicki	"	2-0	Ngog, Gerrard (pen)	31,202
19th Aug	P-O Leg 1	(h)	Trabzonspor	Tur	1-0	Babel	40,941
26th Aug	P-O Leg 2	(a)	Trabzonspor	"	2-1	Kacar (o.g.), Kuyt	21,065
16th Sept	Group K	(h)	Steaua Bucharest	Rom	4-1	Cole, Ngog 2 (1 pen), Lucas	25,605
30th Sept	Group K	(a)	FC Utrecht	Hol	0-0		23,662
21st Oct	Group K	(a)	Napoli	Ita	0-0		55,489
4th Nov	Group K	(h)	Napoli	Ita	3-1	Gerrard 3 (1 pen)	33,895
2nd Dec	Group K	(a)	Steaua Bucharest	Rom	1-1	Jovanovic	20,000
15th Dec	Group K	(h)	FC Utrecht	Hol	0-0		37,800
17th Feb	R. 32 L1	(a(	Sparta Prague	Cze	0-0		17,564
24th Feb	R. 32 L2	(h)	Sparta Prague	Cze	1-0	Kuyt	42,949
10th Mar	R. 16 L1	(a)	Braga	Por	0-1		12,991
17th Mar	R. 16 L2	(h)	Braga	Por	0-0		37,494

BIGGEST EUROPEAN VICTORIES

DATE	OPPONENTS	VENUE	COMPETITION	SCORE
17th Sept 1974	Stromsgodset	Home	European Cup-Winners' Cup	11-0
16th Sept 1969	Dundalk	Home	Inter-Cities Fairs Cup	10-0
1st Oct 1980	Oulu Palloseura	Home	European Cup	10-1
7th Nov 1967	TSV Munich 1860	Home	Inter-Cities Fairs Cup	8-0
6th Nov 2007	Besiktas	Home	Champions League	8-0
30th Sept 1981	Oulu Palloseura	Home	European Cup	7-0
4th Nov 1975	Real Sociedad	Home	UEFA Cup	6-0
6th Dec 1977	SV Hamburg	Home	European Super Cup	6-0
14th Sept 1964	Reykjavik	Home	European Cup	6-1
18th Sept 1991	Kuusysi Lahti	Home	UEFA Cup	6-1
16th Sept 1992	Apollon Limassol	Home	European Cup-Winners' Cup	6-1
17th Aug 1964	Reykjavik	Away	European Cup	5-0
28th Sept 1976	Crusaders	Away	European Cup	5-0
2nd Nov 1982	HJK Helsinki	Home	European Cup	5-0
28th Sept 1983	BK Odense	Home	European Cup	5-0
29th Sept 1998	FC Kosice	Home	UEFA Cup	5-0
8th Aug 2001	FC Haka	Away	European Cup	5-0
2nd Oct 2002	Spartak Moscow	Home	European Cup	5-0

CLUB WORLD CHAMPIONSHIP RESULTS

Date	Round	Venue	Opponents	Opponent Country	Score	Scorers	Att
1981							
13th Dec	Final	Tokyo	Flamengo	Bra	0-3		62,000
1984							
9th Dec	Final	Tokyo	Independiente	Arg	0-1		62,000
2005							
15th Dec	S.F.	Yokohama	Saprissa	CRi	3-0	Crouch 2, Gerrard	43,902
18th Dec	Final	Yokohama	Sao Paulo	Bra	0-1		66,821

MOST SUCCESSIVE HOME WINS IN EUROPE

The Reds' record runs in European competition, including the teams beaten.

ALL-TIME RECORD		
NO. OF WINS	**PERIOD**	**TEAMS BEATEN**
9	1976-1978	Bruges, Crusaders, Trabzonspor, Saint-Etienne, FC Zurich, Dynamo Dresden, Hamburg, Benfica, Borussia Moenchengladbach
9	1983-1991	Benfica, Dinamo Bucharest, Lech Poznan, Benfica, Austria Vienna, Panathinaikos, Kuusysi Lahti, Auxerre, Swarovski Tirol
8	2010	Unirea Urziceni, Lille, Benfica, Atletico Madrid, Rabotnicki, Trabzonspor, Steaua Bucharest, Napoli
7	1968-1971	Athletic Bilbao, Dundalk, Vitoria Setubal, Ferencvaros, Dinamo Bucharest, Hibernian, Bayern Munich
7	1972-1973	Eintracht Frankfurt, AEK Athens, Dynamo Berlin, Dynamo Dresden, Tottenham Hotspur, Borussia Moenchengladbach, Jeunesse D'Esch
7	1981-1983	Oulu Palloseura, AZ '67 Alkmaar, CSKA Sofia, Dundalk, HJK Helsinki, Widzew Lodz, Odense

MOST EUROPEAN SEMI-FINALS – BRITISH CLUBS

CLUB	EURO. CUP/ CHAMP. LGE	EURO. CUP WINNERS' CUP	FAIRS/UEFA CUP/ EUROPA LGE	TOTAL
Liverpool	9	2	5	16
Manchester United	12	2	1	15
Chelsea	5	4	1	10
Leeds United	3	1	5	9
Arsenal	2	3	2	7
Tottenham Hotspur	1	2	4	7
Celtic	3	2	1	6
Rangers	1	2	2	5
Birmingham City	0	0	3	3
Nottingham Forest	2	0	1	3
West Ham United	0	3	0	3
Aberdeen	0	2	0	2
Dundee	1	0	1	2
Dundee United	1	0	1	2
Hibernian	1	0	1	2
Manchester City	0	2	0	2
Newcastle United	0	0	2	2
Wolverhampton W.	0	1	1	2
Aston Villa	1	0	0	1
Derby County	1	0	0	1
Dunfermline Ath.	0	1	0	1
Everton	0	1	0	1
Fulham	0	0	1	1
Ipswich Town	0	0	1	1
London XI	0	0	1	1
Middlesbrough	0	0	1	1

CLASSIC EUROPEAN SEASON – 1980/81

Liverpool's third European Cup-winning campaign in five seasons began in less than impressive fashion. Despite possessing a side full of European experience – only Alan Kennedy, Sammy Lee and David Johnson had not played in the Reds' previous victories in the competition – they were held to a 1-1 draw at Finnish part-timers Oulu Palloseura. However, two weeks later back at Anfield, a record 10-1 victory was recorded, which remains the club's biggest win in the competition. Graeme Souness hit a treble as did Terry McDermott, who had also netted in Finland.

Aberdeen – managed by Alex Ferguson – were next up in what was billed as a 'Battle of Britain'. A brilliant chip from Terry McDermott earned victory at Pittodrie in the first leg, before Willie Miller's own goal set the Reds on the way in the second game at Anfield. Phil Neal added a second before the break, with Kenny Dalglish and Alan Hansen setting the seal on a 5-0 aggregate triumph.

Liverpool hosted CSKA Sofia in the first leg of the quarter-final. The Bulgarian champions had knocked out holders Nottingham Forest in round one but despite the disruption of skipper Phil Thompson going off injured, another Souness hat-trick ensured an impressive 5-1 victory. The second leg proved a formality once David Johnson had steadied any nerves with a 10th-minute strike. Ray Clemence even saved a late penalty from Plamen Markov to ensure a 6-1 aggregate success to set up a last four encounter with Bayern Munich.

Without the injured Souness, the Reds struggled at Anfield in the first leg, and a 0-0 draw meant Bayern were strong favourites in the second leg – particularly when Kenny Dalglish limped off early on in the Olympic Stadium. However, his replacement, young forward Howard Gayle, wreaked havoc with his pace and his near-60 minute cameo helped unsettle the home side. Ray Kennedy hit a vital away goal with seven minutes remaining and despite Karl-Heinz Rummenigge pouncing a few minutes later, Bob Paisley's Liverpool hung on to secure a final berth against Real Madrid in Paris.

The Spanish champions, six-time winners of the competition, were in their first European Cup final for 15 years and included England international Laurie Cunningham, making only his first appearance in the competition having returned from a long-term injury. They had the better of things early on, although as the game wore on Liverpool – with Souness becoming more influential – came back strongly. The Reds were let off when Camacho lobbed over with just Ray Clemence to beat, but with only nine minutes remaining Ray Kennedy's throw-in on the left found namesake Alan, who shook off Cortes' challenge before firing home emphatically into the roof of the net.

The success was not only Liverpool's third European Cup triumph in five seasons: it was the fifth successive year the trophy had been won by an English club, while Paisley became the first manager to win the trophy three times.

EUROPEAN CUP STATISTICS 1980/81

PLAYER	AGE	GAMES	GOALS	PLAYER	AGE	GAMES	GOALS
Jimmy Case	26	2+3	0	Alan Kennedy	25	6	1
Ray Clemence	32	9	0	Ray Kennedy	29	9	2
Avi Cohen	23	2+1	0	Sammy Lee	21	9	2
Kenny Dalglish	29	9	1	Terry McDermott	28	8	6
David Fairclough	23	2	2	Richard Money	24	1	0
Howard Gayle	22	0+1	0	Phil Neal	29	9	1
Alan Hansen	25	9	1	Ian Rush	18	1	0
Steve Heighway	32	1+2	0	Graeme Souness	27	8	6
Colin Irwin	23	2+1	0	Phil Thompson	26	7	0
David Johnson	28	5	1				

* Age at start of 1980/81 season

Team line-ups

Liverpool (4-4-1-1):

Johnson

Dalglish

R. Kennedy   Souness   McDermott   Lee

A. Kennedy   Thompson   Hansen   Neal

Clemence

Sub: Case (Dalglish) 86
Subs not used: Ogrizovic, Irwin, Money, Gayle

Real Madrid (3-4-3):

Santillana

Cunningham   Juanito

Camacho   Angel   del Bosque
Stielike

Sabido   Navajas   Cortes

Agustin

Subs: Pineda (Cortes) 87
Subs not used: Gonzalez, San Jose, Angel, Hernandez

LIVERPOOL FC 1
REAL MADRID 0

European Cup
Final
Parc des Princes, Paris, France
Wednesday May 27, 1981.
Attendance: 48,360

Goal: A. Kennedy (81)
Bookings: R. Kennedy (Liverpool),
Stielike (Real Madrid)
Referee: Karoly Palotai (Hungary)

EUROPEAN PLAYER RECORDS

ALL-TIME EUROPEAN APPEARANCES – Games played includes substitute appearances

PLAYER	LFC CAREER	GAMES	PLAYER	LFC CAREER	GAMES
Jamie Carragher	1997-	139	Chris Lawler	1963-1975	66
Steven Gerrard	1998-	116	Dietmar Hamann	1999-2006	61
Sami Hyypia	1999-2009	94	Dirk Kuyt	2006-	54
Ian Callaghan	1960-1978	89	Kenny Dalglish	1977-1990	51
Tommy Smith	1963-1978	85	Steve Finnan	2003-2008	51
Ray Clemence	1968-1981	80	Ray Kennedy	1974-1981	50
Emlyn Hughes	1967-1979	79	Michael Owen	1997-2004	50
John Arne Riise	2001-2008	79	Phil Thompson	1972-1983	50
Pepe Reina	2005-	76	Xabi Alonso	2004-2009	48
Phil Neal	1974-1985	74	Alan Hansen	1977-1990	46
Steve Heighway	1970-1981	67	Danny Murphy	1997-2004	46

EUROPEAN CUP/UEFA CHAMPIONS LEAGUE APPEARANCES (30+ GAMES)

PLAYER	LFC CAREER	GAMES	PLAYER	LFC CAREER	GAMES
Jamie Carragher	1997-	91	Graeme Souness	1978-1984	36
Steven Gerrard	1998-	81	Alan Kennedy	1978-1985	34
John Arne Riise	2001-2008	68	Ray Clemence	1968-1981	33
Sami Hyypia	1999-2009	67	Sammy Lee	1978-1986	33
Phil Neal	1974-1985	57	Ray Kennedy	1974-1981	32
Pepe Reina	2005-	56	Phil Thompson	1972-1983	32
Xabi Alonso	2004-2009	47	Luis Garcia	2004-2007	31
Kenny Dalglish	1977-1990	47	Terry McDermott	1974-1982	31
Steve Finnan	2003-2008	44	Ian Callaghan	1960-1978	30
Alan Hansen	1977-1990	43	Peter Crouch	2005-2008	30
Dirk Kuyt	2006-	40	Bruce Grobbelaar	1981-1994	30
Dietmar Hamann	1999-2006	37			

INTER-CITIES FAIRS CUP/UEFA CUP/EUROPA LEAGUE APPEARANCES (20+ GAMES)

PLAYER	LFC CAREER	GAMES	PLAYER	LFC CAREER	GAMES
Jamie Carragher	1997-	46	Robbie Fowler	1993-2001 &	24
Emlyn Hughes	1967-1979	45		2006-2007	
Ian Callaghan	1960-1978	41	Danny Murphy	1997-2004	24
Tommy Smith	1963-1978	41	John Toshack	1970-1977	24
Ray Clemence	1968-1981	36	Larry Lloyd	1969-1974	23
Chris Lawler	1963-1975	35	Dietmar Hamann	1999-2006	22
Steven Gerrard	1998-	34	Emile Heskey	2000-2004	22
Michael Owen	1997-2004	33	Kevin Keegan	1971-1977	22
Steve Heighway	1970-1981	30	Alec Lindsay	1969-1977	22
Brian Hall	1969-1976	25	Lucas Leiva	2007-	20
Sami Hyypia	1999-2009	25	Peter Thompson	1963-1972	20
Sami Hyypia	1999-2009	25			

EUROPEAN CUP-WINNERS' CUP APPEARANCES (8+ GAMES)

PLAYER	LFC CAREER	GAMES	PLAYER	LFC CAREER	GAMES
Ian Callaghan	1960-1978	17	Steve McManaman	1990-1999	11
Tommy Smith	1963-1978	16	Jamie Redknapp	1991-2001	11
Chris Lawler	1963-1975	15	Peter Thompson	1963-1972	11

EUROPEAN PLAYER RECORDS

EUROPEAN GOALS

PLAYER	LFC CAREER	GAMES	GOALS	PLAYER	LFC CAREER	GAMES	GOALS
Steven Gerrard	1998-	116	38	Fernando Torres	2007-2011	30	12
Michael Owen	1997-2004	50	22	Kevin Keegan	1971-1977	40	12
Ian Rush	1980-87/88-96	38	20	Ray Kennedy	1974-1981	50	12
Roger Hunt	1959-1969	31	17	Peter Crouch	2005-2008	30	11
Terry McDermott	1974-1982	34	15	Luis Garcia	2004-2007	32	11
Dirk Kuyt	2006-	54	15	Kenny Dalglish	1977-1990	51	11
Robbie Fowler	1993-01/06-07	44	14	Chris Lawler	1963-1975	66	11
Jimmy Case	1975-1981	35	13	Steve Heighway	1970-1981	67	11
Emile Heskey	2000-2004	45	13	Phil Neal	1974-1985	74	11

EUROPEAN CUP/UEFA CHAMPIONS LEAGUE GOALS

PLAYER	LFC CAREER	GAMES	GOALS	PLAYER	LFC CAREER	GAMES	GOALS
Steven Gerrard	1998-	81	28	Fernando Torres	2007-2011	24	8
Ian Rush	1980-87/88-96	25	14	Ian St John	1961-1971	13	7
Terry McDermott	1974-1982	31	12	Jimmy Case	1975-1981	22	7
Dirk Kuyt	2006-	40	12	Djibril Cisse	2004-2006	22	7
Peter Crouch	2005-2008	30	11	Ryan Babel	2007-2011	26	7
Roger Hunt	1959-1969	14	10	Emile Heskey	2000-2004	22	6
Luis Garcia	2004-2007	31	10	Ronnie Whelan	1981-1994	23	6
Kenny Dalglish	1977-1990	47	10	Yossi Benayoun	2007-2010	26	6
Phil Neal	1974-1985	57	10	Ray Kennedy	1974-1981	32	6
Michael Owen	1997-2004	16	9	Graeme Souness	1978-1984	36	6
David Johnson	1976-1982	20	8	Sami Hyypia	1999-2009	67	6
Fernando Torres	2007-2011	24	8	John Wark	1984-1987	9	5

INTER-CITIES FAIRS CUP/UEFA CUP/EUROPA LEAGUE GOALS

PLAYER	LFC CAREER	GAMES	GOALS	PLAYER	LFC CAREER	GAMES	GOALS
Michael Owen	1997-2004	33	12	Emile Heskey	2000-2004	22	6
Steven Gerrard	1998-	34	10	Ian Callaghan	1960-1978	41	6
Dean Saunders	1991-1992	5	9	Emlyn Hughes	1967-1979	45	6
John Toshack	1970-1977	24	8	Jimmy Case	1975-1981	9	5
Kevin Keegan	1971-1977	22	7	Roger Hunt	1959-1969	10	5
Alun Evans	1968-1972	10	6	Steve Heighway	1970-1981	30	5
Phil Boersma	1969-1975	13	6	Tommy Smith	1963-1978	41	5
David Ngog	2008-2011	17	6				

EUROPEAN CUP-WINNERS' CUP GOALS

PLAYER	LFC CAREER	GAMES	GOALS
Robbie Fowler	1993-01/06-07	7	7
Ian Rush	1980-87/88-96	4	5
Chris Lawler	1963-1975	15	5
John Barnes	1987-1997	7	3

**Dean Saunders (right) –
Scorer of nine goals in five
European games in 1991/92**

Terry McDermott (above centre) wheels away in triumph after opening the scoring in the 1977 European Champions Cup final against Borussia Moenchengladbach, while (below) the players enjoy the lap of honour after triumphing again the following year against FC Brugge

Ian Rush and Craig Johnston (above) show off 'old big ears' after victory on penalties in 1984 against Roma in Italy, while (below) Sami Hyypia has his eye on the prize at the pre-match press conference ahead of the 2005 Champions League final against AC Milan in Istanbul

EUROPEAN PLAYER RECORDS

The below list is a rundown of the players to have played in the most games in European competition. Due to the expansion of competitions such as the Champions League, only Norwegian midfielder Roar Strand in the below list appeared in European competition before the first season of the Champions League format, in 1992/93.

Jamie Carragher is the highest-placed Liverpool player in joint-eighth alongside Thierry Henry, with Steven Gerrard joint-20th alongside Iker Casillas. Fernando Morientes is the only other player in the list with Liverpool connections, having appeared for the Reds during the 2005/06 Champions League. The totals include substitute appearances and UEFA Super Cup games, and is up-to-date at the end of the 2010/11 season.

EUROPEAN APPEARANCES – ALL-TIME RECORD

PLAYER	APPS	CLUB(S) REPRESENTED IN EUROPEAN COMPS.
Paolo Maldini	168	AC Milan
Clarence Seedorf	148	Ajax, Real Madrid, Inter Milan, AC Milan
Raul	147	Real Madrid, Schalke
Oliver Kahn	142	Karlsruhe, Bayern Munich
Ryan Giggs	141	Manchester United
Javier Zanetti	141	Inter Milan
Roberto Carlos	140	Inter Milan, Real Madrid, Fenerbahce
Jamie Carragher	**139**	**Liverpool**
Thierry Henry	139	Monaco, Arsenal, Barcelona
Andriy Shevchenko	138	Dynamo Kiev, AC Milan, Chelsea
Edwin van der Sar	138	Ajax, Juventus, Fulham, Manchester United
Luis Figo	134	Sporting Lisbon, Barcelona, Real Madrid, Inter Milan
Paul Scholes	132	Manchester United
Xavi	132	Barcelona
Roar Strand	127	Rosenborg, Molde
A'sandro Del Piero	126	Juventus
Gary Neville	119	Manchester United
Carles Puyol	117	Barcelona
Iker Casillas	116	Real Madrid
Steven Gerrard	**116**	**Liverpool**
David Beckham	114	Manchester United, Real Madrid, AC Milan
Filippo Inzaghi	114	Parma, Juventus, AC Milan
F'nando Morientes	113	Real Zaragoza, Real Madrid, Monaco, Liverpool, Valencia, Marseille

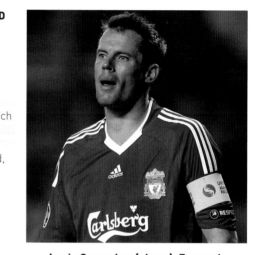

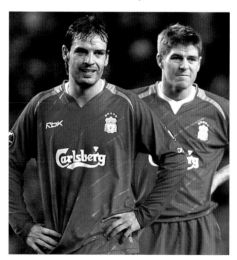

Jamie Carragher (above), Fernando Morientes and Steven Gerrard (below) – Members of the European 100 club

EUROPEAN PLAYER RECORDS

A hat-trick against Napoli in 2010/11 and a goal against FK Rabotnicki ensured that Steven Gerrard added to his lead as the leading British goalscorer for an English club in Europe. With a total of 38 goals, it is a record that should be safe – for at least another season. Michael Owen, John Wark and Ian Rush are the other players in the list with Liverpool connections.

MOST GOALS BY A BRITISH PLAYER FOR AN ENGLISH CLUB IN EUROPE

PLAYER	CLUB (S)	GOALS	EUROPEAN CAREER
Steven Gerrard	Liverpool	38	1998-
Alan Shearer	Blackburn, Newcastle	32	1994-2006
Peter Lorimer	Leeds United	30	1962-1978
Ryan Giggs	Manchester United	29	1991-
Denis Law	Manchester United	28	1962-1972
Michael Owen	Liverpool, Man. Utd	26	1997-
Paul Scholes	Manchester United	26	1994-2011
Wayne Rooney	Manchester United	25	2004-
Andy Cole	Newcastle, Man. Utd	23	1994-2001
John Wark	Ipswich T, Liverpool	23	1974-1985
Bobby Charlton	Manchester United	22	1956-1972
Martin Chivers	Tottenham Hotspur	22	1967-1975
Frank Lampard	West Ham, Chelsea	22	1999-
Ray Kennedy	Arsenal, Liverpool	20	1969-1981
Ian Rush	Liverpool	20	1981-1985 & 1991-1996

Due to Liverpool being without European competition in 2011/12, Steven Gerrard must wait at least another campaign before being able to challenge the top two – both prolific forwards – in the most goals in Europe for one English club list.

MOST GOALS IN EUROPE FOR ONE ENGLISH CLUB

PLAYER	CLUB	GOALS	EUROPEAN CAREER
Thierry Henry	Arsenal	42	1999-2007
Steven Gerrard	Liverpool	38	1998-
Ruud van Nistelrooy	Manchester United	38	2001-2006
Peter Lorimer	Leeds United	30	1962-1978
Alan Shearer	Newcastle United	30	1996-2006
Ryan Giggs	Manchester United	29	1991-
Denis Law	Manchester United	28	1962-1972
Didier Drogba	Chelsea	28	2004-
Paul Scholes	Manchester United	26	1994-2011
Wayne Rooney	Manchester United	25	2004-
Bobby Charlton	Manchester United	22	1956-1972
Martin Chivers	Tottenham Hotspur	22	1967-1975
Michael Owen	Liverpool	22	1997-2004
Frank Lampard	Chelsea	21	2001-
Ian Rush	Liverpool	20	1981-1985 & 1991-1996
Ole Gunnar Solskjaer	Manchester United	20	1996-2007
Andy Cole	Manchester United	19	1994-2001
John Wark	Ipswich Town	18	1974-1983
Roger Hunt	Liverpool	17	1959-1969
Mick Jones	Leeds United	17	1967-1973

EUROPEAN PLAYER RECORDS

Joe Cole created a new Liverpool record in 2010/11 with his quick-fire strike against Steaua Bucharest in the Europa League. His goal after only 27 seconds is recognised as the fastest ever by a Reds player, beating the previous best set by Phil Boersma nearly 38 years previously.

FASTEST LIVERPOOL FC GOALS IN EUROPE

PLAYER	TIME OF GOAL	DATE	OPPOSITION	COMPETITION
Joe Cole	27 seconds	16th Sept 2010	Steaua Bucharest	Europa League
Phil Boersma	57 seconds	13th Dec 1972	Dynamo Berlin	UEFA Cup
Alun Evans	59 seconds	16th Sept 1969	Dundalk	Inter-Cities Fairs Cup
Chris Lawler	2 minutes	1st Dec 1965	Standard Liege	Euro Cup-Winners' Cup
Kevin Keegan	2 minutes	16th Mar 1977	Saint-Etienne	European Cup
F. Sin-Pongolle	2 minutes	13th Sept 2005	Real Betis	European Cup
Gordon Wallace	3 minutes	17th Aug 1964	Reykjavik	European Cup
Alec Lindsay	3 minutes	17th Sept 1974	Stromsgodset	Euro Cup-Winners' Cup
Roger Hunt	4 minutes	4th May 1965	Inter Milan	European Cup
Jan Molby	4 minutes	6th Nov 1991	Auxerre	UEFA Cup
Paul Stewart	4 minutes	16th Sept 1992	Apollon Limassol	Euro Cup-Winners' Cup
Markus Babbel	4 minutes	16th May 2001	Alaves	UEFA Cup
Luis Garcia	4 minutes	3rd May 2005	Chelsea	European Cup
Steven Gerrard	4 minutes	11th Dec 2007	Marseille	European Cup
Dirk Kuyt	4 minutes	1st Oct 2008	PSV Eindhoven	European Cup
David Ngog	4 minutes	24th Nov 2009	Debreceni	European Cup

Robbie Fowler leads the Liverpool FC record standings in terms of the quickest to reach double figures for the club in European competition. Jimmy Case, in joint-third with Ian Rush, is the best of the non-strikers, whilst Steven Gerrard's rise up the Liverpool record goalscoring charts came about later in his Reds career based on how long he took to reach 10 goals.

FASTEST TO 10 EUROPEAN GOALS FOR LIVERPOOL FC

PLAYER	GAMES TAKEN	PLAYER	GAMES TAKEN
Robbie Fowler	16	Steve Heighway	49
Roger Hunt	18	Steven Gerrard	55
Jimmy Case	20	Phil Neal	56
Ian Rush	20	Chris Lawler	61
Terry McDermott	22	Emlyn Hughes	79
Michael Owen	22	Ian Callaghan	88
Ian St John	24		
Fernando Torres	26		
Peter Crouch	27		
Dirk Kuyt	27		
Luis Garcia	30		
Emile Heskey	31		
John Toshack	32		
Kevin Keegan	36		
Kenny Dalglish	37		
Ray Kennedy	39		

Robbie Fowler – First to 10

LIVERPOOL FC MANAGERS – EUROPE

Although Roy Hodgson's tenure as Liverpool boss was brief, he did rise to second amongst the club's men in charge for a positive reason. His 10-match unbeaten run in Europa League competition sees him lie second behind Joe Fagan in the list of the club's managers and how many games in European competition they went unbeaten.

MOST GAMES UNBEATEN AT START OF MANAGERIAL CAREER

MANAGER	MATCHES	YEAR OF FIRST UNBEATEN GAME – YEAR OF FIRST DEFEAT
Joe Fagan	12	1983-1985
Roy Hodgson	10	2010
Bill Shankly	8	1964-1965
Bob Paisley	4	1974-1975
Roy Evans/Gerard Houllier	4	1998
Roy Evans	3	1995
Kenny Dalglish	2	2011
Graeme Souness	1	1991
Gerard Houllier	0	1998

Roy Hodgson lies third for the most impressive win ratio enjoyed by a Reds boss in Europe. Kenny Dalglish is bottom having only enjoyed 1 win in his first 4 games in charge of the club in continental competition, with Joe Fagan well ahead following his success during two seasons in charge.

BIGGEST WIN RATIO ENJOYED BY LIVERPOOL FC MANAGERS IN EUROPEAN COMPETITION

MANAGER	P	W	D	L	F	A	% WINS
Joe Fagan	19	14	2	3	34	10	73.7
Bob Paisley	61	39	11	11	140	49	63.9
Roy Hodgson	10	6	4	0	15	4	60.0
Rafael Benitez	85	49	16	20	140	68	57.7
Bill Shankly	65	34	13	18	114	54	52.3
Gerard Houllier	52	26	17	9	78	45	50.0
Roy Evans	16	8	5	3	24	16	50.0
Graeme Souness	12	6	0	6	26	16	50.0
Roy Evans/Gerard Houllier	4	2	2	0	10	2	50.0
Kenny Dalglish	4	1	2	1	1	1	25.0

Joint-managers - Houllier and Evans

LFC IN EUROPE: CLUB-BY-CLUB RECORD

OPPOSITION	PLAYED	WON	DRAWN	LOST	FOR	AGAINST
Aberdeen	2	2	0	0	5	0
AC Milan	2	1	0	1	4	5
AEK Athens	2	2	0	0	6	1
Ajax Amsterdam	2	0	1	1	3	7
Alaves	1	1	0	0	5	4
Anderlecht	6	5	0	1	11	4
Apollon Limassol	2	2	0	0	8	2
Arsenal	2	1	1	0	5	3
AS Monaco	2	1	0	1	2	1
AS Roma	5	3	1	1	5	2
Athletic Bilbao	4	2	1	1	4	3
Atletico Madrid	4	1	2	1	4	4
Austria Vienna	2	1	1	0	5	2
Auxerre	4	3	0	1	6	2
AZ '67 Alkmaar	2	1	1	0	5	4
Basel FC	2	0	2	0	4	4
Bayer Leverkusen	4	3	0	1	9	6
Bayern Munich	7	2	4	1	9	7
Benfica	10	6	0	4	19	11
Besiktas	2	1	0	1	9	2
Boavista	2	0	2	0	2	2
Bordeaux	2	2	0	0	4	0
Borussia Dortmund	3	1	1	1	3	2
Borussia Moenchengladbach	5	3	0	2	10	5
Braga	2	0	1	0	0	1
Brann Bergen	2	1	1	0	4	1
Brondby	2	0	1	1	0	1
Celta Vigo	2	0	0	2	1	4
Celtic	6	1	3	2	5	6
Chelsea	10	2	5	3	10	12
Club Brugge KV	3	2	1	0	5	3
Crusaders	2	2	0	0	7	0
CSKA Moscow	1	1	0	0	3	1
CSKA Sofia	6	4	0	2	10	5
Debreceni VSC	2	2	0	0	2	0
Deportivo La Coruna	2	1	1	0	1	0
Dinamo Bucharest	4	3	1	0	7	2
Dundalk	4	4	0	0	19	1
Dynamo Berlin	2	1	1	0	3	1
Dynamo Dresden	6	4	1	1	11	4
Dynamo Kiev	2	2	0	0	3	1
Dynamo Tblisi	2	1	0	1	2	4
Eintracht Frankfurt	2	1	1	0	2	0
FC Barcelona	8	3	3	2	6	6
FC Cologne	3	0	3	0	2	2
FC Porto	4	2	2	0	7	2
FC Utrecht	2	0	2	0	0	0
Ferencvaros	6	1	3	2	3	4
Fiorentina	2	0	0	2	1	4
FK Rabotnicki	2	2	0	0	4	0
Galatasaray	4	1	2	1	6	6
Genoa	2	0	0	2	1	4
Graz AK	2	1	0	1	2	1
Haka FC	2	2	0	0	9	1
Hamburg	2	1	1	0	7	1
Hibernian	4	3	0	1	6	2
HJK Helsinki	2	1	0	1	5	1
Honved	2	1	1	0	2	0
Inter Milan	4	3	0	1	6	4

LFC IN EUROPE: CLUB-BY-CLUB RECORD

OPPOSITION	PLAYED	WON	DRAWN	LOST	FOR	AGAINST
Jeunesse D'Esch	2	1	1	0	3	1
Juventus	6	2	1	3	4	5
Kaunas FBK	2	2	0	0	5	1
Kosice FC	2	2	0	0	8	0
Kuusysi Lahti	2	1	0	1	6	2
Lech Poznan	2	2	0	0	5	0
Leeds United	2	0	1	1	0	1
Levski Sofia	2	2	0	0	6	2
Lille	2	1	0	1	3	1
Maccabi Haifa	2	1	1	0	3	2
Malmo	2	2	0	0	4	1
Munich 1860	2	1	0	1	9	2
MyPa 47	2	2	0	0	4	1
Napoli	2	1	1	0	3	1
Nottingham Forest	2	0	1	1	0	2
Odense	2	2	0	0	6	0
Olimpija Ljubljana	2	1	1	0	4	1
Olympiakos	4	2	1	1	7	4
Olympique Lyon	2	0	1	1	2	3
Olympique Marseille	6	3	1	2	9	5
Oulu Palloseura	4	3	1	0	19	2
Panathinaikos	2	2	0	0	5	0
Paris St Germain	2	1	0	1	2	3
Petrolul Ploesti	3	2	0	1	5	3
PSV Eindhoven	6	5	1	0	12	2
Rapid Bucharest	2	1	1	0	1	0
RC Strasbourg	2	1	0	1	2	3
Real Betis	2	1	1	0	2	1
Real Madrid	3	3	0	0	6	0
Real Sociedad	2	2	0	0	9	1
Red Star Belgrade	2	0	0	2	2	4
Reykjavik	2	2	0	0	11	1
Saint-Etienne	2	1	0	1	3	2
Servette Geneva	2	1	0	1	3	2
Sion FC	2	2	0	0	8	4
Slask Wroclaw	2	2	0	0	5	1
Slovan Liberec	2	2	0	0	4	2
Sparta Prague	2	1	0	0	1	0
Spartak Moscow	4	2	0	2	10	7
Spartak Vladikavkaz	2	1	1	0	2	1
Standard Liege	4	3	1	0	6	2
Steaua Bucharest	4	2	2	0	7	3
Stromsgodset	2	2	0	0	12	0
Swarowski Tirol	2	2	0	0	6	0
Total Network Solutions	2	2	0	0	6	0
Tottenham Hotspur	2	1	0	1	2	2
Toulouse	2	2	0	0	5	0
Trabzonspor	4	3	0	1	6	2
Unirea Urziceni	2	2	0	0	4	1
Valencia	4	0	2	2	2	5
Vitesse Arnhem	2	2	0	0	2	0
Vitoria Setubal	2	1	0	1	3	3
Widzew Lodz	2	1	0	1	3	4
Zurich FC	2	2	0	0	6	1
OVERALL	**328**	**185**	**72**	**71**	**582**	**265**

Games decided on toss of coin (Petrolul) in a third game counted as a draw.
One-game ties decided on penalties count as wins or losses.
Statistics correct at end of 2009/10 season.

LIVERPOOL FC EUROPEAN OPPONENTS

FK Rabotnicki, Napoli, FC Utrecht and Braga were the newcomers to Liverpool's all-time list of opponents in competitive European competition during 2010/11. FK Rabotnicki became the 37th country the club had visited in competitive European action (excluding England), whilst Napoli became the seventh Italian side the Reds have faced.

Liverpool have now faced 114 clubs in all, with the 18 countries the club have yet to visit in European competition being: Albania, Andorra, Armenia, Azerbaijan, Belarus, Bosnia-Herzegovina, Croatia, Estonia, Faroe Islands, Georgia, Kazakhstan, Latvia, Liechtenstein, Malta, Moldova, Montenegro, San Marino and Serbia.

The countries, and the clubs, that Liverpool have faced are listed below and opposite:

AUSTRIA (3)
AK Graz, Austria Vienna, Swarovski Tirol

BELGIUM (3)
Anderlecht, FC Bruges, Standard Liege

BULGARIA (2)
CSKA Sofia, Levski Sofia

CYPRUS (1)
Apollon Limassol

CZECH REPUBLIC (2)
Slovan Liberec, Sparta Prague

DENMARK (2)
Brondby, Odense

EAST GERMANY (2)
Dynamo Berlin, Dynamo Dresden

ENGLAND (5)
Arsenal, Chelsea, Leeds United, Nottingham Forest, Tottenham Hotspur

FINLAND (5)
FC Haka, HJK Helsinki, Kuusysi Lahti, MyPa 47, Oulu Palloseura

FRANCE (10)
Auxerre, Bordeaux, Lille, Lyon, Marseille, Monaco, Paris St Germain, RC Strasbourg, St Etienne, Toulouse

GERMANY (2)
Bayer Leverkusen, Borussia Dortmund

GREECE (3)
AEK Athens, Olympiakos, Panathinaikos

HOLLAND (5)
Ajax Amsterdam, AZ '67 Alkmaar, FC Utrecht, PSV Eindhoven, Vitesse Arnhem

HUNGARY (3)
Debreceni VSC, Ferencvaros, Honved

ICELAND (1)
Reykjavik

ISRAEL (1)
Maccabi Haifa

ITALY (7)
AC Milan, AS Roma, Fiorentina, Genoa, Inter Milan, Juventus, Napoli

LIVERPOOL FC EUROPEAN OPPONENTS

LITHUANIA (1)
FBK Kaunas

LUXEMBOURG (1)
Jeunesse D'Esch

MACEDONIA (1)
FK Rabotnicki

NORTHERN IRELAND (1)
Crusaders

NORWAY (2)
Brann Bergen, Stromsgodset

POLAND (3)
Lech Poznan, Slask Wroclaw, Widzew Lodz

PORTUGAL (5)
Benfica, Boavista, Braga, FC Porto, Vitoria Setubal

REPUBLIC OF IRELAND (1)
Dundalk

ROMANIA (5)
Dinamo Bucharest, Petrolul Ploesti, Rapid Bucharest, Steaua Bucharest, Unirea Urziceni

RUSSIA (4)
CSKA Moscow, Dynamo Tblisi, Spartak Moscow, Spartak Vladikavkaz

SCOTLAND (3)
Aberdeen, Celtic, Hibernian

SLOVAKIA (1)
FC Kosice

SLOVENIA (1)
Olimpija Ljubljana

SPAIN (10)
Alaves, Athletic Bilbao, Atletico Madrid, Barcelona, Celta Vigo, Deportivo La Coruna, Real Betis, Real Madrid, Real Sociedad, Valencia

SWEDEN (1)
Malmo

SWITZERLAND (4)
FC Basel, FC Sion, FC Zurich, Servette Geneva

TURKEY (3)
Besiktas, Galatasaray, Trabzonspor

UKRAINE (1)
Dynamo Kiev

WALES (1)
Total Network Solutions

WEST GERMANY (7)
Bayern Munich, Borussia Moenchengladbach, Borussia Dortmund, FC Cologne, Eintracht Frankfurt, Hamburg, 1860 Munich

YUGOSLAVIA (1)
Red Star Belgrade

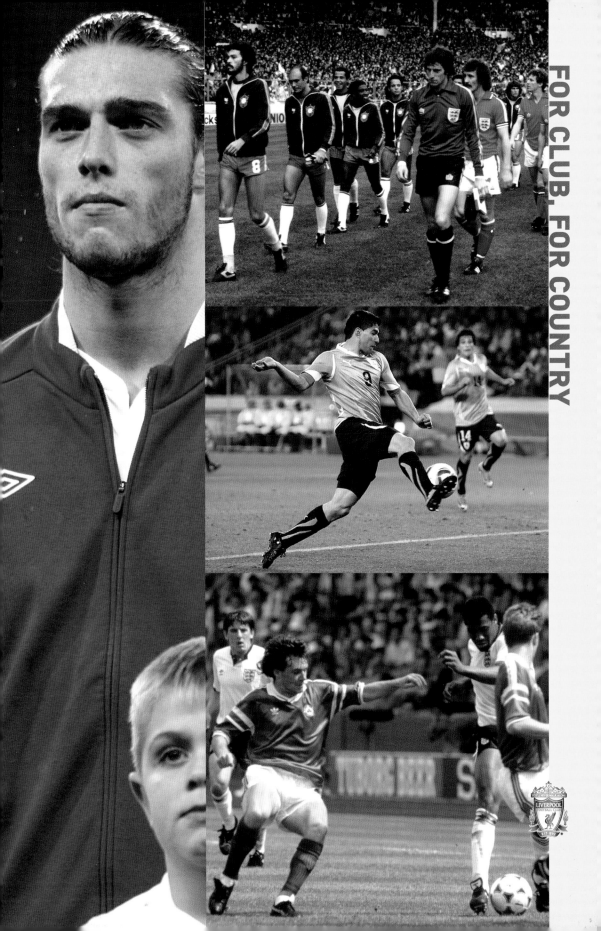

ENGLAND

There are 59 Liverpool players to have represented England. Andy Carroll became the 59th member of the club, celebrating the feat with his first international goal in a 1-1 draw with Ghana back in March 2011. Stewart Downing, a summer signing from Aston Villa, became No. 60 early in the 2011/12 campaign.

LIVERPOOL FC PLAYERS CAPPED BY ENGLAND (AT END OF AUGUST 2011)					
PLAYER	CAPS WON AT LIVERPOOL	TOTAL CAPS	PLAYER	CAPS WON AT LIVERPOOL	TOTAL CAPS
Steven Gerrard	89	89	John Scales	3	3
Michael Owen	60	89	Phil Taylor	3	3
Emlyn Hughes	59	62	Gerry Byrne	2	2
Ray Clemence	56	61	Scott Carson	2	3
Phil Neal	50	50	Bill Jones	2	2
John Barnes	48	79	Alan Kennedy	2	2
Phil Thompson	42	42	Jimmy Melia	2	2
Jamie Carragher	38	38	Jack Parkinson	2	2
Emile Heskey	35	62	John Bamber	1	1
Peter Beardsley	34	59	Frank Becton	1	2
Roger Hunt	34	34	Thomas Bradshaw	1	1
Peter Crouch	28	40	Andy Carroll	1	2
Kevin Keegan	28	63	Raby Howell	1	2
Terry McDermott	25	25	David James	1	53
Steve McManaman	24	37	Chris Kirkland	1	1
Robbie Fowler	22	26	Neil Ruddock	1	1
Glen Johnson	19	34	Tommy Smith	1	1
Ray Kennedy	17	17			
Steve McMahon	17	17			
Jamie Redknapp	17	17			
Peter Thompson	16	16			
Sam Hardy	14	21			
Sammy Lee	14	14			
Gordon Milne	14	14			
Paul Ince	12	53			
Danny Murphy	9	9			
Nick Barmby	8	23			
Harry Chambers	8	8			
Rob Jones	8	8			
Alan A'Court	5	5			
Tom Bromilow	5	5			
David Johnson	5	8			
Ephraim Longworth	5	5			
Mark Wright	5	45			
Ian Callaghan	4	4			
Chris Lawler	4	4			
Alec Lindsay	4	4			
Jack Cox	3	3			
Gordon Hodgson	3	3			
Laurie Hughes	3	3			
Larry Lloyd	3	4			
Tommy Lucas	3	3			

**Peter Crouch and Steven Gerrard –
Past and present England Reds**

HOME NATIONS

Charlie Adam became Liverpool's 23rd Scottish international in history when he appeared against Denmark in August 2011. Signed from Blackpool, the midfielder had already won 11 caps before his summer move from Blackpool. Danny Wilson won three Scotland caps in his debut season in England, a tally also added to in the same match.

Craig Bellamy and Robbie Keane were the last Liverpool players to represent Wales and Republic of Ireland respectively earlier this century, although Bellamy's return to the club at the end of the summer 2011 transfer window will ensure he adds to his tally. No Reds player has turned out for Northern Ireland since before World War II.

LIVERPOOL FC PLAYERS CAPPED BY SCOTLAND (AT END OF AUGUST 2011)

PLAYER	CAPS WON AT LIVERPOOL	TOTAL CAPS	PLAYER	CAPS WON AT LIVERPOOL	TOTAL CAPS
Kenny Dalglish	55	102	John Wark	3	29
Graeme Souness	37	54	Jimmy McDougall	2	2
Billy Liddell	28	28	Frank McGarvey	2	7
Steve Nicol	27	27	Donald MacKinlay	2	2
Alan Hansen	26	26	Ron Yeats	2	2
Tommy Younger	16	24	Charlie Adam	1	12
Ian St John	14	21	George Allan	1	1
Gary Gillespie	13	13	Billy Dunlop	1	1
Alex Raisbeck	8	8	Jock McNab	1	1
Danny Wilson	4	4	Tom Miller	1	3
Ken Campbell	3	8	Hugh Morgan	1	2
Tommy Lawrence	3	3			

LIVERPOOL FC PLAYERS CAPPED BY WALES (AT END OF AUGUST 2011)

PLAYER	CAPS WON AT LIVERPOOL	TOTAL CAPS	PLAYER	CAPS WON AT LIVERPOOL	TOTAL CAPS
Ian Rush	67	73	Cyril Sidlow	7	7
John Toshack	26	40	Ray Lambert	5	5
Joey Jones	18	72	Richard Morris	5	11
Maurice Parry	16	16	Edward Parry	5	5
Craig Bellamy	11	62	John Hughes	3	3
Ernest Peake	10	11	Lee Jones	1	2
George Lathom	8	10	Robert Matthews	1	3
Dean Saunders	8	75			

LIVERPOOL FC PLAYERS CAPPED BY NORTHERN IRELAND & REPUBLIC OF IRELAND (AT END OF AUGUST 2011)

PLAYER	CAPS WON AT LIVERPOOL	TOTAL CAPS	PLAYER	CAPS WON AT LIVERPOOL	TOTAL CAPS
Ronnie Whelan	51	53	Mark Kennedy	17	34
Steve Staunton	38	102	Jim Beglin	15	15
Ray Houghton	34	73	Jason McAteer	14	52
Steve Heighway	33	34	Billy Lacey (NI)	12	23
Steve Finnan	28	53	Michael Robinson	5	24
Elisha Scott (NI)	27	31	Robbie Keane	4	109
Phil Babb	25	35	David McMullan (NI)	3	3
Mark Lawrenson	24	39	Ken De Mange	1	2
John Aldridge	19	69			

INTERNATIONAL CAPS

LFC PLAYERS CAPPED FOR THEIR COUNTRIES – HOME NATIONS (AT END OF AUGUST 2011)

PLAYER	COUNTRY	CAPS	PLAYER	COUNTRY	CAPS
Steven Gerrard	England	89	Alex Raisbeck	Scotland	=
Ian Rush	Wales	67	Dean Saunders	Wales	=
Michael Owen	England	60	Cyril Sidlow	Wales	7
Emlyn Hughes	England	59	Alan A'Court	England	5
Ray Clemence	England	56	Tom Bromilow	England	=
Kenny Dalglish	Scotland	55	David Johnson	England	=
Ronnie Whelan	Republic of Ireland	51	Ray Lambert	Wales	=
Phil Neal	England	50	Ephraim Longworth	England	=
John Barnes	England	48	Richard Morris	Wales	=
Phil Thompson	England	42	Edward Parry	Wales	=
Jamie Carragher	England	38	Michael Robinson	Republic of Ireland	=
Steve Staunton	Republic of Ireland	=	Mark Wright	England	=
Graeme Souness	Scotland	37	Ian Callaghan	England	4
Emile Heskey	England	35	Robbie Keane	Republic of Ireland	=
Peter Beardsley	England	34	Chris Lawler	England	=
Ray Houghton	Republic of Ireland	=	Alec Lindsay	England	=
Roger Hunt	England	=	Danny Wilson	Scotland	=
Steve Heighway	Republic of Ireland	33	Ken Campbell	Scotland	3
Peter Crouch	England	28	Jack Cox	England	=
Steve Finnan	Republic of Ireland	=	Gordon Hodgson	England	=
Kevin Keegan	England	=	John Hughes	Wales	=
Billy Liddell	Scotland	=	Laurie Hughes	England	=
Steve Nicol	Scotland	27	Tommy Lawrence	Scotland	=
Elisha Scott	Northern Ireland	=	Larry Lloyd	England	=
Alan Hansen	Scotland	26	Tommy Lucas	England	=
John Toshack	Wales	=	David McMullan	Northern Ireland	=
Phil Babb	Republic of Ireland	25	John Scales	England	=
Terry McDermott	England	=	Phil Taylor	England	=
Mark Lawrenson	Republic of Ireland	24	John Wark	Scotland	=
Steve McManaman	England	=	Gerry Byrne	England	2
Robbie Fowler	England	22	Scott Carson	England	=
John Aldridge	Republic of Ireland	19	Bill Jones	England	=
Glen Johnson	England	=	Alan Kennedy	England	=
Joey Jones	Wales	18	Donald MacKinlay	Scotland	=
Mark Kennedy	Republic of Ireland	17	Jimmy McDougall	Scotland	=
Ray Kennedy	England	=	Frank McGarvey	Scotland	=
Steve McMahon	England	=	Jimmy Melia	England	=
Jamie Redknapp	England	=	Jack Parkinson	England	=
Maurice Parry	Wales	16	Ron Yeats	Scotland	=
Peter Thompson	England	=	Charlie Adam	Scotland	1
Tommy Younger	Scotland	=	George Allan	Scotland	=
Jim Beglin	Republic of Ireland	15	John Bamber	England	=
Sam Hardy	England	14	Frank Becton	England	=
Sammy Lee	England	=	Thomas Bradshaw	England	=
Jason McAteer	Republic of Ireland	=	Andy Carroll	England	=
Gordon Milne	England	=	Ken De Mange	Republic of Ireland	=
Ian St John	Scotland	=	Billy Dunlop	Scotland	=
Gary Gillespie	Scotland	13	Raby Howell	England	=
Paul Ince	England	12	David James	England	=
Billy Lacey	Northern Ireland	=	Lee Jones	Wales	=
Craig Bellamy	Wales	11	Chris Kirkland	England	=
Ernest Peake	Wales	10	Robert Matthews	Wales	=
Danny Murphy	England	9	Jock McNab	Scotland	=
Nick Barmby	England	8	Tom Miller	Scotland	=
Harry Chambers	England	=	Hugh Morgan	Scotland	=
Rob Jones	England	=	Neil Ruddock	England	=
George Lathom	Wales	8	Tommy Smith	England	=

INTERNATIONAL GOALS

LFC PLAYERS WHO'VE SCORED FOR THEIR COUNTRIES – HOME NATIONS (AT 31 JULY 2011)

PLAYER	COUNTRY	GOALS	PLAYER	COUNTRY	GOALS
Michael Owen	England	26	Ronnie Whelan	Republic of Ireland	3
Ian Rush	Wales	=	Robbie Keane	Republic of Ireland	2
Steven Gerrard	England	19	Billy Lacey	Northern Ireland	=
Roger Hunt	England	18	Sammy Lee	England	=
Peter Crouch	England	14	Tom Miller	Scotland	=
Kenny Dalglish	Scotland	13	Dean Saunders	Wales	=
John Barnes	England	8	Steve Staunton	Republic of Ireland	=
Ian St John	Scotland	=	Alan A'Court	England	1
John Toshack	Wales	=	John Aldridge	Republic of Ireland	=
Kevin Keegan	England	7	Nick Barmby	England	=
Peter Beardsley	England	6	Andy Carroll	England	=
Billy Liddell	Scotland	=	Steve Finnan	Republic of Ireland	=
Harry Chambers	England	5	Gordon Hodgson	England	=
Robbie Fowler	England	=	Emlyn Hughes	England	=
Emile Heskey	England	=	Glen Johnson	England	=
Phil Neal	England	=	Chris Lawler	England	=
Craig Bellamy	Wales	4	Jason McAteer	Republic of Ireland	=
Graeme Souness	Scotland	=	Jimmy Melia	England	=
Ray Houghton	Republic of Ireland	3	Danny Murphy	England	=
David Johnson	England	=	Ernest Peake	Wales	=
Ray Kennedy	England	=	Jamie Redknapp	England	=
Mark Lawrenson	Republic of Ireland	=	Phil Thompson	England	=
Terry McDermott	England	=	Danny Wilson	Scotland	=

Andy Carroll – England scorer while at Liverpool

NATIONALITIES

At the end of the 2010/11 season, around 100 overseas players had represented the club in competitive first-team games. Note that Gordon Hodgson, Craig Johnston (both South Africa) and John Barnes (Jamaica) have represented England at the minimum of Under-21 level.

OVERSEAS LIVERPOOL FC FIRST-TEAM PLAYERS

COUNTRY	NO. OF PLAYERS	PLAYERS
France	13	Jean-Michel Ferri, Pegguy Arphexad, Bernard Diomede, Gregory Vignal, Nicolas Anelka, Bruno Cheyrou, Patrice Luzi, Anthony Le Tallec, Florent Sinama-Pongolle, Djibril Cisse, Charles Itandje, Damien Plessis, David Ngog
Spain	=	Josemi, Luis Garcia, Xabi Alonso, Antonio Nunez, Fernando Morientes, Pepe Reina, Antonio Barragan, Miki Roque, Alvaro Arbeloa, Fernando Torres, Albert Riera, Daniel Ayala, Daniel Pacheco
South Africa	8	Lance Carr, Hugh Gerhadi, Dirk Kemp, Berry Nieuwenhuys, Robert Priday, Arthur Riley, Doug Rudham, Harman Van Den Berg
Holland	6	Erik Meijer, Sander Westerveld, Bolo Zenden, Jan Kromkamp, Dirk Kuyt, Ryan Babel
Norway	=	Stig Inge Bjornebye, Oyvind Leonhardsen, Bjorn Tore Kvarme, Vegard Heggem, Frode Kippe, John Arne Riise
Argentina	=	Mauricio Pellegrino, Gabriel Paletta, Javier Mascherano, Emiliano Insua, Sebastian Leto, Maxi Rodriguez
Germany	5	Karlheinz Riedle, Dietmar Hamann, Markus Babbel, Christian Ziege, Sean Dundee
Denmark	4	Jan Molby, Torben Piechnik, Daniel Agger, Christian Poulsen
Brazil	3	Fabio Aurelio, Lucas Leiva, Diego Cavalieri
Israel	=	Avi Cohen, Ronny Rosenthal, Yossi Benayoun
Italy	=	Daniele Padelli, Andrea Dossena, Alberto Aquilani
Finland	=	Sami Hyypia, Jari Litmanen, Lauri Dalla Valle
Australia	2	Harry Kewell, Brad Jones
Mali	=	Djimi Traore, Mohamed Sissoko
Portugal	=	Abel Xavier, Raul Meireles
Senegal	=	El-Hadji Diouf, Salif Diao
Switzerland	=	Stephane Henchoz, Philipp Degen
USA	=	Brad Friedel, Zak Whitbread
Cameroon	1	Rigobert Song
Chile	=	Mark Gonzalez
Croatia	=	Igor Biscan
Greece	=	Sotirios Kyrgiakos
Guinea	=	Titi Camara
Hungary	=	Istvan Kozma
Morocco	=	Nabil El Zhar
Poland	=	Jerzy Dudek
Serbia	=	Milan Jovanovic
Slovakia	=	Martin Skrtel
Sweden	=	Glenn Hysen
Ukraine	=	Andriy Voronin
Uruguay	=	Luis Suarez
Zimbabwe	=	Bruce Grobbelaar

COPA AMERICA

The globalisation of the game in the modern era has meant Liverpool can now add player representation in South America's major international tournament, the Copa America.

Javier Mascherano became the first Liverpool player to compete in the competition in 2007. The competition's policy of host rotation meant that Venezuela were hosts, and the defensive midfielder enjoyed an unchacteristically goalscoring tournament. Mascherano netted the only goal in a group victory over Paraguay, and in a 4-0 success over Peru at the quarter-final phase. However, as impressive as Argentina were throughout the competition – having won all 5 of their games – they came up short in the final, losing out 3-0 to a Brazil side who included new Liverpool goalkeeper Alexander Doni in their line-up. It was to prove a second successive defeat in a Copa America final for Mascherano.

There was success in 2011 for one of Liverpool's two representatives at the finals in Argentina. **Luis Suarez**, so impressive since joining the club, helped guide Uruguay to glory, a year after he helped them reach the World Cup semi-finals. A goalscorer during the group phase, Suarez really made his mark when it mattered most – in the knockout phase. The forward converted a penalty during the quarter-final shootout triumph over the hosts, before scoring both goals in the last four victory over Peru. In the final, Suarez opened the scoring in the 3-0 victory over Paraguay, helping his country to a record 15th Copa America title.

For midfielder **Lucas Leiva**, his Brazil side endured a tournament to forget. The midfielder was an ever-present as his side scraped through to the quarter-finals. A failure to score in a third game in four proved key, while Lucas was also sent off as this country were beaten on penalties by Paraguay – who did not record a shot on target during 120 minutes.

LIVERPOOL FC PLAYERS AT THE COPA AMERICA					
YEAR	**HOSTS**	**PLAYER**	**COUNTRY**	**APPS**	**GOALS**	**HOW COUNTRY FARED**
2007	Venezuela	Javier Mascherano	Argentina	6	2	Runners-Up
2011	Argentina	Lucas Leiva	Brazil	4	0	Quarter-Finals
		Luis Suarez	Uruguay	6	4	Winners

Luis Suarez (left) and Lucas Leiva enjoyed contrasting emotions at the Copa America in 2011

LFC PLAYERS AT OTHER MAJOR TOURNAMENTS

Players who have represented their national sides in other international competitions, while affiliated with Liverpool, are noted below. Goalkeeper Brad Friedel is the most prominent name, having appeared for the USA at the Confederations Cup, at the Olympics and in the CONCACAF Gold Cup. Rigobert Song is the only player to have tasted success, captaining and scoring the clinching penalty in the shoot-out to lead Cameroon to the African Cup of Nations in 2000 – although Lucas Leiva did return from Beijing with Olympic bronze, in 2008.

LIVERPOOL FC PLAYERS AT THE FIFA CONFEDERATIONS CUP

YEAR	HOSTS	PLAYER	COUNTRY	APPS	GOALS	HOW COUNTRY FARED
1999	Mexico	Brad Friedel	USA	2	0	3rd place
2009	South Africa	Andrea Dossena	Italy	1	0	Group phase
2009	South Africa	Xabi Alonso	Spain	4	1	3rd place
2009	South Africa	Alvaro Arbeloa	Spain	3	0	3rd place
2009	South Africa	Pepe Reina	Spain	1	0	3rd place
2009	South Africa	Albert Riera	Spain	4	0	3rd place
2009	South Africa	Fernando Torres	Spain	5	3	3rd place

LIVERPOOL FC PLAYERS AT THE OLYMPICS

YEAR	HOSTS	PLAYER	COUNTRY	APPS	GOALS	HOW COUNTRY FARED
2000	Sydney, Australia	Brad Friedel	USA	6	0	4th place
2008	Beijing, China	Ryan Babel	Holland	4	1	Quarter-finals
2008	Beijing, China	Lucas Leiva	Brazil	5	0	Bronze medal

LIVERPOOL FC PLAYERS AT THE AFRICAN CUP OF NATIONS

YEAR	HOSTS	PLAYER	COUNTRY	APPS	GOALS	HOW COUNTRY FARED
2000	Ghana/Nigeria	Rigobert Song	Cameroon	6	0	Winners
2004	Tunisia	Salif Diao	Senegal	4	0	Quarter-finals
2004	Tunisia	El-Hadji Diouf	Senegal	4	0	Quarter-finals
2008	Ghana	Mohamed Sissoko	Mali	2	0	Group phase

LIVERPOOL FC PLAYERS AT THE AFC ASIAN CUP

YEAR	HOSTS	PLAYER	COUNTRY	APPS	GOALS	HOW COUNTRY FARED
2007	Indonesia/Malaysia/ Thailand/Vietnam	Harry Kewell	Australia	4	1	Quarter-finals
2011	Qatar	Brad Jones	Australia	0	0	Runners-up

LIVERPOOL FC PLAYERS AT THE CONCACAF GOLD CUP

YEAR	HOSTS	PLAYER	COUNTRY	APPS	GOALS	HOW COUNTRY FARED
1998	USA	Brad Friedel	USA	2	0	Runners-up
2000	USA	Brad Friedel	USA	3	0	Quarter-finals

YOUTH INTERNATIONALS

Six Liverpool players were in England Under-17s World Cup squad for the finals, held in Mexico during the summer of 2011. Goalkeeper Tyrell Belford, defenders Matthew Regan and Brad Smith, midfielders Raheem Sterling and Jack Dunn, plus striker Adam Morgan all represented the club.

Jordan Henderson played at the 2011 European Championships as a Liverpool player, having signed days before the tournament began from Sunderland, while Michael Ngoo appeared for England Under-20s in the 2011 U20 World Cup, held in Colombia.

Jamie Carragher holds the club record of 27 for most Under-21 caps won whilst being a Liverpool player, with Scott Carson having made his 29 appearances at other clubs, including the Reds. The below list includes home nation Reds players to have appeared in competitive and friendly encounters for the Under-21s (from 1976 onwards – English unless stated).

LIVERPOOL FC PLAYERS AT INTERNATIONAL UNDER-21 LEVEL

PLAYER	CAPS	YEAR OF DEBUT	COUNTRY	PLAYER	CAPS	YEAR OF DEBUT	COUNTRY
Gary Ablett	1	1988		Jim Magilton	1	1990	N. Ireland
David Burrows	7	1989		Dominic Matteo	4	1994	
Roman Calliste	15	2005	Wales	Lleyton Maxwell	14	1999	Wales
Jamie Carragher	27	1997		Steve McManaman	7	1991	
Scott Carson	29	2004		Danny Murphy	4	1998	
David Fairclough	1	1977		Steve Nicol	14	1981	Scotland
Robbie Fowler	8	1994		Michael Owen	1	1998	
Robbie Foy	5	2004	Scotland	Jamie Redknapp	19	1993	
Sean Friars	21	1997	N Ireland	Gareth Roberts	11	1997	Wales
Steven Gerrard	4	2000		Ian Rush	2	1981	Wales
Jordan Henderson	10	2010		David Thompson	7	1997	
Emile Heskey	16	1997		John Welsh	8	2004	
Lee Jones	12	1992	Wales	Danny Williams	9	1998	Wales
Rob Jones	2	1993		Paul Willis	1	2006	N. Ireland
Martin Kelly	2	2010		Danny Wilson	5	2010	Scotland
Chris Kirkland	8	2001		Stephen Wright	10	2001	
Sammy Lee	6	1981					

Steve McManaman (left) and Jamie Carragher on England Under-21 duty

YOUTH INTERNATIONALS

The following two pages include a list of Liverpool players to have represented their country at major youth championships, from Under-20 level through to Under-16 level. Jamie Carragher, Michael Owen and Martin Kelly are the most high-profile names, although Stephen Wright also played Premier League football for the Reds and Sunderland.

LIVERPOOL FC PLAYERS AT INTERNATIONAL UNDER-20 LEVEL

PLAYER	COUNTRY	MAJOR CHAMPIONSHIP
Dean Bouzanis	Australia	2009 World Cup
Jamie Carragher	England	1997 World Cup
Michael Foley	Republic of Ireland	2003 World Cup
Peter Gulacsi	Hungary	2009 World Cup
Martin Kelly	England	2009 World Cup
Neil Murphy	England	1999 World Cup
Krisztian Nemeth	Hungary	2009 World Cup
Michael Ngoo	England	2011 World Cup
Michael Owen	England	1997 World Cup
Darren Potter	Republic of Ireland	2003 World Cup
Andras Simon	Hungary	2009 World Cup
John Welsh	England	2003 World Cup
Zak Whitbread	USA	2003 World Cup
Stephen Wright	England	1999 World Cup

LIVERPOOL FC PLAYERS AT INTERNATIONAL UNDER-19 LEVEL

PLAYER	COUNTRY	MAJOR CHAMPIONSHIP(S)
Dean Bouzanis	Greece	2008 European Championship
Peter Gulacsi	Hungary	2008 European Championship
Chris Mavinga	France	2010 European Championship
Krisztian Nemeth	Hungary	2008 European Championship
Jon Otsemobor	England	2002 European Championship
Daniel Pacheco	Spain	2010 European Championship
Mikel San Jose	Spain	2008 European Championship
Andras Simon	Hungary	2008 European Championship
John Welsh	England	2002, 2003 European Championship
Paul Willis	Northern Ireland	2003 European Championship

Stephen Wright (left) and Jon Otsemobor – Liverpool and England youth defenders

YOUTH INTERNATIONALS

LIVERPOOL FC PLAYERS AT INTERNATIONAL UNDER-17 LEVEL

LIVERPOOL FC PLAYERS AT INTERNATIONAL UNDER-17 LEVEL

PLAYER	COUNTRY	PERIOD AT LIVERPOOL	MAJOR CHAMPIONSHIP
Tyrell Belford	England	Present	2011 World Cup
Christopher Buchtmann	Germany	2009-2010	2009 European Championship
Conor Coady	England	Present	2010 European Championship
Jack Dunn	England	Present	2011 World Cup
David Mannix	England	2004-2007	2002 European Championship
Adam Morgan	England	Present	2011 World Cup
David Raven	England	2004-2006	2002 European Championship
Matthew Regan	England	Present	2011 World Cup
Brad Smith	England	Present	2011 World Cup
Mark Smyth	England	2002-2005	2002 European Championship
Raheem Sterling	England	2011-	2011 World Cup
Andre Wisdom	England	Present	2010 European Championship

LIVERPOOL FC PLAYERS AT INTERNATIONAL UNDER-16 LEVEL

PLAYER	COUNTRY	PERIOD AT LIVERPOOL	MAJOR CHAMPIONSHIP
John Welsh	England	1994-2006	2001 European Championship

 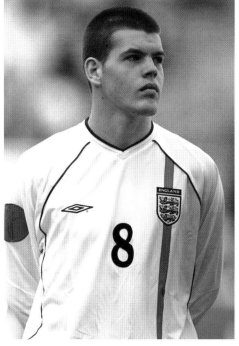

Adam Morgan (left) and John Welsh – Young Reds at major tournaments

THE COMPLETE FIRST-TEAM RECORD

A statistical breakdown of every competitive first-team game the club have played, correct at the end of the 2010/11 season.

LIVERPOOL FOOTBALL CLUB 1892-2011

COMPETITION	P	W	D	L	F	A
FA Premier League Home	367	230	86	51	708	283
FA Premier League Away	367	136	98	133	481	430
FA Premier League	734	366	184	184	1189	713
First Division Home	1548	924	354	270	3164	1570
First Division Away	1548	483	415	650	1930	2386
First Division	3096	1407	769	920	5094	3956
FA Premier League/First Division Home	1915	1154	440	321	3872	1853
FA Premier League/First Division Away	1915	619	513	783	2411	2816
FA Premier League/First Division	3830	1773	953	1104	6283	4669
Second Division Home	214	162	32	20	614	223
Second Division Away	214	81	50	83	363	348
Second Division	428	243	82	103	977	571
All League Games Home	2129	1316	472	341	4486	2076
All League Games Away	2129	700	563	866	2774	3164
All League Games	4258	2016	1035	1207	7260	5240
Test Matches Home	3	3	0	0	8	0
Test Matches Away	2	0	1	1	0	2
Test Matches Neutral	1	0	0	1	0	1
Test Matches	6	3	1	2	8	3
FA Cup Home	179	120	31	28	364	141
FA Cup Away	178	74	47	57	239	185
FA Cup Neutral	48	20	11	17	68	57
FA Cup	405	214	89	102	671	383
League Cup Home	100	71	20	9	248	86
League Cup Away	91	42	19	30	148	98
League Cup Neutral	14	8	3	3	19	13
League Cup	205	121	42	42	415	197
European Cup/Champions League Home	83	59	13	11	191	50
European Cup/Champions League Away	83	36	23	24	112	84
European Cup/Champions League Neutral	9	6	1	2	14	10
European Cup/Champions League	175	101	37	37	317	144
European Cup-Winners' Cup Home	14	11	2	1	43	9
European Cup-Winners' Cup Away	14	5	3	6	13	18
European Cup-Winners' Cup Neutral	1	0	0	1	1	2
European Cup-Winners' Cup	29	16	5	8	57	29
Fairs Cup/UEFA Cup/Europa Lge Home	58	43	8	7	124	25
Fairs Cup/UEFA Cup/Europa Lge Away	58	20	21	17	63	53
Fairs Cup/UEFA Cup/Europa Lge Neutral	1	1	0	0	5	4
Fairs Cup/UEFA Cup/Europa Lge	117	64	29	24	192	82
European/UEFA Super Cup Home	2	2	0	0	8	1
European/UEFA Super Cup Away	3	0	1	2	2	6
European/UEFA Super Cup Neutral	2	2	0	0	6	3
European/UEFA Super Cup	7	4	1	2	16	10
All European Competitions Home	157	115	23	19	366	85
All European Competitions Away	158	61	48	49	190	161
All European Competitions Neutral	13	9	1	3	26	19
All European Competitions	328	185	72	71	582	265
World Club Championships	4	1	0	3	3	5

THE COMPLETE FIRST-TEAM RECORD

LIVERPOOL FOOTBALL CLUB 1892-2011					
COMPETITION	**P**	**W**	**D**	**L**	**F**	**A**
FA Charity/Community Shield Home	1	0	1	0	2	2
FA Charity/Community Shield Away	3	1	1	1	3	3
FA Charity/Community Shield Neutral	17	9	3	5	19	16
FA Charity/Community Shield	21	10	5	6	24	21
Screen Sport Super Cup Home	4	4	0	0	10	3
Screen Sport Super Cup Away	4	2	2	0	9	3
Screen Sport Super Cup	8	6	2	0	19	6
F. League Centenary Tournament Home	1	1	0	0	4	1
F. League Centenary Tournament Away	1	0	0	1	1	2
Football League Centenary Tournament	2	1	0	1	5	3
Overall Home	2574	1630	547	397	5488	2394
Overall Away	2566	880	681	1005	3364	3618
Overall Neutral	97	47	18	32	135	111
TOTAL	**5237**	**2557**	**1246**	**1434**	**8987**	**6123**

The players – plus retiring boss Bill Shankly – line up after victory in the 1974 Charity Shield

MOST POINTS WON IN TOP-FLIGHT FOOTBALL

The Reds top the list for most points achieved by a side in the highest level of England football. The below table shows the top-15 clubs, with Liverpool nearly 100 points better off than Arsenal – who have also played the same number of games in the First Division/Premier League.

MOST POINTS WON IN TOP-FLIGHT LEAGUE FOOTBALL – AT END OF 2010/11 SEASON

CLUB	TOTAL POINTS WON	GAMES PLAYED	AVERAGE POINTS PER GAME	SEASONS IN TOP LEAGUE
Liverpool	5118	3830	1.34	96
Arsenal	5030	3830	1.31	94
Everton	4944	4214	1.17	108
Manchester United	4806	3474	1.38	86
Aston Villa	4540	3880	1.17	100
Chelsea	3715	3094	1.20	76
Tottenham Hotspur	3700	3090	1.20	76
Newcastle United	3603	3198	1.13	61
Manchester City	3590	3316	1.08	82
Sunderland	3282	3112	1.05	80
Blackburn Rovers	2916	2682	1.09	71
West Bromwich Albion	2842	2842	1.00	73
Bolton Wanderers	2788	2764	1.01	72
Sheffield Wednesday	2781	2582	1.08	66
Derby County	2510	2468	1.02	65

ALL-TIME LEAGUE WINS

The top 13 'most successful' sides in terms of victories is listed below, with Liverpool rated second having played one season less than Manchester United in top spot. The two sides are the only English clubs to break the 2000 wins barrier, with Arsenal in third unlikely to reach that landmark for a few seasons. Incidentally, more of the Reds' successes came at the top level.

ALL-TIME LEAGUE WINS – AT END OF 2010/11 SEASON

CLUB	TOTAL LEAGUE WINS	GAMES PLAYED	WIN %	SEASONS IN LEAGUE (TOP FLIGHT)
Manchester United	2040	4290	47.55	108 (86)
Liverpool	2016	4258	47.35	107 (96)
Arsenal	1931	4258	45.35	107 (94)
Wolverhampton Wanderers	1835	4540	40.42	112 (61)
Aston Villa	1833	4394	41.72	112 (100)
Everton	1794	4382	40.94	112 (108)
Sunderland	1791	4424	40.48	110 (80)
Preston North End	1783	4592	38.83	112 (46)
Sheffield United	1766	4446	39.72	108 (60)
Newcastle United	1760	4290	41.03	107 (80)
Burnley	1759	4568	38.51	112 (52)
Manchester City	1754	4332	40.49	108 (82)
West Bromwich Albion	1749	4514	38.75	112 (73)

MOST POINTS WON BY TEAMS IN PREMIER LEAGUE HISTORY

10/11 POS.		POS.	CLUB	POINTS	HIGHEST POSITION	SEASONS IN PREMIERSHIP
1		1	Manchester United	1574	1st (12 times)	19
2		2	Arsenal	1379	1st (3 times)	19
3		3	Chelsea	1338	1st (3 times)	19
4		4	Liverpool	1282	2nd (2 times)	19
5		5	Aston Villa	1051	2nd (1992/1993)	19
6		6	Tottenham Hotspur	1017	4th (2009/2010)	19
7		7	Everton	978	4th (2004/2005)	19
8		8	Newcastle United	952	2nd (2 times)	17
9		9	Blackburn Rovers	939	1st (1994/1995)	17
10		10	West Ham United	764	5th (1998/1999)	16
13	↑	11	Manchester City	695	3rd (2010/2011)	14
11	↑	12	Leeds United	692	3rd (1999/2000)	12
12	↓	13	Middlesbrough	633	7th (2004/2005)	14
14		14	Southampton	587	8th (2002/2003)	13
15		15	Bolton Wanderers	539	6th (2004/2005)	12
16		16	Fulham	459	7th (2008/2009)	10
17		17	Coventry City	409	11th (2 times)	9
21	↑	18	Sunderland	395	7th (2 times)	10
18	↓	19	Sheffield Wednesday	392	7th (3 times)	8
19	↓	20	Wimbledon (MK Dons)	391	6th (1993/1994)	8
20	↓	21	Charlton Athletic	361	7th (2003/2004)	8
22		22	Leicester City	342	8th (1999/2000)	8
25	↑	23	Birmingham City	301	9th (2009/2010)	7
23	↓	24	Portsmouth	293*	8th (2007/2008)	7
24	↓	25	Derby County	274	8th (1998/1999)	7
29	↑	26	Wigan Athletic	252	10th (2005/2006)	6
26	↓	27	Nottingham Forest	239	3rd (1994/1995)	5
27	↓	28	Ipswich Town	224	5th (2000/2001)	5
28	↓	29	Queens Park Rangers	216	5th (1992/1993)	4
30		30	Norwich City	201	3rd (1992/1993)	4
33	↑	31	West Bromwich Albion	169	11th (2010/2011)	5
31	↓	32	Crystal Palace	160	18th (2004/2005)	4
34	↑	33	Stoke City	138	11th (2009/2010)	3
32	↓	34	Sheffield United	132	14th (1992/1993)	3
37	↑	35	Wolverhampton Wanderers	111	15th (2009/2010)	3
35	↓	36	Reading	91	8th (2006/2007)	2
36	↓	37	Oldham Athletic	89	19th (1992/1993)	2
38		38	Hull City	65	17th (2008/09)	2
39		39	Bradford City	62	17th (1999/2000)	2
40		40	Watford	52	20th (1999/2000)	2
-	↑	41	Blackpool	39	19th (2010/2011)	1
41	↓	42	Barnsley	35	19th (1997/1998)	1
42	↓	43	Burnley	30	18th (2009/2010)	1
=	↓	=	Swindon Town	30	22nd (1994/1995)	1

* Portsmouth docked 9 points after going into administration during 2009/10 season*

FULL PREMIER LEAGUE RECORD - CLUB-BY-CLUB

		HOME					AWAY					
	PLD	W	D	L	F	A	W	D	L	F	A	PTS
Arsenal	38	9	6	4	36	19	5	7	7	15	22	55
Aston Villa	38	12	3	4	40	19	8	5	6	22	17	68
Barnsley	2	0	0	1	0	1	1	0	0	3	2	3
Birmingham City	14	2	4	1	13	7	1	4	2	9	9	16
Blackburn Rovers	34	11	5	1	31	11	5	6	6	23	27	59
Blackpool	2	0	0	1	1	2	0	0	1	1	2	0
Bolton Wanderers	24	11	1	0	29	6	6	3	3	19	15	55
Bradford City	4	2	0	0	4	1	1	0	1	2	1	9
Burnley	2	1	0	0	4	0	1	0	0	4	0	6
Charlton Athletic	16	4	3	1	14	7	4	0	4	13	9	27
Chelsea	38	12	3	4	33	19	3	4	12	8	27	52
Coventry City	18	6	1	2	17	6	3	2	4	10	11	30
Crystal Palace	8	3	1	0	10	3	2	1	1	10	3	17
Derby County	14	5	1	1	18	4	5	0	2	12	5	31
Everton	38	8	9	2	23	15	8	4	7	23	22	61
Fulham	20	6	4	0	17	2	6	0	4	19	14	40
Hull City	4	1	1	0	8	3	1	1	0	3	1	8
Ipswich Town	10	2	1	2	6	2	3	2	0	14	5	18
Leeds United	24	8	1	3	28	11	6	3	3	20	12	46
Leicester City	16	4	1	3	8	7	3	3	2	11	7	25
Manchester City	28	10	3	1	28	11	3	8	3	15	15	50
Manchester United	38	7	3	9	28	26	4	4	11	17	30	40
Middlesbrough	28	10	4	0	28	8	3	5	6	12	16	48
Newcastle United	34	14	2	1	42	15	6	4	7	28	23	66
Norwich City	8	3	0	1	11	2	2	1	1	6	5	16
Nottingham Forest	10	4	1	0	14	5	0	3	2	4	6	16
Oldham Athletic	4	2	0	0	3	1	1	0	1	5	3	9
Portsmouth	14	5	2	0	16	3	3	1	3	9	9	27
Queens Park Rangers	8	3	1	0	6	3	3	0	1	7	4	19
Reading	4	2	0	0	4	1	1	0	1	3	4	9
Sheffield United	6	2	0	1	7	3	0	2	1	1	2	8
Sheffield Wednesday	16	7	0	1	16	4	2	4	2	11	12	31
Southampton	26	7	4	2	28	14	5	3	5	17	19	43
Stoke City	6	2	1	0	6	0	0	2	1	1	3	9
Sunderland	20	5	5	0	14	4	7	1	2	14	5	42
Swindon Town	2	0	1	0	2	2	1	0	0	5	0	4
Tottenham Hotspur	38	12	5	2	38	17	5	5	9	24	26	61
Watford	4	1	0	1	2	1	2	0	0	6	2	9
West Bromwich Alb.	10	5	0	0	10	0	4	0	1	16	2	27
West Ham United	32	12	4	0	33	4	7	3	6	22	20	64
Wigan Athletic	12	4	2	0	12	5	3	2	1	8	3	25
Wimbledon	16	4	3	1	17	8	1	3	4	5	9	21
Wolverhampton W.	6	2	0	1	3	1	1	2	0	4	1	11

THE PREMIER/FOOTBALL LEAGUE FINISHES

PREMIER LEAGUE/DIVISION ONE – 96 SEASONS

POSITION	NUMBER OF FINISHES	MOST RECENT FINAL POSITION	POSITION	NUMBER OF FINISHES	MOST RECENT FINAL POSITION
1st	18	1989/90	12th	4	1948/49
2nd	12	2008/09	13th	2	1914/15
3rd	7	2006/07	14th	1	1932/33
4th	8	2007/08	15th	1	1906/07
5th	9	2004/05	16th	4	1927/28
6th	3	2010/11	17th	3	1952/53
7th	5	2009/10	18th	2	1936/37
8th	4	1993/94	19th	1	1935/36
9th	4	1950/51	20th	0	–
10th	2	1931/32	21st	0	–
11th	5	1951/52	22nd	1	1953/54

DIVISION TWO – 11 SEASONS

POSITION	NUMBER OF FINISHES	MOST RECENT FINAL POSITION	POSITION	NUMBER OF FINISHES	MOST RECENT FINAL POSITION
1st	4	1961/62	4th	2	1958/59
3rd	4	1960/61	11th	1	1954/55

PREMIER LEAGUE RECORD

LEAGUE STATISTICS 1992-2011

SEASON	P	W	D	L	F	A	PTS	POS
1992/1993	42	16	11	15	62	55	59	6
1993/1994	42	17	9	16	59	55	60	8
1994/1995	42	21	11	10	65	37	74	4
1995/1996	38	20	11	7	70	34	71	3
1996/1997	38	19	11	8	62	37	68	4
1997/1998	38	18	11	9	68	42	65	3
1998/1999	38	15	9	14	68	49	54	7
1999/2000	38	19	10	9	51	30	67	4
2000/2001	38	20	9	9	71	39	69	3
2001/2002	38	24	8	6	67	30	80	2
2002/2003	38	18	10	10	61	41	64	5
2003/2004	38	16	12	10	55	37	60	4
2004/2005	38	17	7	14	52	41	58	5
2005/2006	38	25	7	6	57	25	82	3
2006/2007	38	20	8	10	57	27	68	3
2007/2008	38	21	13	4	67	28	76	4
2008/2009	38	25	11	2	77	27	86	2
2009/2010	38	18	9	11	61	35	63	7
2010/2011	38	17	7	14	59	44	58	6

FOOTBALL LEAGUE RECORD - CLUB-BY-CLUB

TEAM	PLAYED	WON	DRAWN	LOST	FOR	AGAINST
Arsenal	174	68	46	60	246	222
Aston Villa	172	81	38	53	303	248
Barnsley	12	7	2	3	23	15
Birmingham City	100	47	25	28	167	137
Blackburn Rovers	126	53	38	35	223	170
Blackpool	42	18	9	15	74	66
Bolton Wanderers	116	52	29	35	187	138
Bradford City	26	18	2	6	45	22
Bradford Park Avenue	6	3	1	2	10	8
Brentford	10	4	3	3	16	16
Brighton & Hove Albion	16	8	6	2	36	20
Bristol City	30	16	3	11	52	39
Bristol Rovers	16	10	1	5	32	21
Burnley	76	31	19	26	125	95
Burton Swifts	4	3	1	0	17	3
Burton United	2	1	0	1	3	2
Burton Wanderers	2	1	0	1	5	3
Bury	48	26	14	8	92	53
Cardiff City	26	8	2	16	35	51
Carlisle United	2	2	0	0	3	0
Charlton Athletic	56	29	8	19	93	70
Chelsea	136	62	28	46	209	187
Chesterfield	2	1	1	0	7	2
Coventry City	68	39	16	13	113	45
Crewe Alexandra	4	4	0	0	20	1
Crystal Palace	26	15	6	5	57	17
Darwen	2	1	1	0	4	0
Derby County	126	66	28	32	248	156
Doncaster Rovers	10	5	2	3	19	13
Everton	184	70	57	57	249	218
Fulham	48	27	13	8	90	46
Gainsborough Trinity	2	2	0	0	8	2
Glossop	4	3	1	0	11	5
Grimsby Town	36	18	10	8	87	47
Huddersfield Town	68	25	17	26	113	113
Hull City	10	7	3	0	26	11
Ipswich Town	60	28	19	13	110	59
Leeds United	100	51	25	24	164	101
Leicester City	88	36	19	33	143	121
Leyton Orient	14	9	2	3	37	15
Lincoln City	20	11	4	5	42	28
Loughborough Town	2	2	0	0	5	2
Luton Town	28	13	9	6	52	33
Manchester City	150	75	37	38	268	196
Manchester United	156	53	43	60	206	217
Middlesbrough	134	57	39	38	229	172
Middlesbrough Ironopolis	2	2	0	0	8	0
Millwall	4	3	1	0	6	3
Newcastle United	150	72	37	41	263	187
Northampton Town	2	1	1	0	5	0

FOOTBALL LEAGUE RECORD - CLUB-BY-CLUB

TEAM	PLAYED	WON	DRAWN	LOST	FOR	AGAINST
Northwich Victoria	2	2	0	0	7	2
Norwich City	46	24	11	11	84	47
Nottingham Forest	100	50	24	26	167	99
Notts County	60	34	12	14	110	63
Oldham Athletic	24	14	4	6	39	30
Oxford United	6	5	1	0	20	3
Plymouth Argyle	10	5	3	2	22	15
Portsmouth	60	25	15	20	106	90
Port Vale	12	7	3	2	38	20
Preston North End	64	26	17	21	114	99
Queens Park Rangers	40	28	6	6	68	34
Reading	4	3	0	1	7	5
Rotherham United	20	14	3	3	57	21
Scunthorpe United	8	6	2	0	17	8
Sheffield United	118	55	27	36	192	153
Sheffield Wednesday	116	54	26	36	197	165
Southampton	74	35	18	21	112	86
Stoke City	112	55	30	27	183	116
Sunderland	148	66	32	50	249	213
Swansea City	20	10	4	6	51	27
Swindon Town	2	1	1	0	7	2
Tottenham Hotspur	136	63	34	39	215	154
Walsall	4	2	2	0	11	3
Watford	16	12	1	3	37	16
West Bromwich Albion	118	56	33	29	183	129
West Ham United	108	57	29	22	179	98
Wigan Athletic	12	7	4	1	20	8
Wimbledon	28	11	10	7	41	31
Wolverhampton Wanderers	92	45	17	30	141	107

Kenny Dalglish – A goalscorer v QPR in the league

BIGGEST-EVER VICTORIES

The top-28 Liverpool wins is included below, with the most recent having occurred in 2008 – an 8-0 victory over Besiktas. Another 8-0 and a 7-0 have also been achieved during the 21st century, while the 7-1 success over Southampton remains the most recent biggest league win, in January 1999.

LIVERPOOL FC'S HIGHEST SCORES – 1892-2011 (ALL COMPETITIONS)

DATE	OPPONENTS	VENUE	COMPETITION	SCORE
17th Sept 1974	Stromsgodset	Home	European Cup-Winners' Cup	11-0
16th Sept 1969	Dundalk	Home	Inter Cities' Fairs Cup	10-0
23rd Sept 1986	Fulham	Home	League Cup	10-0
18th Feb 1896	Rotherham Town	Home	League	10-1
1st Oct 1980	Oulu Palloseura	Home	European Cup	10-1
29th Oct 1892	Newtown	Home	FA Cup	9-0
12th Sept 1989	Crystal Palace	Home	League	9-0
26th Dec 1928	Burnley	Home	League	8-0
7th Nov 1967	TSV Munich 1860	Home	Inter Cities' Fairs Cup	8-0
9th Jan 1990	Swansea City	Home	FA Cup	8-0
29th Nov 2000	Stoke City	Away	League Cup	8-0
6th Nov 2007	Besiktas	Home	Champions League	8-0
6th Dec 1902	Grimsby Town	Home	League	9-2
8th Apr 1905	Burslem Port Vale	Home	League	8-1
29th Feb 1896	Burton Swifts	Away	League	7-0
28th Mar 1896	Crewe Alexandra	Away	League	7-0
4th Jan 1902	Stoke City	Home	League	7-0
26th Nov 1955	Fulham	Home	League	7-0
2nd Sept 1978	Tottenham Hotspur	Home	League	7-0
30th Sept 1981	Oulu Palloseura	Home	European Cup	7-0
20th Feb 1985	York City	Home	FA Cup	7-0
6th Jan 1996	Rochdale	Home	FA Cup	7-0
21st Mar 2006	Birmingham City	Away	FA Cup	7-0
1st Oct 1927	Portsmouth	Home	League	8-2
12th Oct 1895	Newton Heath	Home	League	7-1
12th Sept 1936	Grimsby Town	Home	League	7-1
23rd Mar 1991	Derby County	Away	League	7-1
16th Jan 1999	Southampton	Home	League	7-1

Big wins – Fowler and Crouch, on target in 1999 and 2007 respectively

2000TH LEAGUE WIN

The Reds' first victory of the 2010/11 season provided the landmark 2000th victory in league football for the first team. The 1-0 victory over West Bromwich Albion marked a consistent sequence of a little over five years since the previous three landmark successes. The full list of landmark wins are noted below – with the "1-0" scoreline the most common result to mark another century of wins (7 of the 20 victories).

LANDMARK LIVERPOOL FC LEAGUE VICTORIES

LANDMARK VICTORY	OPPONENT	VENUE	DATE	SCORE	LIVERPOOL SCORERS
1st	Middlesbrough Ironopolis	Away	2nd Sept 1893	2-0	McVean, McQue
100th	Manchester City	Home	3rd Mar 1900	5-2	Raybould 2 (1 pen), Walker, Satterthwaite, Cox
200th	Sheffield United	Away	16th Dec 1905	2-1	Parry, Cox
300th	Manchester City	Away	6th Jan 1912	3-2	Parkinson, Bovill, Stuart
400th	Birmingham City	Home	11th Feb 1922	1-0	Forshaw
500th	Tottenham Hotspur	Home	30th Apr 1927	1-0	Edmed
600th	Birmingham City	Away	4th Nov 1933	2-1	English, Hodgson
700th	Preston North End	Home	7th Apr 1947	3-0	Stubbins 2, Balmer
800th	Sunderland	Home	3rd Apr 1954	4-3	Jackson, Evans, Liddell (pen), Anderson
900th	Charlton Athletic	Away	31st Jan 1959	3-2	Twentyman, Morris, Melia
1000th	West Bromwich Albion	Home	19th Oct 1963	1-0	Milne
1100th	Fulham	Home	27th Apr 1968	4-1	Callaghan, Hunt 2, Hateley
1200th	Tottenham Hotspur	Away	25th Nov 1972	2-1	Heighway, Keegan
1300th	Ipswich Town	Home	30th Apr 1977	2-1	R. Kennedy, Keegan
1400th	Leeds United	Home	10th Oct 1981	3-0	Rush 2, Cherry (o.g.)
1500th	Leicester City	Home	2nd Nov 1985	1-0	Rush
1600th	Charlton Athletic	Home	30th Dec 1989	1-0	Barnes
1700th	Southampton	Home	5th Apr 1995	3-1	Rush 2, Fowler (pen)
1800th	Leicester City	Home	21st Oct 2000	1-0	Heskey
1900th	Newcastle United	Home	26th Dec 2005	2-0	Gerrard, Crouch
2000th	West Bromwich Albion	Home	29th Aug 2010	1-0	Torres

2000-up – Victory over West Brom in August 2010 was another landmark occasion

CONSECUTIVE SCORING GAMES

The current list of the longest home team scoring sequences at Anfield, with the most recent run, between 2008-2010, having fallen just three short of the all-time record.

CONSECUTIVE SCORING GAMES AT HOME – ALL COMPETITIONS		
NO. OF GAMES	**PERIOD**	**TEAM THAT ENDED THE RUN**
40	22nd February 1904-24th February 1906	Manchester City
37	13th December 2008-8th April 2010	Fulham
34	25th September 1979-5th November 1980	Nottingham Forest
33	20th January 1968-1st February 1969	Nottingham Forest
31	29th September 1956-11th January 1958	Middlesbrough
30	19th November 1932-3rd February 1934	Bolton Wanderers
30	26th December 1989-9th February 1991	Everton
29	19th February 1972-20th January 1973	Manchester City
28	10th April 1985-22nd February 1986	Everton
27	16th March 1991-26th February 1992	Southampton

HOME DEFEATS

The Reds have suffered 341 defeats since their first campaign as part of the Football League in 1893/94. They have been beaten by 50 different teams since then, with their most common opposition inflicting the most defeats, namely Everton, Arsenal and Manchester United. The full list is noted below.

LEAGUE ONLY – CORRECT AT END OF 2010/11			
NUMBER OF DEFEATS	**OPPOSITION**	**NUMBER OF DEFEATS**	**OPPOSITION**
23	Everton	2	Bradford City, Ipswich Town, Lincoln City, Notts County, Oldham Athletic
22	Arsenal, Man Utd		
18	Sunderland		
15	Aston Villa	1	Barnsley, Bradford PA, Brentford, Brighton & HA, Bristol Rovers, Bury, Crystal Palace, Doncaster Rovers, QPR, Watford
13	Man City, Middlesbrough, Sheffield Wednesday		
12	Huddersfield Town		
11	Leicester City, Newcastle Utd		
10	Bolton Wanderers		
9	Blackburn Rovers, Chelsea, Sheffield United, West Brom, Wolves		
8	Burnley		
7	Birmingham City, Cardiff City, Leeds United, Nottingham F		
6	Blackpool, Charlton Athletic, Derby County, Preston NE, Tottenham Hotspur		
4	Norwich City, Portsmouth, Southampton		
3	Bristol City, Coventry City, Stoke, West Ham, Wimbledon		

Anfield derby action from 2010/11

PLAYER RECORDS – APPEARANCES

Jamie Carragher moved up to second in the Liverpool all-time appearance holder table towards the end of the 2010/11 season. The Reds vice-captain went clear behind Ian Callaghan when making his 666th appearance, in the 5-2 victory at Fulham, in May 2011.

Although Steven Gerrard endured some injury problems, he did reach the top 10 by vitue of making a goalscoring 550th appearance, at Blackburn Rovers, in January 2011.

TOTAL APPEARANCES – ALL COMPETITIONS

	PLAYER	FIRST-TEAM CAREER	GAMES
1	Ian Callaghan	1960-1978	857
2	Jamie Carragher	1997-	668
3	Ray Clemence	1968-1981	665
=	Emlyn Hughes	1967-1979	665
5	Ian Rush	1980-1987 & 1988-1996	660
6	Phil Neal	1974-1985	650
7	Tommy Smith	1963-1978	638
8	Bruce Grobbelaar	1981-1994	628
9	Alan Hansen	1977-1990	620
10	Steven Gerrard	1998-	556
11	Chris Lawler	1963-1975	549
12	Billy Liddell	1946-1960	534
13	Kenny Dalglish	1977-1990	515
14	Ronnie Whelan	1981-1994	493
15	Roger Hunt	1959-1969	492
16	Phil Thompson	1972-1983	477
17	Steve Heighway	1970-1981	475
18	Steve Nicol	1982-1994	468
=	Elisha Scott	1913-1934	468
20	Sami Hyypia	1999-2009	464
21	Ron Yeats	1961-1971	454
22	Donald MacKinlay	1910-1928	434
23	Ian St John	1961-1971	425
24	Peter Thompson	1963-1972	416
25	Arthur Goddard	1902-1914	414

PLAYER RECORDS – CONSECUTIVE APPEARANCES

MOST CONSECUTIVE APPEARANCES – ALL COMPETITIONS

	PLAYER	TIME SPAN	GAMES
1	Phil Neal	Oct 1976-Sept 1983	417
2	Ray Clemence	Sept 1972-Mar 1978	336
3	Bruce Grobbelaar	Aug 1981-Aug 1986	317
4	Chris Lawler	Oct 1965-Apr 1971	316
5	David James	Feb 1994-Feb 1998	213
6	Alan Kennedy	Jan 1982-Mar 1985	205
7	Ian Callaghan	Aug 1971-Sept 1974	185
8	Kenny Dalglish	Aug 1977-Aug 1980	180
9	Emlyn Hughes	Oct 1972-Oct 1975	177
10	Peter Thompson	Sept 1965-Apr 1968	153

PLAYER RECORDS – CUP APPEARANCES

Twenty-three Liverpool players have made 100 or more appearances in domestic and overseas cup competitions. Jamie Carragher is only 12 behind Ian Callaghan, while Steven Gerrard is the only other player currently in the squad in the below list. Note that the 'others' column includes appearances in the Screen Sport Super Cup, Centenary Trophy, FA Charity Shield/FA Community Shield and World Club Championship.

TOP 20 PLAYERS WHO HAVE PLAYED MOST CUP TIES FOR LIVERPOOL FC

	PLAYER	TOTAL	FA CUP	LGE CUP	EUROPE	OTHERS
1	Ian Callaghan	217	79	42	89	7
2	Jamie Carragher	205	34	28	139	4
3	Ray Clemence	195	54	55	80	6
=	Phil Neal	195	45	66	74	10
5	Emlyn Hughes	191	62	46	79	4
=	Ian Rush	191	61	78	38	14
7	Bruce Grobbelaar	188	62	70	38	18
8	Alan Hansen	186	58	68	46	14
9	Tommy Smith	171	52	30	85	4
10	Steven Gerrard	169	29	20	116	4
11	Kenny Dalglish	160	37	59	51	13
12	Sami Hyypia	146	29	19	94	4
13	Steve Heighway	144	36	38	67	3
14	Chris Lawler	143	47	27	66	3
15	Phil Thompson	137	36	43	50	8
16	Ronnie Whelan	131	41	50	24	16
17	Steve Nicol	125	50	42	20	13
18	Ray Kennedy	118	28	35	50	5
19	Mark Lawrenson	115	24	50	28	13
20	John Arne Riise	114	17	13	79	5

Top man – Ian Callaghan

PREMIER LEAGUE APPEARANCES

Jamie Carragher has moved to second having featured in the first few games of 2011/12.

MOST PREMIER LEAGUE APPEARANCES FOR ONE CLUB (AT END OF 2010/11 SEASON)

PLAYER	APPEARANCES	CLUB
Ryan Giggs	573*	Manchester United
Paul Scholes	466	Manchester United
Jamie Carragher	**463***	**Liverpool**
Gary Neville	400	Manchester United
Steven Gerrard	**387***	**Liverpool**
Gareth Barry	365	Aston Villa
Jussi Jaaskelainen	361*	Bolton Wanderers
Shay Given	354	Newcastle United
Frank Lampard	344*	Chelsea
John Terry	342*	Chelsea
Ray Parlour	333	Arsenal
Mark Schwarzer	332	Middlesbrough
Jason Dodd	329	Southampton
Roy Keane	326	Manchester United
Gary Kelly	325	Leeds United
David Seaman	325	Arsenal
Sami Hyypia	**318**	**Liverpool**

Jamie Carragher – Closing in on 500 league games

* Still at club at end of 2010/11 season

MOST PREMIER LEAGUE APPEARANCES IN CAREER (AT END OF 2010/11 SEASON)

PLAYER	APPEARANCES	CLUB(S)
Ryan Giggs	573*	Manchester United
David James	572	Liverpool, Aston Villa, West Ham, Man. City, Portsmouth
Gary Speed	535	Leeds United, Everton, Newcastle United, Bolton Wanderers
Sol Campbell	503	Tottenham, Arsenal, Portsmouth, Newcastle United
Frank Lampard	492*	West Ham, Chelsea
Emile Heskey	488*	Leicester C., Liverpool, Birmingham C., Wigan A., Aston Villa
Paul Scholes	466	Manchester United
Jamie Carragher	**463***	**Liverpool**
Phil Neville	460*	Manchester United, Everton
Alan Shearer	441	Blackburn Rovers, Newcastle United
Mark Schwarzer	438*	Middlesbrough, Fulham
Gareth Barry	432*	Aston Villa, Manchester City
Gareth Southgate	426	Crystal Palace, Aston Villa, Middlesbrough
Rio Ferdinand	421*	West Ham, Leeds United, Manchester United
Teddy Sheringham	418	Nottingham Forest, Tottenham Hotspur (x2), Manchester United, Portsmouth, West Ham United
Andy Cole	414	Newcastle United, Manchester United, Blackburn Rovers, Fulham, Manchester City, Portsmouth, Sunderland
Kevin Davies	413*	Southampton, Blackburn Rovers, Bolton Wanderers
Nicky Butt	411	Manchester United, Newcastle United, Birmingham City
Shay Given	406*	Blackburn Rovers, Newcastle United, Manchester City
Gary Neville	400	Manchester United
Brad Friedel	400*	Liverpool, Blackburn Rovers, Aston Villa

* Still playing in Premier League at start of 2011/12 season

MOST APPEARANCES IN PREMIER LEAGUE

POS.	PLAYER	GAMES	POS.	PLAYER	GAMES
1	Jamie Carragher	463	24	Ian Rush	130
2	Steven Gerrard	387	25	Phil Babb	128
3	Sami Hyypia	318	26	Jerzy Dudek	127
4	Robbie Fowler	266	=	Dominic Matteo	127
5	Steve McManaman	240	28	Vladimir Smicer	121
6	John Arne Riise	234	29	Neil Ruddock	115
7	Jamie Redknapp	231	30	Lucas Leiva	111
8	Pepe Reina	220	31	Michael Thomas	107
9	Michael Owen	216	32	Fernando Torres	102
10	David James	214	33	Jason McAteer	100
11	Dietmar Hamann	191			
12	Dirk Kuyt	174			
13	Danny Murphy	170			
14	John Barnes	162			
15	Rob Jones	155			
16	Emile Heskey	150			
17	Patrik Berger	148			
18	Steve Finnan	145			
19	Xabi Alonso	143			
20	Dirk Kuyt	141			
21	Stig Inge Bjornebye	139			
22	Mark Wright	137			
23	Stephane Henchoz	135			

Steven Gerrard – Closing in on 400

MOST GOALS IN PREMIER LEAGUE

POS.	PLAYER	GOALS
1	Robbie Fowler	128
2	Michael Owen	118
3	Steven Gerrard	84
4	Fernando Torres	65
5	Dirk Kuyt	49
6	Ian Rush	45
7	Steve McManaman	41
8	Emile Heskey	39
9	Jamie Redknapp	29
=	Own Goals	29
11	Patrik Berger	28
12	Stan Collymore	26
13	Danny Murphy	25
14	John Barnes	22
=	Peter Crouch	22
=	Sami Hyypia	22
17	John Arne Riise	21
18	Milan Baros	19
19	Yossi Benayoun	18
=	Luis Garcia	18
21	Xabi Alonso	15
22	Paul Ince	14
23	Djibril Cisse	13
24	Harry Kewell	12

Robbie Fowler – Premier League No.1

PREMIER LEAGUE PLAYERS' RECORD (A-G)

PLAYER	FIRST GAME- LAST GAME	LEAGUE		FA CUP		LEAGUE CUP		EUROPE		OTHER GAMES		LFC CAREER	
		A	G	A	G	A	G	A	G	A	G	A	G
Daniel Agger	2006-2011	93	3	4	0	5	2	33	2	1	0	136	7
Xabi Alonso	2004-2009	143	15	12	2	4	0	48	2	3	0	210	19
David Amoo	2010-2010	0	0	0	0	0	0	1	0	0	0	1	0
Nicolas Anelka	2001-2002	20	4	2	1	0	0	0	0	0	0	22	5
Alberto Aquilani	2009-2010	18	1	2	0	1	0	7	1	0	0	28	2
Alvaro Arbeloa	2007-2009	66	2	3	0	3	0	26	0	0	0	98	2
Pegguy Arphexad	2000-2002	2	0	0	0	2	0	2	0	0	0	6	0
Fabio Aurelio	2006-2011	85	3	5	0	5	0	35	1	1	0	131	4
Daniel Ayala	2009-2010	5	0	0	0	0	0	0	0	0	0	5	0
Phil Babb	1994-1999	128	1	12	0	16	0	14	0	0	0	170	1
Markus Babbel	2000-2002	42	3	5	1	7	1	17	1	2	0	73	6
Ryan Babel	2007-2010	91	12	9	1	7	0	39	9	0	0	146	22
Nick Barmby	2000-2002	32	2	5	1	7	1	13	4	1	0	58	8
John Barnes	1987-1997	314	84	51	16	26	3	12	3	4	2	407	108
Milan Baros	2002-2005	68	19	3	0	8	4	28	4	1	0	108	27
Antonio Barragan	2005-2005	0	0	0	0	0	0	1	0	0	0	1	0
Craig Bellamy	2006-2007	27	7	0	0	2	0	12	2	1	0	42	9
Yossi Benayoun	2007-2010	92	18	6	3	4	1	32	7	0	0	134	29
Patrik Berger	1996-2003	148	28	8	0	11	3	28	4	1	0	196	35
Igor Biscan	2000-2005	72	2	7	0	15	1	23	0	1	0	118	3
Stig I. Bjornebye	1992-1999	139	2	13	0	16	0	16	2	0	0	184	4
David Burrows	1988-1993	146	3	17	0	16	0	11	0	3	0	193	3
Titi Camara	1999-2000	33	9	2	1	2	0	0	0	0	0	37	10
Jamie Carragher	1997-2011	463	4	34	0	28	0	139	1	4	0	668	5
Andy Carroll	2011-2011	7	2	0	0	0	0	2	0	0	0	9	2
Scott Carson	2005-2006	4	0	1	0	1	0	3	0	0	0	9	0
Diego Cavalieri	2008-2010	0	0	2	0	4	0	2	0	0	0	8	0
Phil Charnock	1992-1992	0	0	0	0	1	0	1	0	0	0	2	0
Bruno Cheyrou	2002-2004	31	2	6	2	2	0	8	1	1	0	48	5
Djibril Cisse	2004-2006	49	13	6	2	0	0	23	9	1	0	79	24
Nigel Clough	1993-1995	39	7	2	0	3	2	0	0	0	0	44	9
Joe Cole	2010-2011	20	2	0	0	0	0	12	1	0	0	32	3
Stan Collymore	1995-1997	61	26	9	7	4	0	7	2	0	0	81	35
Peter Crouch	2005-2008	85	22	11	5	5	1	30	11	3	3	134	42
Stephen Darby	2008-2010	1	0	1	0	1	0	3	0	0	0	6	0
Philipp Degen	2008-2010	7	0	1	0	4	0	1	0	0	0	13	0
Salif Diao	2002-2005	37	1	2	0	8	1	14	1	0	0	61	3
Julian Dicks	1993-1994	24	3	1	0	3	0	0	0	0	0	28	3
Bernard Diomede	2000-2001	2	0	0	0	0	0	3	0	0	0	5	0
El-Hadji Diouf	2002-2004	55	3	4	0	7	3	13	0	1	0	80	6
Andrea Dossena	2008-2009	18	1	2	0	2	0	9	1	0	0	31	2
Jerzy Dudek	2001-2007	127	0	9	0	11	0	38	0	1	0	186	0
Sean Dundee	1998-1999	3	0	0	0	1	0	1	0	0	0	5	0
Nathan Eccleston	2009-2010	2	0	0	0	2	0	5	0	0	0	9	0
Nabil El Zhar	2006-2009	21	0	1	0	4	1	6	0	0	0	32	1
Jean Michel Ferri	1999-1999	2	0	0	0	0	0	0	0	0	0	2	0
Steve Finnan	2003-2008	145	1	13	0	6	0	51	0	2	0	217	1
Jon Flanagan	2011-2011	7	0	0	0	0	0	0	0	0	0	7	0
Robbie Fowler	1993-2007	266	128	24	12	35	29	44	14	0	0	369	183
Brad Friedel	1998-1999	25	0	0	0	4	0	2	0	0	0	31	0
Luis Garcia	2004-2007	77	18	4	1	5	0	32	11	3	0	121	30
Steven Gerrard	1998-2011	387	84	29	10	20	7	116	38	4	1	556	140
Mark Gonzalez	2006-2007	25	2	0	0	2	0	8	1	1	0	36	3
Bruce Grobbelaar	1981-1994	440	0	62	0	70	0	38	0	18	0	628	0
Danny Guthrie	2006-2007	3	0	0	0	3	0	1	0	0	0	7	0

PREMIER LEAGUE PLAYERS' RECORD (H-N)

PLAYER	FIRST GAME-LAST GAME	LEAGUE		FA CUP		LEAGUE CUP		EUROPE		OTHER GAMES		LFC CAREER	
		A	G	A	G	A	G	A	G	A	G	A	G
Dietmar Hamann	1999-2006	191	8	16	1	12	0	61	2	3	0	283	11
Steve Harkness	1991-1999	102	2	6	0	15	1	16	0	0	0	139	3
Vegard Heggem	1998-2000	54	3	1	0	4	0	6	0	0	0	65	3
Stephane Henchoz	1999-2004	135	0	15	0	16	0	37	0	2	0	205	0
Emile Heskey	2000-2004	150	39	14	6	12	2	45	13	2	0	223	60
Jack Hobbs	2007-2007	2	0	0	0	3	0	0	0	0	0	5	0
Mike Hooper	1986-1993	51	0	5	0	10	0	4	0	3	0	73	0
Don Hutchison	1992-1994	45	7	3	0	8	2	3	1	1	0	60	10
Sami Hyypia	1999-2009	318	22	29	2	19	3	94	8	4	0	464	35
Paul Ince	1997-1999	65	14	3	1	6	1	7	1	0	0	81	17
Thomas Ince	2010-2010	0	0	0	0	0	0	1	0	0	0	1	0
Emiliano Insua	2007-2010	46	0	3	0	3	1	10	0	0	0	62	1
Charles Itandje	2007-2008	0	0	4	0	3	0	0	0	0	0	7	0
David James	1992-1999	214	0	19	0	22	0	22	0	0	0	277	0
Glen Johnson	2009-2011	53	5	0	0	1	0	16	0	0	0	70	5
Brad Jones	2010-2010	0	0	0	0	1	0	1	0	0	0	2	0
Lee Jones	1994-1996	3	0	0	0	1	0	0	0	0	0	4	0
Paul Jones	2004-2004	2	0	0	0	0	0	0	0	0	0	2	0
Rob Jones	1991-1998	183	0	27	0	22	0	11	0	0	0	243	0
Josemi	2004-2005	21	0	0	0	1	0	12	0	1	0	35	0
Milan Jovanovic	2010-2011	10	0	0	0	1	1	7	1	0	0	18	2
Robbie Keane	2008-2009	19	5	1	0	1	0	7	2	0	0	28	7
Martin Kelly	2008-2011	12	0	1	0	1	0	13	0	0	0	27	0
Mark Kennedy	1995-1998	16	0	1	0	2	0	2	0	0	0	21	0
Harry Kewell	2003-2008	93	12	10	2	5	1	30	3	1	0	139	16
Frode Kippe	1999-2001	0	0	0	0	2	0	0	0	0	0	2	0
Chris Kirkland	2001-2004	25	0	3	0	6	0	11	0	0	0	45	0
Paul Konchesky	2010-2011	15	0	0	0	0	0	3	0	0	0	18	0
Istvan Kozma	1992-1992	6	0	2	0	1	0	0	0	1	0	10	0
Jan Kromkamp	2006-2006	14	0	4	0	0	0	0	0	0	0	18	0
Dirk Kuyt	2006-2011	174	49	10	2	3	0	54	15	0	0	241	66
Bjorn Tore Kvarme	1997-1999	45	0	2	0	2	0	5	0	0	0	54	0
Sotiros Kyrgiakos	2009-2011	30	3	0	0	3	0	16	0	0	0	49	3
Lucas Leiva	2007-2011	111	1	9	1	6	1	42	3	0	0	168	6
O. Leonhardsen	1997-1999	37	7	1	0	6	0	5	0	0	0	49	7
Anthony Le Tallec	2003-2005	17	0	4	0	2	0	9	1	0	0	32	1
Sebastian Leto	2007-2007	0	0	0	0	2	0	2	0	0	0	4	0
Jari Litmanen	2001-2002	26	5	3	1	3	0	11	3	0	0	43	9
Patrice Luzi	2004-2004	1	0	0	0	0	0	0	0	0	0	1	0
Gary McAllister	2000-2002	55	5	5	0	6	1	20	2	1	1	87	9
Jason McAteer	1995-1999	100	3	12	3	13	0	14	0	0	0	139	6
Steve McManaman	1990-1999	272	46	29	5	33	10	30	5	0	0	364	66
Mike Marsh	1989-1993	69	2	8	0	11	3	12	1	1	0	101	6
Javier Mascherano	2007-2010	94	2	5	0	2	0	38	1	0	0	139	3
Dominic Matteo	1993-2000	127	1	8	1	9	0	11	0	0	0	155	2
Layton Maxwell	1999-1999	0	0	0	0	1	1	0	0	0	0	1	1
Erik Meijer	1999-2000	24	0	0	0	3	2	0	0	0	0	27	2
Raul Meireles	2010-2011	33	5	1	0	0	0	7	0	0	0	41	5
Neil Mellor	2002-2005	12	2	2	0	6	3	2	1	0	0	22	6
Jan Molby	1984-1995	218	44	28	4	28	9	7	1	11	3	292	61
F. Morientes	2005-2006	41	8	5	1	3	0	11	3	1	0	61	12
Danny Murphy	1997-2004	170	25	15	3	16	11	46	5	2	0	249	44
Jon Newby	1999-2000	1	0	2	0	1	0	0	0	0	0	4	0
David Ngog	2008-2011	63	9	3	0	5	2	23	8	0	0	94	19
Steve Nicol	1982-1994	343	36	50	3	42	4	20	2	13	1	468	46
Antonio Nunez	2004-2005	18	0	1	0	3	1	5	0	0	0	27	1

PREMIER LEAGUE PLAYERS' RECORD (O-Z)

PLAYER	FIRST GAME-LAST GAME	LEAGUE		FA CUP		LEAGUE CUP		EUROPE		OTHER GAMES		LFC CAREER	
		A	G	A	G	A	G	A	G	A	G	A	G
Jon Otsemobor	2002-2003	4	0	0	0	2	0	0	0	0	0	6	0
Michael Owen	1997-2004	216	118	15	8	14	9	50	22	2	1	297	158
Daniel Pacheco	2009-2010	5	0	0	0	1	0	8	0	0	0	14	0
Daniele Padelli	2007-2007	1	0	0	0	0	0	0	0	0	0	1	0
Gabriel Paletta	2006-2007	3	0	0	0	3	1	2	0	0	0	8	1
Richie Partridge	2000-2004	0	0	0	0	3	0	0	0	0	0	3	0
M. Pellegrino	2005-2005	12	0	0	0	1	0	0	0	0	0	13	0
Lee Peltier	2006-2007	0	0	0	0	3	0	1	0	0	0	4	0
Jermaine Pennant	2006-2008	55	3	3	0	3	0	19	0	1	0	81	3
Torben Piechnik	1992-1993	17	0	2	0	5	0	0	0	0	0	24	0
Damien Plessis	2008-2009	3	0	0	0	3	1	2	0	0	0	8	1
Darren Potter	2004-2005	2	0	1	0	5	0	9	0	0	0	17	0
Christian Poulsen	2010-2011	12	0	0	0	0	0	9	0	0	0	21	0
David Raven	2004-2005	1	0	1	0	2	0	0	0	0	0	4	0
Jamie Redknapp	1991-2001	237	30	18	2	27	5	26	4	0	0	308	41
Pepe Reina	2005-2011	220	0	9	0	1	0	76	0	3	0	309	0
Karlheinz Riedle	1997-1999	60	11	2	0	7	2	7	2	0	0	76	15
Albert Riera	2008-2010	40	3	3	1	1	0	12	1	0	0	56	5
John Arne Riise	2001-2008	234	21	17	3	13	2	79	4	5	1	348	31
Jack Robinson	2010-2011	3	0	0	0	0	0	0	0	0	0	3	0
Maxi Rodriguez	2010-2011	45	11	1	0	0	0	6	0	0	0	52	11
Miki Roque	2006-2006	0	0	0	0	0	0	1	0	0	0	1	0
Ronny Rosenthal	1990-1993	74	21	8	0	9	1	4	0	2	0	97	22
Neil Ruddock	1993-1997	115	11	11	0	20	1	6	0	0	0	152	12
Ian Rush	1980-1996	469	229	61	39	78	48	38	20	14	10	660	346
Dean Saunders	1991-1992	42	11	8	2	5	2	5	9	1	1	61	25
John Scales	1994-1996	65	2	14	0	10	2	5	0	0	0	94	4
Jonjo Shelvey	2010-2011	15	0	1	0	1	0	4	0	0	0	21	0
F. S-Pongolle	2003-2006	38	4	5	2	8	1	12	2	3	0	66	9
Mohamed Sissoko	2005-2007	51	1	6	0	4	0	23	0	3	0	87	1
Martin Skrtel	2008-2011	92	3	6	0	2	0	28	0	0	0	128	3
Vladimir Smicer	1999-2005	121	10	10	1	15	5	37	3	1	0	184	19
Jamie Smith	2006-2006	0	0	0	0	1	0	0	0	0	0	1	0
Mark Smyth	2004-2004	0	0	0	0	1	0	0	0	0	0	1	0
Rigobert Song	1999-2000	34	0	1	0	2	0	1	0	0	0	38	0
Jay Spearing	2008-2011	14	0	0	0	3	0	10	0	0	0	27	0
Steve Staunton	1988-2000	109	0	18	1	13	5	7	0	1	1	148	7
Paul Stewart	1992-1993	32	1	1	0	6	0	2	2	1	0	42	3
Luis Suarez	2011-2011	13	4	0	0	0	0	0	0	0	0	13	4
Nick Tanner	1989-1992	40	1	2	0	8	0	8	0	1	0	59	1
Michael Thomas	1991-1998	124	9	17	2	10	1	12	0	0	0	163	12
David Thompson	1996-2000	48	5	1	0	5	0	2	0	0	0	56	5
Fernando Torres	2007-2011	102	65	7	1	3	3	30	12	0	0	142	81
Djimi Traore	1999-2006	88	0	5	0	14	0	32	0	2	0	141	1
Gregory Vignal	2001-2003	11	0	1	0	3	0	5	0	0	0	20	0
Andriy Voronin	2007-2009	27	5	1	0	2	0	10	1	0	0	40	6
Mark Walters	1991-1995	94	14	9	0	12	4	8	1	1	0	124	19
Stephen Warnock	2004-2007	40	1	3	0	8	0	15	0	1	0	67	1
John Welsh	2002-2005	4	0	1	0	3	0	2	0	0	0	10	0
Sander Westerveld	1999-2001	75	0	8	0	5	0	14	0	1	0	103	0
Ronnie Whelan	1981-1994	362	46	41	7	50	14	24	6	16	0	493	73
Zak Whitbread	2004-2005	0	0	1	0	4	0	2	0	0	0	7	0
Danny Wilson	2010-2011	2	0	0	0	1	0	5	0	0	0	8	0
Mark Wright	1991-1997	158	5	18	0	16	2	17	2	1	0	210	9
Stephen Wright	2000-2002	14	0	2	0	2	0	3	1	0	0	21	1
Abel Xavier	2002-2002	14	1	0	0	1	0	5	1	1	0	21	2
Boudewijn Zenden	2005-2007	23	2	0	0	2	0	21	0	1	0	47	2
Christian Ziege	2000-2001	16	1	3	0	4	1	9	0	0	0	32	2

PREMIER LEAGUE NUMBERS GAME

SHIRT	PLAYERS (PREMIER LEAGUE APPEARANCES IN BRACKETS)				
1	Grobbelaar (29),	James (171),	Westerveld (75),	Dudek (92)	
2	R.Jones (125),	Henchoz (135),	Kromkamp (14),	Arbeloa (9),	Dossena (16),
	Johnson (53)				
3	Burrows (4),	Dicks (24),	Scales (3),	Kvarme (45),	Ziege (16),
	Xavier (14),	Finnan (145),	Konchesky (15)		
4	Nicol (35),	McAteer (100),	Song (34),	Hyypia (245),	Aquilani (18),
	Meireles (33)				
5	M.Wright (104),	Staunton (44),	Baros (68),	Agger (93)	
6	Hutchison (11),	Babb (128),	Babbel (42),	Riise (131),	Aurelio (14)
7	Clough (39),	McManaman (101),	Smicer (91),	Kewell (93),	Keane (19),
	Suarez (13)				
8	Stewart (8),	Collymore (61),	Leonhardsen (37),	Heskey (150),	Gerrard (217)
9	Rush (98),	Fowler (144),	Anelka (20),	Diouf (55),	Cisse (49),
	Torres (102),	Carroll (7)			
10	Barnes (135),	Owen (178),	Garcia (77),	Voronin (27),	Cole (20)
11	Walters (35),	Redknapp (103),	Smicer (30),	Fowler (14),	Gonzalez (25),
	Benayoun (30),	Riera (40)			
12	Whelan (23),	Scales (62),	Harkness (38),	Hyypia (73),	Dudek (35),
	P.Jones (2),	Pellegrino (12),	Aurelio (71),	Pacheco (1)	
13	James (14),	Riedle (60),	Murphy (130),	Le Tallec (4)	
14	Molby (25),	Ruddock (19),	Heggem (54),	Alonso (143),	Jovanovic (10)
15	Redknapp (99),	Berger (148),	Diao (11),	Crouch (85),	Benayoun (62)
16	Thomas (99),	Dundee (3),	Hamann (191),	Pennant (55),	Kyrgiakos (30)
17	McManaman (108),	Ince (65),	Gerrard (129),	Josemi (21),	Bellamy (27),
	Arbeloa (57),	Rodriguez (45)			
18	Rosenthal (3),	Owen (38),	Ferri (2),	Meijer (24),	Riise (103),
	Nunez (18),	Kuyt (174)			
19	Piechnik (1),	Kennedy (16),	Friedel (14),	Arphexad (2),	Morientes (41),
	Babel (91)				
20	Bjornebye (128),	Barmby (32),	Le Tallec (13),	Carson (4),	Mascherano (94)
21	Marsh (2),	Matteo (127),	McAllister (55),	Diao (26),	Traore (48),
	Lucas (111)				
22	Harkness (43),	Camara (33),	Kirkland (25),	Sissoko (51),	Insua (41),
	Wilson (2)				
23	Fowler (108),	Carragher (463)			
24	L.Jones (3),	Murphy (40),	Diomede (2),	S-Pongolle (38),	Ngog (63)
25	Ruddock (96),	Thompson (48),	Biscan (72),	Reina (220)	
26	Spearing (14)				
27	Vignal (11),	Degen (7)			
28	Gerrard (41),	Cheyrou (31),	Warnock (40),	Plessis (1),	Poulsen (12)
29	Friedel (11),	S.Wright (14),	Luzi (1),	Paletta (3)	
30	Traore (40),	Zenden (7),	Padelli (1)		
31	Raven (1),	El Zhar (18)			
32	Newby (1),	Welsh (4),	Zenden (16),	Darby (1)	
33	Mellor (12),	Shelvey (15)			
34	Potter (2),	Kelly (12)			
35	Guthrie (3)				
36	Otsemobor (4)				
37	Litmanen (26),	Skrtel (92)			
38	Dossena (2),	Flanagan (7)			
39	Eccleston (2)				
40	Ayala (5)				
42	El Zhar (3)				
46	Hobbs (2)				
47	Plessis (2),	Pacheco (4)			
48	Insua (5)				
49	Robinson (3)				

NUMBERS GAME

Larger squads – and the use of bigger squad numbers – means that keeping tabs on Liverpool's spiralling number wearers continues to be more problematic with the continual shift further away from the traditional 1-11. Pepe Reina has continued to add to his growing appearance tally in the No. 25 shirt, while the No. 37 is likely to remain synonymous with Martin Skrtel for years to come.
*Note that the asterix denotes continuing sequence of games played (at end of August 2011).

MOST CONSECUTIVE APPEARANCES IN A NUMBER SHIRT (LEAGUE ONLY)

SHIRT	PLAYER	APPEARANCES
1	Ray Clemence	232
2	Phil Neal	253
3	Alan Kennedy	131
4	Steve Nicol	87
5	Larry Lloyd	85
6	Alan Hansen	78
7	Kenny Dalglish	147
8	Roger Hunt	104
9	Ian Rush	73
10	Jimmy Melia	90
11	Ian Callaghan	162
12	Sami Hyypia	42
13	Danny Murphy	39
14	Neil Ruddock	42
15	Jamie Redknapp	48
16	Dietmar Hamann	42
17	Steve McManaman	61
18	John Arne Riise	41
19	Ryan Babel	15
20	Stig Inge Bjornebye	55
21	Dominic Matteo	24
22	Steve Harkness	27
23	Robbie Fowler	91
24	Danny Murphy	14
25	Pepe Reina	154*
26	Jay Spearing	9
27	Gregory Vignal	4
28	Steven Gerrard	12
29	Brad Friedel	11
30	Djimi Traore	14
31	Nabil El Zhar	4
32	Bolo Zenden	5
33	Jonjo Shelvey	6
34	Martin Kelly	8
35	Danny Guthrie	2
36	Jon Otsemobor	4
37	Martin Skrtel	38
38	Jon Flanagan	8
39	Nathan Eccleston	1
40	Daniel Ayala	2
42	Nabil El Zhar	2
46	Jack Hobbs	2
47	Damien Plessis	1
	Daniel Pacheco	1
48	Emiliano Insua	3
49	Jack Robinson	2

Most consistent – Phil Neal

Ray Clemence – Main man in 1

CONSISTENT REDS

Goalkeeper Pepe Reina continues to climb up the Liverpool ever-present charts having again played all 38 league games in season 2010/11. The Spain international was seventh in the all-time list going into 2011/12 and with David James and Ian Callaghan within 10 matches of his 152-game total, he is on course to reach the top five should he remain injury-free before 2011 is out.

100 OR MORE CONSECUTIVE LEAGUE APPEARANCES FOR LIVERPOOL FC

GAMES	PLAYER	FIRST APPEARANCE-LAST APPEARANCE
365	Phil Neal	14th December 1974-24th September 1983
241	Chris Lawler	2nd October 1965-24th April 1971
232	Ray Clemence	9th September 1972-4th March 1978
210	Bruce Grobbelaar	29th August 1981-3rd May 1986
162	Ian Callaghan	17th January 1971-29th March 1975
159	David James	19th February 1994-22nd February 1998
152	Pepe Reina	11th August 2007-
147	Kenny Dalglish	20th August 1977-6th December 1980
141	Alan Kennedy	26th December 1981-31st March 1985
124	Emlyn Hughes	4th November 1972-25th October 1975
119	William Goldie	23rd December 1899-27th April 1903
119	Elisha Scott	17th December 1921-25th October 1924
116	Tommy Lawrence	22nd April 1967-17th January 1970
114	Tommy Smith	21st August 1965-2nd March 1968
104	Roger Hunt	18th November 1961-4th April 1964
102	Chris Lawler	1st May 1971-24th November 1973

Pepe Reina – A consistent Reds presence in the modern era

LONG-SERVING

Steven Gerrard and Jamie Carragher feature in the LFC records for goalscoring and time spent in the first team. It is no surprise to see Gerrard amongst the regular scorers for the club, with a goal in the 2011/12 campaign set to take the skipper to third for getting on the scoresheet for 13 consecutive season in red.

Carragher made his first-team bow at Middlesbrough in the League Cup on 8th January 1997, with his appearance against Bolton on 27th August 2011 taking him to 14 years and 231 days.

PLAYERS TO SCORE FOR LIVERPOOL FC IN AT LEAST 10 SUCCESSIVE SEASONS

PLAYER	NO. OF SEASONS	SEASONS
Billy Liddell	15	1946-1960
Ronnie Whelan	14	1981-1994
Jack Cox	12	1898-1909
Steven Gerrard	12	2000-2011
Arthur Goddard	12	1902-1913
Emlyn Hughes	12	1968-1979
Gordon Hodgson	11	1926-1936
Alan A'Court	11	1953-1963
Roger Hunt	11	1960-1970
Donald MacKinlay	11	1913-1927
Phil Neal	11	1976-1986
Jack Parkinson	11	1904-1914
Tommy Smith	11	1965-1975
Jack Balmer	10	1936-1951
John Barnes	10	1988-1997
Kenny Dalglish	10	1978-1987
Chris Lawler	10	1965-1974
Ian St John	10	1962-1971
Sami Hyypia	10	2000-2009

Ronnie Whelan and (below) Tommy Smith

LONGEST-SERVING LIVERPOOL FC PLAYERS

PLAYER	LFC CAREER	TIME SPAN
Elisha Scott	1913-1934	21 yrs, 51 days
Donald MacKinlay	1910-1928	18 yrs, 134 days
Ian Callaghan	1960-1978	17 yrs, 347 days
Phil Taylor	1936-1954	17 yrs, 287 days
Ephraim Longworth	1910-1928	17 yrs, 215 days
Jack Balmer	1935-1952	16 yrs, 155 days
Tommy Smith	1963-1978	14 yrs, 352 days
Billy Liddell	1946-1960	14 yrs, 239 days
Jamie Carragher	1997-2011	14 yrs, 216 days
Ian Rush	1980-1987 1988-1996	14 yrs, 40 days
Billy Dunlop	1895-1909	14 yrs, 23 days

PREMIER LEAGUE CAPTAINS

The updated table of Liverpool's most successful captains in Premier League games. The list is ordered in win percentage value first, with Steven Gerrard the club's most prolific – and successful – skipper taking into account 25+ games as skipper.

LIVERPOOL FC CAPTAINS IN PREMIER LEAGUE GAMES (MOST SUCCESSFUL FIRST)							
CAPTAIN	PLD	W	D	L	PTS	WIN %	AVE PTS. PER GAME
Steve Nicol	9	6	2	1	20	66.67	2.22
Steve McManaman	8	5	1	2	16	62.50	2.00
Robbie Fowler	22	12	4	6	40	54.55	1.82
Steven Gerrard	237	126	58	53	436	53.16	1.84
Sami Hyypia	131	69	32	30	239	52.67	1.82
Jamie Carragher	39	20	11	8	71	51.28	1.82
Pepe Reina	6	3	1	2	10	50.00	1.67
John Barnes	87	43	25	19	154	49.43	1.77
Ian Rush	87	40	20	27	140	45.98	1.61
Jamie Redknapp	22	10	5	7	35	45.45	1.59
Paul Ince	65	28	18	19	102	43.08	1.57
Mark Wright	17	4	4	9	16	23.53	0.94
Neil Ruddock	2	0	2	0	2	0.00	1.00
Dirk Kuyt	1	0	1	0	1	0.00	1.00
Phil Babb	1	0	0	1	0	0.00	0.00
TOTAL	**734**	**366**	**184**	**184**	**1282**	**49.86**	**1.75**

Steven Gerrard and Jamie Carragher – Over 250 games between them as captains

SHORT CAREERS

Thomas Ince's departure in the summer of 2011 leaves him at No. 6 in the list of shortest Liverpool careers. The midfielder made a cameo appearance during the League Cup in 2010/11. Note that the list is compiled with the assumption that players who appeared before the introduction of subs in 1965/66 played a full 90 minutes.

SHORTEST LIVERPOOL FC FIRST-TEAM CAREERS

PLAYER	MINUTES	APPS	APPEARANCES SPAN
Miki Roque	6	1	2006
Lauri Dalla Valle	7	1	2010
Dave Wilson	10	1	1967
Antonio Barragan	11	1	2005
Patrice Luzi	13	1	2004
Thomas Ince	15	1	2010
James Smith	16	1	2006
Brian Mooney	30	1	1986
Lee Jones	33	4	1994-1996
Colin Russell	33	1	1981
Jon Newby	34	4	1999-2000
Mark Smyth	50	1	2004
Jean-Michel Ferri	51	2	1999
Sean Dundee	56	5	1998-1999
Barry Jones	68	1	1991
Derek Brownbill	71	1	1973

Short spells – Thomas Ince (left) and Sean Dundee

CLEAN SHEETS – GOALKEEPERS

The statistical record for Liverpool's most effective goalkeepers in terms of clean sheets and fewest goals conceded. Pepe Reina currently stands second in the all-time list in terms of the percentage of games he averages a clean sheet, with only Ray Clemence ahead of him. Reina is also already third behind Clem and Bruce Grobbelaar in the most clean sheets kept for the club.

Note on all the below tables, that for a goalkeeper to be awarded a clean sheet he must have played the full match. However, if injured, subbed or sent off having conceded during that game the appearance counts.

LIVERPOOL FC CAREER STATISTICS – AT END OF 2010/11 SEASON

PLAYER	GAMES PLAYED	GOALS CONCEDED	GOALS PER GAME	CLEAN SHEETS	CLEAN SHEET %
Ray Clemence	665	488	0.73	323	48.57
Pepe Reina	309	248	0.80	146	47.25
Bruce Grobbelaar	628	532	0.85	266	42.36
David James	275	273	0.99	102	37.09
Tommy Lawrence	390	404	1.04	133	34.10
Elisha Scott	468	647	1.38	137	29.27
Sam Hardy	239	340	1.42	63	26.36
Arthur Riley	338	608	1.80	69	20.41

Pepe Reina surpasses Ray Clemence in the table below, having kept more clean sheets for the Reds in his first 200 league games. The Spain international reached 100 in the 3-0 victory against Aston Villa in December 2010.

CLEAN SHEETS IN FIRST 200 FULL LEAGUE GAMES

PLAYER	CLEAN SHEETS	DATE OF 200TH START UNDER CRITERIA
Pepe Reina	100	29th December 2010
Ray Clemence	93	7th December 1974
Bruce Grobbelaar	86	8th March 1986
Elisha Scott	75	6th December 1924
David James	70	28th December 1998
Tommy Lawrence	63	9th September 1967
Sam Hardy	52	11th November 1911
Arthur Riley	32	23rd February 1935

Ray Clemence kept four more clean sheets than Reina in his first 300 games for the club, having also conceded 13 fewer goals during that period. The top three, as in each of the tables on this page, are proven to have by far the greatest all-time record of the club's goalkeepers.

CLEAN SHEETS IN FIRST 300 FULL GAMES

PLAYER	CLEAN SHEETS	GOALS AGAINST	DATE OF 300TH APPEARANCE
Ray Clemence	146	225	8th March 1975
Pepe Reina	142	238	17th March 2011
Bruce Grobbelaar	135	241	5th March 1986
Elisha Scott	107	335	25th December 1926
Tommy Lawrence	97	329	4th May 1968
Arthur Riley	61	552	18th April 1938

CLEAN SHEETS – PEPE REINA

Pepe Reina's complete clean sheet record for Liverpool is noted below, correct up until the end of the 2010/11 season. Although not noted in the table below, Reina can now at least add a clean sheet to his tally against Arsenal, courtesy of the Reds' 2-0 early season win at the Emirates in 2011/12.

CLUB-BY-CLUB – AT END OF 2010/11 SEASON

OPPOSITION	CLEAN SHEETS	GAMES PLAYED	CLEAN SHEET %	OPPOSITION	CLEAN SHEETS	GAMES PLAYED	CLEAN SHEET %
Chelsea	9	22	41	Hull City	1	4	25
Sunderland	8	10	80	Reading	1	6	17
Manchester City	8	12	67	AC Milan	0	1	0
Bolton Wanderers	7	12	58	CSKA Moscow	0	1	0
Fulham	7	12	58	CSKA Sofia	0	1	0
Newcastle United	6	10	60	FBK Kaunas	0	1	0
Aston Villa	6	12	50	Fiorentina	0	1	0
Tottenham Hotspur	6	12	50	Galatasaray	0	1	0
West Ham United	6	12	50	Sao Paulo	0	1	0
West Bromwich Alb	5	6	83	Sheffield United	0	1	0
Blackburn Rovers	5	12	42	Barcelona	0	2	0
Everton	5	14	36	Blackpool	0	2	0
PSV Eindhoven	4	5	80	Lyon	0	2	0
Stoke City	4	6	67	Maccabi Haifa	0	2	0
Middlesbrough	4	8	50	FC Porto	0	2	0
Birmingham City	4	9	44	Steaua Bucharest	0	2	0
Portsmouth	4	9	44	Atletico Madrid	0	4	0
Wigan Athletic	4	11	36	Benfica	0	4	0
Wolverhampton W	3	4	75	Arsenal	0	13	0
Manchester United	3	14	21	**TOTAL**	**146**	**309**	**47**
Anderlecht	2	2	100				
Bordeaux	2	2	100				
Burnley	2	2	100				
Charlton Athletic	2	2	100				
Debrenci VSC	2	2	100				
Inter Milan	2	2	100				
Real Madrid	2	2	100				
Sparta Prague	2	2	100				
Standard Liege	2	2	100				
TNS	2	2	100				
Toulouse	2	2	100				
Watford	2	2	100				
Marseille	2	4	50				
Deportivo Saprissa	1	1	100				
Utrecht	1	1	100				
Besiktas	1	2	50				
Derby County	1	2	50				
Lille	1	2	50				
Napoli	1	2	50				
Real Betis	1	2	50				
Sporting Braga	1	2	50				
Trabzonspor	1	2	50				
Unirea Urziceni	1	2	50				

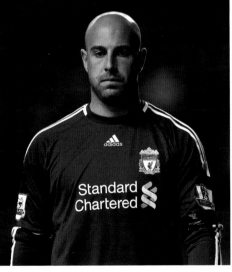

Pepe Reina appears unimpressed by another clean sheet against Manchester City

JAMIE CARRAGHER'S LIVERPOOL FC APPEARANCES

The complete breakdown of Liverpool's second-highest appearance holder's games is included here. Note that 'Other' includes FA Community Shield and Club World Cup appearances. Statistics are correct at the end of the 2010/11 season.

CLUB-BY-CLUB						CLUB-BY-CLUB				
TEAM	PRM LGE	DOM. CUPS	EURO. COMPS	OTH.	TOTAL	TEAM	PRM LGE	DOM. CUPS	EURO. COMPS	OTH.	TOTAL
Chelsea	26	4	10	1	41	B Dortmund	–	–	2	–	2
Arsenal	27	4	2	–	33	Burnley	2	–	–	–	2
Man Utd	26	3	–	1	30	Celta Vigo	–	–	2	–	2
Aston Villa	27	1	–	–	28	Debreceni	–	–	2	–	2
Tottenham H	26	1	–	–	27	D La Coruna	–	–	2	–	2
Everton	24	2	–	–	26	Dynamo Kiev	–	–	2	–	2
West Ham	22	1	–	–	23	Graz	–	–	2	–	2
Blackburn R	21	1	–	–	22	Inter Milan	–	–	2	–	2
Middlesboro	20	2	–	–	22	Juventus	–	–	2	–	2
Newcastle U	21	1	–	–	22	Kosice	–	–	2	–	2
Man City	17	2	–	–	19	Levski Sofia	–	–	2	–	2
Fulham	16	2	–	–	18	Lille	–	–	2	–	2
Bolton W	17	–	–	–	17	Lyon	–	–	2	–	2
Sunderland	16	–	–	–	16	Monaco	–	–	2	–	2
Charlton Ath	15	–	–	–	15	Napoli	–	–	2	–	2
Portsmouth	12	3	–	–	15	Norwich City	2	–	–	–	2
Leeds United	12	2	–	–	14	Notts Forest	2	–	–	–	2
Southampton	13	1	–	–	14	Real Betis	–	–	2	–	2
Birmingham	10	3	–	–	13	Real Madrid	–	–	2	–	2
Wigan Athletic	12	–	–	–	12	Slovan Liberec	–	–	2	–	2
West Brom	10	1	–	–	11	Sparta Prague	–	–	2	–	2
Derby County	9	–	–	–	9	Spa Moscow	–	–	2	–	2
Leicester City	9	–	–	–	9	Spo Braga	–	–	2	–	2
Crystal Palace	3	4	–	–	7	Standard Liege	–	–	2	–	2
Reading	4	3	–	–	7	TNS	–	–	2	–	2
Barcelona	–	–	6	–	6	Trabzonspor	–	–	2	–	2
Coventry City	6	–	–	–	6	Uni Urziceni	–	–	2	–	2
Marseille	–	–	6	–	6	Alaves	–	–	1	–	1
Stoke City	5	1	–	–	6	Barnsley	–	1	–	–	1
Watford	4	2	–	–	6	Bayern Munich	–	–	1	–	1
Hull City	4	1	–	–	5	Blackpool	1	–	–	–	1
PSV E'hoven	–	–	5	–	5	Cardiff City	–	1	–	–	1
Sheffield Wed	5	–	–	–	5	Crewe Alex	–	1	–	–	1
Ath Madrid	–	–	4	–	4	CSKA Moscow	–	–	1	–	1
B Leverkusen	–	–	4	–	4	CSKA Sofia	–	–	1	–	1
Benfica	–	–	4	–	4	Dep Saprissa	–	–	–	1	1
Bradford City	4	–	–	–	4	Fiorentina	–	–	1	–	1
Galatasaray	–	–	4	–	4	Grimsby Town	–	1	–	–	1
Ipswich Town	3	1	–	–	4	Haka	–	–	1	–	1
Olympiakos	–	–	4	–	4	Havant & W	–	1	–	–	1
Porto	–	–	4	–	4	Huddersfield	–	1	–	–	1
Roma	–	–	4	–	4	Kaunas	–	–	1	–	1
Sheffield Utd	2	2	–	–	4	Macc Haifa	–	–	1	–	1
Valencia	–	–	4	–	4	Port Vale	–	1	–	–	1
Wimbledon	4	–	–	–	4	Preston NE	–	1	–	–	1
Wolves	4	–	–	–	4	Rabotnicki	–	–	1	–	1
Celtic	–	–	3	–	3	R Bucharest	–	–	1	–	1
Luton Town	–	3	–	–	3	Rotherham U	–	1	–	–	1
AC Milan	–	–	2	–	2	Sao Paulo	–	–	–	1	1
Anderlecht	–	–	2	–	2	Toulouse	–	–	1	–	1
Auxerre	–	–	2	–	2	Tranmere Rov	–	1	–	–	1
Basel	–	–	2	–	2	Utrecht	–	–	1	–	1
Besiktas	–	–	2	–	2	Vit Arnhem	–	–	1	–	1
Boavista	–	–	2	–	2	Wycombe W	–	1	–	–	1
Bordeaux	–	–	2	–	2	**TOTAL**	**463**	**62**	**139**	**4**	**668**

PLAYER RECORDS – GOALS

Steven Gerrard remains the only member of Liverpool's squad in the top 25 for goals. Dirk Kuyt is the next-best of the 2011/12 squad, having reached 66 goals in all competitions.

TOTAL GOALS – ALL COMPETITIONS

	PLAYER	FIRST-TEAM CAREER	GOALS
1	Ian Rush	1980-1987 & 1988-1996	346
2	Roger Hunt	1959-1969	286
3	Gordon Hodgson	1926-1935	241
4	Billy Liddell	1946-1960	228
5	Robbie Fowler	1993-2001 & 2006-2007	183
6	Kenny Dalglish	1977-1990	172
7	Michael Owen	1997-2004	158
8	Harry Chambers	1919-1928	151
9	Steven Gerrard	1998-	140
10	Sam Raybould	1900-1907	129
11	Jack Parkinson	1903-1914	128
12	Dick Forshaw	1919-1927	124
13	Ian St John	1961-1971	118
14	Jack Balmer	1935-1952	110
15	John Barnes	1987-1997	108
16	Kevin Keegan	1971-1977	100
17	John Toshack	1970-1977	96
18	Albert Stubbins	1946-1953	83
19	Fernando Torres	2007-2011	81
=	Terry McDermott	1974-1982	81
21	Jack Cox	1898-1909	80
22	Berry Nieuwenhuys	1933-1947	79
=	Jimmy Melia	1955-1964	79
24	David Johnson	1976-1982	78
25	Arthur Goddard	1902-1914	77

PLAYER RECORDS – CONSECUTIVE GOALS

GOALSCORERS IN SUCCESSIVE LEAGUE GAMES

GAMES	PLAYER	SEASON	GAMES	PLAYER	SEASON
10	John Aldridge	1986/87-87/88	5	Sam Raybould	1906/07
8	Dick Forshaw	1924/25	5	Dick Forshaw	1925/26
8	John Aldridge	1988/89	5	Gordon Hodgson	1930/31
7	Jack Balmer	1946/47	5	Gordon Hodgson	1931/32
6	Robert Robinson	1904/05	5	Sam English	1933/34
6	Gordon Hodgson	1933/34	5	Sam English	1933/34
6	Berry Nieuwenhuys	1934/35	5	Albert Stubbins	1946/47
6	Tony Rowley	1957/58	5	Billy Liddell	1949/50
6	Roger Hunt	1962/63	5	Billy Liddell	1954/55
6	Roger Hunt	1964/65	5	Dave Hickson	1959/60-60/61
5	Jimmy Ross	1895/96	5	Kevin Lewis	1960/61
5	George Allan	1895/96-96/97	5	Alf Arrowsmith	1963/64
5	John Walker	1899/00	5	Michael Owen	2000/01-01/02
5	Sam Raybould	1902/03	5	Dirk Kuyt	2010/11

PLAYER RECORDS – TOP SCORERS

MOST GOALS IN A SEASON

MOST GOALS IN A SEASON – ALL COMPS

NAME	SEASON	GAMES	GOALS
Ian Rush	1983/84	65	47
Roger Hunt	1961/62	46	42
Ian Rush	1986/87	57	40
Roger Hunt	1964/65	58	37
Gordon Hodgson	1930/31	41	36
Robbie Fowler	1995/96	53	36
John Evans	1954/55	42	33
Billy Liddell	1955/56	44	33
Roger Hunt	1963/64	46	33
Roger Hunt	1965/66	46	33
Fernando Torres	2007/08	46	33
Ian Rush	1985/86	56	33
Sam Raybould	1902/03	34	32
Gordon Hodgson	1928/29	41	32
Billy Liddell	1954/55	44	31
Robbie Fowler	1996/97	44	31
John Aldridge	1988/89	47	31
Ian Rush	1982/83	51	31
Robbie Fowler	1994/95	57	31
Kenny Dalglish	1977/78	62	31
Jack Parkinson	1909/10	32	30
Ian Rush	1981/82	49	30
Roger Hunt	1967/68	57	30

MOST GOALS IN A LEAGUE SEASON

NAME	SEASON	DIV	GA	GLS
Roger Hunt	1961/62	2	41	41
Gordon Hodgson	1930/31	1	40	36
Ian Rush	1983/84	1	41	32
Sam Raybould	1902/03	1	33	31
Roger Hunt	1963/64	1	41	31
Jack Parkinson	1909/10	1	31	30
Gordon Hodgson	1928/29	1	38	30
Billy Liddell	1954/55	2	40	30
Ian Rush	1986/87	1	42	30
Roger Hunt	1965/66	1	37	29
John Evans	1954/55	2	38	29
Robbie Fowler	1995/96	Prem	38	28
Dick Forshaw	1925/26	1	32	27
Gordon Hodgson	1934/35	1	34	27
Billy Liddell	1955/56	2	39	27
John Aldridge	1987/88	1	36	26
Gordon Hodgson	1931/32	1	39	26
George Allan	1895/96	2	20	25
Roger Hunt	1964/65	1	40	25
Roger Hunt	1967/68	1	40	25
Robbie Fowler	1994/95	Prem	42	25

John Aldridge and Roger Hunt – Top goalscorers for the Reds

PLAYER RECORDS – CUP GOALS

Ian Rush is well ahead in the top cup goalscorers for the club, with Steven Gerrard having moved up to second courtesy of his Europa League goals in 2010/11. However, the table gives a slightly misleading picture in terms of the goalscoring contribution of players pre-1960s. The FA Cup and FA Charity Shield were the only 'cup' competitions played by the club before then that qualifies for this table (Liverpool Senior Cup is discounted, for example). The League Cup was introduced during this decade, while the Reds' first season of European competition was in 1964/65.

	PLAYERS WHO HAVE SCORED MORE THAN 20 CUP GOALS OR MORE FOR LIVERPOOL					
	PLAYER	**TOTAL**	**FA CUP**	**LGE CUP**	**EUROPE**	**OTHERS**
1	Ian Rush	117	39	48	20	10
2	Steven Gerrard	56	10	7	38	1
3	Robbie Fowler	55	12	29	14	0
4	Kenny Dalglish	54	13	27	11	3
5	Roger Hunt	41	18	5	17	1
6	Michael Owen	40	8	9	22	1
7	Kevin Keegan	32	14	6	12	0
8	Terry McDermott	27	4	5	15	3
=	Ronnie Whelan	27	7	14	6	0
10	Steve Heighway	26	8	7	11	0
11	John Barnes	24	16	3	3	2
12	Jimmy Case	23	7	3	13	0
=	David Johnson	23	6	9	8	0
=	Ian St John	23	12	1	10	0
15	John Toshack	22	8	3	10	1
16	David Fairclough	21	4	10	7	0
=	Emile Heskey	21	6	2	13	0
=	Ray Kennedy	21	3	6	12	0
=	Steve McMahon	21	7	13	0	1
20	Peter Crouch	20	5	1	11	3
=	Chris Lawler	20	4	5	11	0
=	Steve McManaman	20	5	10	5	0

Ian Rush – Record cup goalscorer for Liverpool

GOALSCORERS – HAT-TRICK MEN

Maxi Rodriguez's stunning late-season goalscoring run saw him join the hat-trick hall of fame.

FULL RECORD OF LIVERPOOL FC HAT-TRICKS

17	Gordon Hodgson
16	Ian Rush
12	Roger Hunt
10	Robbie Fowler, Michael Owen
8	Dick Forshaw
7	Jack Parkinson
6	Sam Raybould
5	Harry Chambers, Billy Liddell
4	George Allan, Joe Hewitt, Steven Gerrard, Fernando Torres
3	John Aldridge, Jack Balmer, Yossi Benayoun, Kenny Dalglish, Tony Hateley, Fred Howe, Robert Robinson, Albert Stubbins, John Toshack, John Wark
2	John Barnes, Harold Barton, Frank Becton, Jimmy Case, William Devlin, Cyril Done, John Evans, Dick Johnson, Terry McDermott, Steve McMahon, Malcolm McVean, Fred Pagnam, Henry Race, Maxi Rodriguez, Jimmy Ross, Antonio Rowley, Ian St John, Dean Saunders, Graeme Souness, Paul Walsh
1	Alan Arnell, Alf Arrowsmith, Milan Baros, Peter Beardsley, Patrik Berger, Louis Bimpson, Phil Boersma, Ian Callaghan, Stan Collymore, Peter Crouch, Alun Evans, David Fairclough, Gary Gillespie, Bobby Graham, Jimmy Harrower, Emile Heskey, Dave Hickson, 'Sailor' Hunter, David Johnson, Kevin Keegan, Dirk Kuyt, Kevin Lewis,
1	Andy McGuigan, William McPherson, Arthur Metcalfe, Jan Molby, Steve Nicol, Ronald Orr, Tom Reid, Michael Robinson, Ronny Rosenthal, Danny Shone, Jimmy Smith, Steve Staunton, James Stewart, James Stott, John Walker, Jimmy Walsh, Mark Walters, Johnny Wheeler, Ronnie Whelan, Jack Whitham, Dave Wright

Maxi Rodriguez – Hat-trick double

87 players have scored a total of 225 hat-tricks

WHERE HAT-TRICKS HAVE BEEN SCORED

	AT ANFIELD	AWAY	TOTAL
League	132	44	176
FA Cup	12	5	17
League Cup	8	6	14
Europe	15	2	17
Other Games	0	1	1
TOTAL	**167**	**58**	**225**

PENALTY KINGS

Steven Gerrard added three spot-kicks to his all-time tally in 2010/11 to go up to 4th in Liverpool's most successful penalty taker list. Dirk Kuyt hit five from the spot to take his tally to eight – all scored in the Premier League.

COMPLETE RECORD – SCORERS IN SHOOT-OUTS NOT INCLUDED

PLAYER	LEAGUE	OTHER COMPS	TOTAL
Jan Molby	30	12	42
Phil Neal	28	10	38
Billy Liddell	34	0	34
Steven Gerrard	15	9	24
Tommy Smith	15	7	22
Robbie Fowler	14	6	20
John Aldridge	15	2	17
Terry McDermott	13	3	16
Gordon Hodgson	15	0	15
Michael Owen	11	2	13
Kevin Keegan	10	1	11
John Barnes	7	3	10
Willie Fagan	7	2	9
Arthur Goddard	7	1	8
Dirk Kuyt	8	0	=
Alec Lindsay	6	2	=
Ronnie Moran	6	2	=
Danny Murphy	5	3	=
Sam Raybould	8	0	=
Willie Stevenson	7	1	=
Jackie Sheldon	7	0	7
Robert Done	6	0	6
Jack Parkinson	6	0	=
Mark Walters	6	0	=
Gary McAllister	1	4	5
Jack Balmer	4	0	4
Peter Beardsley	2	2	=
Tom Chorlton	4	0	=
Donald MacKinlay	3	1	=
Alec Raisbeck	4	0	=
Alf West	4	0	=
Xabi Alonso	2	1	3
Frank Becton	2	1	=
Djibril Cisse	3	0	=
Dick Edmed	2	1	=
Kevin Lewis	3	0	=
Jari Litmanen	1	2	=
Tommy Lucas	3	0	=
Mike Marsh	0	3	=
Jamie Redknapp	3	0	=
Tommy Robertson	3	0	=
Jimmy Ross	3	0	=
Ian Rush	2	1	=
Graeme Souness	1	2	=
John Wark	3	0	=

Dirk Kuyt adds to his LFC penalty haul

PLAYER	LEAGUE	OTHER COMPS	TOTAL
Milan Baros	2	0	2
Patrik Berger	2	0	=
Harry Chambers	2	0	=
Julian Dicks	2	0	=
John Evans	2	0	=
Dick Forshaw	2	0	=
Alf Hanson	2	0	=
Ray Lambert	2	0	=
Andrew McCowie	2	0	=
Duncan McLean	2	0	=
Jimmy Melia	2	0	=
George Allan	1	0	1
Lance Carr	1	0	=
Robert Crawford	1	0	=
El-Hadji Diouf	0	1	=
George Fleming	1	0	=
Gary Gillespie	1	0	=
Gordon Gunson	1	0	=
Brian Hall	0	1	=
Jimmy Harrower	1	0	=
Roger Hunt	1	0	=
Harry Kewell	1	0	=
Fred Morris	1	0	=
David Ngog	0	1	=
Ronald Orr	1	0	=
Robert Robinson	1	0	=
Florent S-Pongolle	0	1	=
Vladimir Smicer	0	1	=
Geoff Strong	1	0	=
Albert Stubbins	1	0	=
Geoff Twentyman	0	1	=

GOALSCORERS – DEBUTANTS

Luis Suarez added his name to the list of goalscoring Liverpool debutants. The 2011 Copa America winner became the 21st player to achieve the feat for the club – and the first since 2006 – since the Reds established themselves back at the top table of English football.

LIVERPOOL FC DEBUT GOALSCORERS (1962-2011)

PLAYER	DATE	OPPONENTS	COMPETITION	GOALS	RESULT
Bobby Graham	14/09/1964	Reykjavik	European Cup	1	6-1
John Sealey	26/04/1965	Wolves	League	1	3-1
Alun Evans	21/09/1968	Leicester City	League	1	4-0
Alec Lindsay	16/09/1969	Dundalk	Fairs Cup	1	10-0
Kevin Keegan	14/08/1971	Nottingham Forest	League	1	3-1
Ray Kennedy	31/08/1974	Chelsea	League	1	3-0
Sammy Lee	08/04/1978	Leicester City	League	1	3-2
Ronnie Whelan	03/04/1981	Stoke City	League	1	3-0
John Wark	31/03/1984	Watford	League	1	2-0
David Speedie	03/02/1991	Manchester United	League	1	1-1
Nigel Clough	14/08/1993	Sheffield Wednesday	League	2	2-0
Robbie Fowler	22/09/1993	Fulham	League Cup	1	3-1
Stan Collymore	19/08/1995	Sheffield Wednesday	League	1	1-0
Michael Owen	06/05/1997	Wimbledon	League	1	1-2
Titi Camara	07/08/1999	Sheffield Wednesday	League	1	2-1
Leyton Maxwell	21/09/1999	Hull City	League Cup	1	4-2
Abel Xavier	09/02/2002	Ipswich Town	League	1	6-0
Craig Bellamy	09/08/2006	Maccabi Haifa	European Cup	1	2-1
Mark Gonzalez	09/08/2006	Maccabi Haifa	European Cup	1	2-1
Gabriel Paletta	25/10/2006	Reading	League Cup	1	4-3
Luis Suarez	02/02/2011	Stoke City	League	1	2-0

GOALSCORERS – SUPER SUBS

LIVERPOOL FC SUBSTITUTES SCORING MORE THAN ONCE IN A GAME

PLAYER	SEASON	OPPOSITION	COMPETITION	RESULT
Steve Staunton (3)	1989/90	Wigan Athletic	League Cup	3-0
Roger Hunt	1969/70	Southampton	League	4-1
Alun Evans	1969/70	Leicester City	FA Cup	2-0
Phil Boersma	1972/73	Carlisle United	League Cup	5-1
David Fairclough	1975/76	Burnley	League	2-0
David Fairclough	1977/78	Derby County	League Cup	2-0
David Johnson	1978/79	Tottenham Hotspur	League	7-0
David Fairclough	1979/80	Exeter City	League Cup	2-0
David Fairclough	1979/80	Bury	FA Cup	2-0
Kenny Dalglish	1986/87	West Ham United	League	5-2
Ian Rush	1988/89	Everton	FA Cup	3-2 aet
Mark Walters	1992/93	Blackburn Rovers	League	2-1
Patrik Berger	1996/97	Leicester City	League	3-0
Milan Baros	2004/05	Millwall	League Cup	3-0
Steven Gerrard	2005/06	TNS	European Cup	3-0
Djibril Cisse	2005/06	CSKA Moscow	Euro. Super Cup	3-1 aet
Florent Sinama-Pongolle	2005/06	Luton Town	FA Cup	5-3
Ryan Babel	2007/08	Besiktas	European Cup	8-0
Ryan Babel	2009/10	Hull City	League	6-1
Steven Gerrard (3)	2010/11	Napoli	Europa League	3-1

GOALSCORERS – SUPER SUBS

LIVERPOOL FC'S MOST PROLIFIC GOALSCORING SUBSTITUTES

	LEAGUE	FA CUP	LGE CUP	EUROPE	OTHERS	TOTAL
David Fairclough	7	2	7	2	0	18
Ryan Babel	6	0	0	6	0	12
Djibril Cisse	2	1	0	4	0	7
Steven Gerrard	1	0	0	6	0	7
Michael Owen	4	0	1	1	0	6
Ian Rush	2	3	0	1	0	6
Vladimir Smicer	4	0	1	1	0	6
Robbie Fowler	3	1	0	1	0	5

MOST GOALS IN A SEASON BY A LIVERPOOL FC SUBSTITUTE

PLAYER	SEASON	SUB APPS	GOALS
Ryan Babel	2007/08	20	7
Djibril Cisse	2005/06	25	7
David Fairclough	1979/80	14	6
David Fairclough	1975/76	12	5
Steven Gerrard	2010/11	2	3
Alun Evans	1969/70	4	3
Steven Gerrard	2005/06	4	3
Phil Boersma	1972/73	5	3
Roger Hunt	1969/70	5	3
Steve Staunton	1989/90	6	3
Kenny Dalglish	1986/87	8	3
David Fairclough	1977/78	8	3
Milan Baros	2004/05	11	3
Vladimir Smicer	2001/02	12	3
Jari Litmanen	2001/02	19	3
Robbie Fowler	2000/01	19	3
Ryan Babel	2009/10	22	3
Luis Garcia	2005/06	22	3

Djibril Cisse – Seven goals in 2005/06

MINUTES OF LIVERPOOL FC SUBSTITUTE GOALS

PERIOD OF MATCH	GOALS
1-10 minutes	0
11-20 minutes	0
21-30 minutes	1
31-40 minutes	3
41-50 minutes	4
51-60 minutes	14
61-70 minutes	23
71-80 minutes	52
81-90 minutes	110
91-120 minutes	9

OVERALL RECORD	GOALS
First half	4
Second half	203
Extra time	9

Earliest – 23 minutes:
Vladimir Smicer v Charlton Athletic (Premier League), 30/03/2003
Latest – 120 minutes:
Nick Barmby v Fulham (Lge Cup), 13/12/2000

Nick Barmby – Late super sub

GOALS SCORED BY OVERSEAS PLAYERS

A total of 50 players of overseas origin have been on the scoresheet for Liverpool in Premier League games. Dirk Kuyt remains the highest-placed current player amongst the list, while Maxi Rodriguez's late-season goal run in 2010/11 sees him on the verge of the top 10.

PREMIER LEAGUE ONLY – CORRECT AT END OF 2010/11

PLAYER	GOALS	PLAYER	GOALS
Fernando Torres	65	Nicolas Anelka	4
Dirk Kuyt	49	Florent Sinama-Pongolle	4
Patrik Berger	28	Luis Suarez	4
Sami Hyypia	22	Daniel Agger	3
John Arne Riise	21	Fabio Aurelio	3
Milan Baros	19	Markus Babbel	3
Yossi Benayoun	18	El-Hadji Diouf	3
Luis Garcia	18	Vegard Heggem	3
Xabi Alonso	15	Sotirios Kyrgiakos	3
Djibril Cisse	13	Albert Riera	3
Ryan Babel	12	Martin Skrtel	3
Harry Kewell	12	Alvaro Arbeloa	2
Karlheinz Riedle	11	Igor Biscan	2
Maxi Rodriguez	11	Stig Inge Bjornebye	2
Vladimir Smicer	10	Bruno Cheyrou	2
Titi Camara	9	Mark Gonzalez	2
David Ngog	9	Javier Mascherano	2
Dietmar Hamann	8	Bolo Zenden	2
Fernando Morientes	8	Alberto Aquilani	1
Oyvind Leonhardsen	7	Salif Diao	1
Jan Molby	7	Andrea Dossena	1
Ronny Rosenthal	6	Lucas Leiva	1
Jari Litmanen	5	Momo Sissoko	1
Raul Meireles	5	Abel Xavier	1
Andriy Voronin	5	Christian Ziege	1

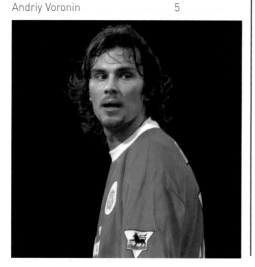 

Patrik Berger (left) and Sami Hyypia – Reached the 20s in the league

AWAY GOALS

The 2010/11 season was not a vintage campaign for scoring in the league away from Anfield, with the Reds improving by only four goals on their total the season before – one of only two seasons in which the team has failed to average a goal a game in the Premier League.

PREMIER LEAGUE ONLY – CORRECT AT END OF 2010/11

SEASON	GAMES PLAYED	GOALS SCORED	PLAYER	GOALS SCORED
2008/09	19	36	Michael Owen	55
2001/02	19	34	Robbie Fowler	43
2000/01	19	31	Steven Gerrard	35
2002/03	19	31	Steve McManaman	23
1994/95	21	27	Emile Heskey	22
1997/98	19	26	Ian Rush	21
2003/04	19	26	Fernando Torres	20
1993/94	21	26	Dirk Kuyt	19
2005/06	19	25	Danny Murphy	12
1995/96	19	24	John Arne Riise	12
1996/97	19	24	John Barnes	11
1998/99	19	24	Sami Hyypia	11
2007/08	19	24	Jamie Redknapp	11
1999/00	19	23	Milan Baros	10
2010/11	19	22	Own Goals	10
2004/05	19	21	Peter Crouch	9
1992/93	21	21	Patrik Berger	8
2006/07	19	18	Djibril Cisse	8
2009/10	19	18	Luis Garcia	8

SCORERS AGAINST LIVERPOOL FC

Andy Cole remains the most prolific player against the Reds in Premier League matches. His 11-goal haul was spread between four clubs, while Thierry Henry in second netted his goals for just one club – Arsenal. Own goals is the top scorer, with 26 scored by Liverpool players.

PREMIER LEAGUE 1992-2011

TOTAL	PLAYER	CLUB(S)
11	Andy Cole	Newcastle Utd (4), Man Utd (4), Blackburn R (2), Fulham (1)
8	Thierry Henry	Arsenal
7	Jimmy Floyd Hasselbaink	Leeds United (2), Chelsea (5)
=	Alan Shearer	Blackburn Rovers (2), Newcastle United (5)
6	Dion Dublin	Coventry City (2), Aston Villa (4)
=	Chris Sutton	Norwich City (2), Blackburn Rovers (4)
=	Mark Viduka	Leeds United
5	Nicolas Anelka	Manchester City (4), Chelsea (1)
=	Andriy Arshavin	Arsenal
=	Darren Bent	Charlton Athletic (2), Sunderland (3)
=	Tim Cahill	Everton
=	Kevin Davies	Southampton (2), Bolton Wanderers (3)
=	Les Ferdinand	QPR (2), Newcastle United (2), Tottenham Hotspur (1)
=	Duncan Ferguson	Everton (4), Newcastle United (1)
=	Mark Hughes	Manchester United (3), Chelsea (2)
=	Robbie Keane	Tottenham Hotspur
=	Matt Le Tissier	Southampton
=	Teddy Sheringham	Nottingham Forest (1), Tottenham Hotspur (4)
=	Dwight Yorke	Aston Villa (4), Manchester United (1)

OPPOSITION

SUPER FRANKIE LAMPARD

Standard Chartered
17

Standard Chartered
tombola

ARSENAL

2010/11 OVERVIEW

Final position: 4th, Premier League
Best cup runs: F Lge Cup; QF, FA Cup
Player of season: Jack Wilshere
Top scorer (all): 22, Robin van Persie

ALL-TIME RECORD

(League matches only)

	PL	W	D	L
Home:	87	48	17	22
Away:	87	20	29	38
Overall:	174	68	46	60

LEADING SCORERS (LEAGUE)

LFC players v Arsenal	Goals
Gordon Hodgson	12
Robbie Fowler	9
Jack Parkinson	9
Roger Hunt	8
Dick Forshaw	7
Current players:	
Steven Gerrard	3
Dirk Kuyt	2

CLUB DETAILS

Nickname: The Gunners
Ground: Emirates Stadium, capacity 60,361 (10/11 away alloc. 2,914)
Manager: Arsene Wenger (app. 01/10/96)
Major signings: Mikel Arteta, Gervinho, Per Mertesacker, A. O-Chamberlain
Year formed: 1886

USEFUL INFORMATION

Website: www.arsenal.com
Address: Highbury House, 75, Drayton Park, N5 1BU
Switchboard: 0207 619 5003

TRAVEL INFORMATION

By Car (from Anfield): 209 miles/3 hours 45 mins.
By Tube: Arsenal (Piccadilly Line) is a three-minute walk. Finsbury Park and Highbury & Islington are also within 10 minutes of the stadium.
By Bus: Main bus stops are located on Holloway Road, Nag's Head, Seven Sisters Road, Blackstock Road and Highbury Corner. Regular services will take you to within 10 minutes walk of the ground.

ASTON VILLA

2010/11 OVERVIEW

Final position: 9th, Premier League
Best cup runs: QF, League Cup; R5, FA Cup
Player of season: Stewart Downing
Top scorer (all): 9, Darren Bent/Ashley Young

ALL-TIME RECORD

(League matches only)

	PL	W	D	L
Home:	86	54	17	15
Away:	86	27	21	38
Overall:	172	81	38	53

LEADING SCORERS (LEAGUE)

LFC players v Aston Villa	Goals
Robbie Fowler	12
Roger Hunt	10
Steven Gerrard	9
Gordon Hodgson	9
Ian Rush	8
Other current player:	
Dirk Kuyt	2

CLUB DETAILS

Nickname: The Villans
Ground: Villa Park, capacity 42,582 (10/11 away allocation 2,416)
Manager: Alex McLeish (app. 17/06/11)
Major signings: Charles N'Zogbia, Shay Given, Alan Hutton, Jermaine Jenas
Year formed: 1874

USEFUL INFORMATION

Website: www.avfc.co.uk
Address: Villa Park, Trinity Road, Birmingham B6 6HE
Switchboard: 0121 327 2299

TRAVEL INFORMATION

By Car (from Anfield): 96 miles/1 hour 50 mins.
By Train: Witton station is a five-minute walk, while Aston is 15 minutes away. From New Street Station, a taxi should take 15 minutes.
By Bus: The number 7 West Midlands Travel Bus runs from Birmingham City Centre to the stadium (Witton). For services check www.travelwm.co.uk

BLACKBURN ROVERS

ARTE ET LABORE

2010/11 OVERVIEW

Final position: 15th, Premier League
Best cup runs: R4, FA Cup; R3, League Cup
Player of season: Chris Samba
Top scorer (all): 6, M. Biram Diouf/Nikola Kalinic

ALL-TIME RECORD

(League matches only)

	PL	W	D	L
Home:	63	38	16	9
Away:	63	15	22	26
Overall:	126	53	38	35

LEADING SCORERS (LEAGUE)

LFC players v Blackburn Rovers	Goals
Billy Liddell	12
Gordon Hodgson	9
Harry Chambers	7
Michael Owen	7
Current player:	
Steven Gerrard	4

CLUB DETAILS

Nickname: Rovers
Ground: Ewood Park, capacity 31,367 (10/11 away allocation 7,099)
Manager: Steve Kean (app. 22/12/10)
Major signings: Scott Dann, David Goodwillie, Ayegbeni Yakubu, Simon Vukcevic
Year formed: 1875

USEFUL INFORMATION

Website: www.rovers.co.uk
Address: Ewood Park, Bolton Road, Blackburn, Lancashire BB2 4JF
Switchboard: 0871 702 1875

TRAVEL INFORMATION

By Car (from Anfield): 40 miles/45 minutes.
By Train: Blackburn station is a mile and a half away, Mill Hill is one mile. Direct trains run from Manchester Victoria, Salford Crescent and Preston.
By Bus: The central bus station is next to the railway station. Services 3, 3A, 3B, 46, and 346 all go from Blackburn to Darwen. Ewood Park is a mile and a half along the journey.

BOLTON WANDERERS

2010/11 OVERVIEW

Final position: 14th, Premier League
Best cup runs: SF, FA Cup; R3, League Cup
Player of season: Stuart Holden
Top scorer (all): 12, Johan Elmander

ALL-TIME RECORD

(League matches only)

	PL	W	D	L
Home:	58	32	16	10
Away:	58	20	13	25
Overall:	116	52	29	35

LEADING SCORERS (LEAGUE)

LFC players v Bolton Wanderers	Goals
Jack Parkinson	11
Steven Gerrard	7
Harry Chambers	6
Dick Edmed	6
Robbie Fowler	6
Gordon Hodgson	6
Other current player:	
Dirk Kuyt	3

CLUB DETAILS

Nickname: The Trotters
Ground: Reebok Stadium, capacity 28,101 (10/11 away alloc. 4,650)
Manager: Owen Coyle (app. 08/01/10)
Major signings: David Ngog, Chris Eagles, Tuncay Sanli, Gael Kakuta
Year formed: 1874

USEFUL INFORMATION

Website: www.bwfc.co.uk
Address: Reebok Stadium, Burnden Way, Lostock, Bolton BL6 6JW
Switchboard: 0844 871 2932

TRAVEL INFORMATION

By Car (from Anfield): 27 miles/40 minutes.
By Train: Horwich Parkway station is a few minutes walk from the stadium. Regular trains run from Bolton, while from Liverpool you can change at Manchester Oxford Road.
By Bus: The club operate regular buses to and from Bolton town centre.

CHELSEA

2010/11 OVERVIEW

Final position: 2nd, Premier League
Best cup runs: QF, Champions Lge; R4 FA Cup
Player of season: Petr Cech
Top scorer (all): 16, Nicolas Anelka

ALL-TIME RECORD

(League matches only)

	PL	W	D	L
Home:	68	45	14	9
Away:	68	17	14	37
Overall:	136	62	28	46

LEADING SCORERS (LEAGUE)

LFC players v Chelsea	Goals
Ian Rush	8
Roger Hunt	7
Willie Fagan	6
Gordon Hodgson	6
Billy Liddell	6
Steve Nicol	6
Current players:	
S. Gerrard, D. Kuyt, R. Meireles	1

CLUB DETAILS

Nickname: The Blues
Ground: Stamford Bridge, capacity 41,841 (10/11 away alloc. 3,089)
Manager: Andre Villas-Boas (app. 22/06/11)
Major signings: Juan Mata, Romelu Lukaku, Raul Meireles, Oriol Romeu,
Year formed: 1905

USEFUL INFORMATION

Website: www.chelseafc.com
Address: Stamford Bridge, Fulham Road, London SW6 1HS
Switchboard: 0871 984 1955

TRAVEL INFORMATION

By Car (from Anfield): 216 miles/4 hours.
By Tube: Fulham Broadway (District Line) is five minutes' walk away. Take a tube to Earls Court and change for Wimbledon-bound tubes. West Brompton overground station is 15 minutes away.
By Bus: Numbers 14, 211 and 414 go along Fulham Road from central London via West Crompton station.

EVERTON

2010/11 OVERVIEW

Final position: 7th, Premier League
Best cup runs: R5, FA Cup; R3, League Cup
Player of season: Leighton Baines
Top scorer (all): 10, J. Beckford/Louis Saha

ALL-TIME RECORD

(League matches only)

	PL	W	D	L
Home:	92	39	30	23
Away:	92	31	27	34
Overall:	184	70	57	57

LEADING SCORERS (LEAGUE)

LFC players v Everton	Goals
Ian Rush	13
Harry Chambers	8
Dick Forshaw	7
Jack Balmer	6
Robbie Fowler	6
Jack Parkinson	6
Current player:	
Dirk Kuyt	5

CLUB DETAILS

Nickname: The Toffees
Ground: Goodison Park, capacity 40,158 (10/11 away allocation 2,881)
Manager: David Moyes (app. 14/03/02)
Major signings: Royston Drenthe, Denis Stracqualursi
Year formed: 1878

USEFUL INFORMATION

Website: www.evertonfc.com
Address: Goodison Park, Goodison Road, Liverpool L4 4EL
Switchboard: 0871 663 1878

TRAVEL INFORMATION

By Car (from Anfield): 0.8 miles/3 minutes.
By Train: From Liverpool Central, take any train heading for Ormskirk or Kirkby and get off at Kirkdale - from there it is a 10-minute walk.
By Bus: From Queen's Square Bus Station in Liverpool city centre, numbers 1, 2, 19, 20, 21, 311, 345 and 350 go past or near the stadium.

FULHAM

2010/11 OVERVIEW

Final position: 8th, Premier League
Best cup runs: R5, FA Cup; R3, League Cup
Player of season: Clint Dempsey
Top scorers (all): 13, Clint Dempsey

ALL-TIME RECORD

(League matches only)

	PL	W	D	L
Home:	24	17	7	0
Away:	24	10	6	8
Overall:	48	27	13	8

LEADING SCORERS (LEAGUE)

LFC players v Fulham	Goals
Billy Liddell	13
Roger Hunt	5
Alan A'Court	4
Ian Callaghan	4
John Evans	4
Current player:	
Maxi Rodriguez	3

CLUB DETAILS

Nickname:	Cottagers
Ground:	Craven Cottage, capacity 26,600 (10/11 away allocation 2,650)
Manager:	Martin Jol (app. 07/06/11)
Major signings:	Bryan Ruiz, John Arne Riise, Pajtim Kasami, Orlando Sa
Year formed:	1879

USEFUL INFORMATION

Website:	www.fulhamfc.com
Address:	Craven Cottage, Stevenage Road, Fulham, London SW6 6HH
Switchboard:	0870 442 1222

TRAVEL INFORMATION

By Car (from Anfield): 216 miles/4 hours.
By Tube: Alight at Putney Bridge (District Line), from central London. The stadium is a 10-minute walk. Bishop's Park, along the Thames is the quickest route – note it's closed after night games.
By Bus: The following run down nearby Fulham Palace Road: 74, 190, 211, 220, 295. London Transport's website is www.tfl.gov.uk

MANCHESTER CITY

2010/11 OVERVIEW

Final position: 3rd, Premier League
Best cup runs: W, FA Cup; L16, Europa League
Player of season: Vincent Kompany
Top scorer (all): 23, Carlos Tevez

ALL-TIME RECORD

(League matches only)

	PL	W	D	L
Home:	75	46	16	13
Away:	75	29	21	25
Overall:	150	75	37	38

LEADING SCORERS (LEAGUE)

LFC players v Manchester City	Goals
Ian Rush	14
Gordon Hodgson	11
Kenny Dalglish	10
Sam Raybould	8
Current players:	
Steven Gerrard	3
Dirk Kuyt	3
Andy Carroll	2

CLUB DETAILS

Nickname:	Blues/The Citizens
Ground:	City of Manchester Stadium, capacity 47,726 (10/11 away allocation 2,560)
Manager:	Roberto Mancini (app. 20/12/09)
Major signings:	Sergio Aguero, Samir Nasri Gael Clichy, Stefan Savic
Year formed:	1887

USEFUL INFORMATION

Website:	www.mcfc.co.uk
Address:	City of Manchester Stadium, SportCity, Rowsley Street, Manchester M11 3FF
Switchboard:	0870 062 1894

TRAVEL INFORMATION

By Car (from Anfield): 36 miles/50 minutes.
By Train: Ashburys station is a 15-minute walk, a five-minute train journey from Manchester Piccadilly (20-25 minutes on foot).
By Bus: The following services run direct from Piccadilly Gardens: 216, 217, 218, 231, 236 and 237.

MANCHESTER UNITED

2010/11 OVERVIEW

Final position: 1st, Premier League
Best cup runs: F, Champions Lge; SF, FA Cup
Player of season: Javier Hernandez
Top scorers (all): 21, Dimitar Berbatov

ALL-TIME RECORD

(League matches only)

	PL	W	D	L
Home:	78	38	18	22
Away:	78	15	25	38
Overall:	156	53	43	60

LEADING SCORERS (LEAGUE)

LFC players v Manchester Utd	Goals
Dick Forshaw	8
Gordon Hodgson	7
J. Parkinson, R. Fowler	6
J. Barnes, H. Chambers, I. St John	5
Current player:	
Steven Gerrard	4

CLUB DETAILS

Nickname: Red Devils
Ground: Old Trafford, capacity 75,769 (10/11 away allocation 2,991)
Manager: Sir Alex Ferguson (app. 06/11/1986)
Major signings: David De Gea, Ashley Young, Phil Jones
Year formed: 1878

USEFUL INFORMATION

Website: www.manutd.com
Address: Sir Matt Busby Way, Old Trafford, Manchester M16 0RA
Switchboard: 0161 868 8000

TRAVEL INFORMATION

By Car (from Anfield): 33 miles/45 minutes.
By Train: Services run from Piccadilly to the club's railway station. There is also a Metrolink service, with the station located next to Lancashire CCC on Warwick Road, which leads to Sir Matt Busby Way.
By Bus: The 250, 255, 256, 263, 290 and 291 run from Piccadilly Gardens in the city centre.

NEWCASTLE UNITED

2010/11 OVERVIEW

Final position: 12th, Premier League
Best cup runs: R4, League Cup; R3 FA Cup
Player of season: Joey Barton
Top scorer (all): 12, Kevin Nolan

ALL-TIME RECORD

(League matches only)

	PL	W	D	L
Home:	75	50	14	11
Away:	75	22	23	30
Overall:	150	72	37	41

LEADING SCORERS (LEAGUE)

LFC players v Newcastle United	Goals
Michael Owen	13
Gordon Hodgson	8
Roger Hunt	8
Ian Rush	7
Current players:	
Steven Gerrard	6
Dirk Kuyt	5

CLUB DETAILS

Nickname: Magpies
Ground: St James' Park, capacity 52,387 (10/11 away allocation 2,747)
Manager: Alan Pardew (app. 09/12/10)
Major signings: Davide Santon, Yohan Cabaye, Sylvain Marveaux, Demba Ba, Gabriel Obertan, Mehdi Abeid
Year formed: 1881

USEFUL INFORMATION

Website: www.nufc.co.uk
Address: St James' Park, Newcastle-upon-Tyne NE1 4ST
Switchboard: 0844 372 1892

TRAVEL INFORMATION

By Car (from Anfield): 173 miles/3 hours.
By Train: The stadium is a 10-minute walk from Newcastle Central Station. It is also served by its own Metro station (St James' Metro).
By Road: Any bus from the town centre heading towards Gallowgate takes you past St James' Park.

NORWICH CITY

Final position: 2nd, Championship
Best cup runs: R3, FA Cup; R2, League Cup
Player of season: Grant Holt
Top scorer (all): 23, Grant Holt

ALL-TIME RECORD

(League matches only)

	PL	W	D	L
Home:	23	15	4	4
Away:	23	9	7	7
Overall:	46	24	11	11

LEADING SCORERS (LEAGUE)

LFC players v Norwich City	Goals
Ian Rush	9
David Fairclough	6
Kenny Dalglish	5
Roger Hunt	5
David Johnson	4

CLUB DETAILS

Nickname: Canaries
Ground: Carrow Road, capacity 26,034
(away allocation 2,500)
Manager: Paul Lambert (app. 18/08/09)
Major signings: Steve Morison, James Vaughan
Year formed: 1902

USEFUL INFORMATION

Website: www.canaries.co.uk
Address: Carrow Road, Norwich
NR1 1JE
Switchboard: 01603 760760

TRAVEL INFORMATION

By Car (from Anfield): 255 miles/4 hrs 50 mins.
By Train: Turn left from Norwich station and head for Morrisons supermarket – the stadium is situated behind that.
By Road: From the end of the M6 connect to the A14, which takes you onto the M11. From the A47 (southern bypass) take the A146 into Norwich, from where Carrow Road is well signposted.

QUEENS PARK RANGERS

Final position: 1st, Championship
Best cup runs: R3, FA Cup; R1, League Cup
Player of season: Paddy Kenny
Top scorers (all): 19, Adel Taarabt

ALL-TIME RECORD

(League matches only)

	PL	W	D	L
Home:	20	17	2	1
Away:	20	11	4	5
Overall:	40	28	6	6

LEADING SCORERS (LEAGUE)

LFC players v QPR	Goals
Ian Rush	10
John Barnes	9
John Toshack	5
John Aldridge	3
Steve Nicol	3

CLUB DETAILS

Nicknames: The Hoops/Rs/Rangers
Ground: Loftus Road, capacity 18,360
(away allocation 1,800-3,400)
Manager: Neil Warnock (app. 01/03/10)
Major signings: Shaun W-Phillips, Joey Barton, Jay Bothroyd, DJ Campbell
Year formed: 1882

USEFUL INFORMATION

Website: www.qpr.co.uk
Address: Loftus Road Stadium,
South Africa Road, London
W12 7PJ
Switchboard: 0208 743 0262

TRAVEL INFORMATION

By Car (from Anfield): 214 miles/3 hours 55 mins.
By Tube: Shepherds Bush tube (Central Line and Hammersmith & City Line) are within a 10-15 minute walk. White City (Central Line) is also nearby.
By Road: From the M1 take the M40 (London), then the A40 (Central London). When the road becomes A40 (M), turn off onto the A40 towards White City/ Shepherds Bush, turn right into Wood Lane and then right into South Africa Road for the stadium.

STOKE CITY

2010/11 OVERVIEW

Final position: 13th, Premier League
Best cup runs: F, FA Cup; R4, League Cup
Player of season: Robert Huth
Top scorers (all): 12, Kenwyne Jones/J. Walters

ALL-TIME RECORD

(League matches only)

	PL	W	D	L
Home:	56	43	10	3
Away:	56	12	20	24
Overall:	112	55	30	27

LEADING SCORERS (LEAGUE)

LFC players v Stoke City	Goals
Roger Hunt	11
Billy Liddell	9
Kenny Dalglish	6
Andy McGuigan	6
Berry Nieuwenhuys	5
Sam Raybould	5

CLUB DETAILS

Nickname: The Potters
Ground: Britannia Stadium, capacity 28,383 (10/11 away all'tion 2,795)
Manager: Tony Pulis (app. 13/06/06)
Major signings: Wilson Palacios, Peter Crouch
Year formed: 1863

USEFUL INFORMATION

Website: www.stokecityfc.com
Address: Stanley Matthews Way, Stoke-on-Trent ST4 4EG
Switchboard: 0871 663 2008

TRAVEL INFORMATION

By Car (from Anfield): 60 miles/1 hour 10 minutes.
By Train: Stoke-on-Trent is two minutes from Glebe Street, where buses to the stadium run. Turn right out of the station and then next right. Follow the road to the end then turn left, down a bank into Glebe Street.
By Bus: From Hanley Bus Station take the 23 to Glebe Street where shuttle bus services to the stadium depart. Service is at 15-minute intervals.

SUNDERLAND

2010/11 OVERVIEW

Final position: 10th, Premier League
Best cup runs: R3, FA Cup & League Cup
Player of season: Phil Bardsley
Top scorers (all): 11, Asamoah Gyan, Darren Bent

ALL-TIME RECORD

(League matches only)

	PL	W	D	L
Home:	74	37	19	18
Away:	74	29	13	32
Overall:	148	66	32	50

LEADING SCORERS (LEAGUE)

LFC players v Sunderland	Goals
Roger Hunt	13
Billy Liddell	10
Harry Chambers	9
Gordon Hodgson	8
Current players:	
Steven Gerrard	3
Dirk Kuyt	2

CLUB DETAILS

Nickname: The Black Cats
Ground: Stadium of Light, capacity 49,000 (10/11 away alloc. 2,340)
Manager: Steve Bruce (app. 03/06/09)
Major signings: Connor Wickham, Craig Gardner, Sebastian Larsson, John O'Shea
Year formed: 1879

USEFUL INFORMATION

Website: www.safc.com
Address: Stadium of Light, Sunderland SR5 1SU
Switchboard: 0871 911 1200

TRAVEL INFORMATION

By Car (from Anfield): 169 miles/3 hours.
By Train: Sunderland mainline station is a 10-15 minute walk. The Metro service also runs from here, with St Peter's or the Stadium of Light stations nearest the stadium.
By Bus: Numbers 2, 3, 4, 12, 13, 15 and 16 stop near ground. All routes connect to the central bus station, Park Lane Interchange.

SWANSEA CITY

2010/11 OVERVIEW

Final position: 3rd, Championship
Best cup runs: R4, FA Cup; R4, League Cup
Player of season: Nathan Dyer
Top scorers (all): 27, Scott Sinclair

ALL-TIME RECORD

(League matches only)

	PL	W	D	L
Home:	10	8	2	0
Away:	10	2	2	6
Overall:	20	10	4	6

LEADING SCORERS (LEAGUE)

LFC players v Swansea City	Goals
Roger Hunt	7
Jimmy Melia	7
Alan A'Court	5
Dave Hickson	3
Tony Rowley	3
Ian Rush	3

CLUB DETAILS

Nickname: Swans
Ground: Liberty Stadium, capacity 20,520 (away allocation 2,000)
Manager: Brendan Rodgers (app. 16/07/10)
Major signings: Danny Graham, Leroy Lita
Year formed: 1912

USEFUL INFORMATION

Website: www.swanseacity.net
Address: Liberty Stadium, Landore, Swansea SA1 2FA
Switchboard: 01792 616600

TRAVEL INFORMATION

By Car (from Anfield): 179 miles/4 hours.
By Train: Swansea High Street station is about two miles from the stadium (30-minute walk). Regular buses are available outside the station (4, 4a, 120, 122, 125, 132); a taxi should cost less than £5.
By Car: Leave the M4 at J45 and take the A4067 towards the city centre (A4067 South). Stay on the road for 2-3 miles and you will reach the stadium.

Swansea City's Liberty Stadium – A new venue for the Reds in 2011/12

TOTTENHAM HOTSPUR

2010/11 OVERVIEW

Final position: 5th, Premier League
Best cup runs: QF, Champions Lge; R4, FA Cup
Player of season: Luka Modric
Top scorer (all): 15, Rafael van der Vaart

ALL-TIME RECORD

(League matches only)

	PL	W	D	L
Home:	68	43	19	6
Away:	68	20	15	33
Overall:	136	63	34	39

LEADING SCORERS (LEAGUE)

LFC players v Tottenham H.	Goals
Roger Hunt	9
Kenny Dalglish	8
Ian Rush	8
Robbie Fowler	6
Billy Liddell	6
Current player:	
Dirk Kuyt	4

CLUB DETAILS

Nicknames: Spurs, Lilywhites
Ground: White Hart Lane, capacity 36,534 (10/11 away alloc. 2,929)
Manager: Harry Redknapp (app. 26/10/08)
Major signings: Emmanuel Abebayor, Scott Parker Brad Friedel, Cristian Ceballos
Year formed: 1882

USEFUL INFORMATION

Website: www.tottenhamhotspur.com
Address: Bill Nicholson Way, 748, High Road, Tottenham, London N17 0AP
Switchboard: 0844 499 5000

TRAVEL INFORMATION

By Car (from Anfield): 214 miles/3 hours 45 mins.
By Tube: The nearest tube station is Seven Sisters (Victoria – a 25-minute walk), with trains running to Liverpool Street. The nearest mainline station is White Hart Lane, approx 5 minutes walk.
By Bus: A regular service runs from Seven Sisters past the stadium (numbers 149, 259, 279).

WEST BROMWICH ALBION

2010/11 OVERVIEW

Final position: 11th, Premier League
Best cup runs: R5, League Cup; R3, FA Cup
Player of season: Youssouf Mulumbu
Top scorer (all): 15, Peter Odemwingie

ALL-TIME RECORD

(League matches only)

	PL	W	D	L
Home:	59	33	17	9
Away:	59	23	16	20
Overall:	118	56	33	29

LEADING SCORERS (LEAGUE)

LFC players v West Brom	Goals
Gordon Hodgson	10
Kenny Dalglish	8
Roger Hunt	8
Current player:	
Steven Gerrard	3

CLUB DETAILS

Nickname: Baggies
Ground: The Hawthorns, capacity 28,003 (10/11 away allocation 2,440)
Manager: Roy Hodgson (app. 11/02/11)
Major signings: Shane Long, Zoltan Gera
Year formed: 1878

USEFUL INFORMATION

Website: www.wba.co.uk
Address: The Hawthorns, West Bromwich, West Midlands B71 4LF
Switchboard: 0871 271 1100

TRAVEL INFORMATION

By Car (from Anfield): 94 miles/1 hour 45 mins.
By Train: The Hawthorns Metro stop is 10 minutes away, served by a service from Birmingham Snow Hill. Smethwick Rolf Street is 15 minutes from the stadium, served by Birmingham New Street trains.
By Bus: The 74 (between Birmingham and Dudley), 79 (Birmingham and Wolverhampton) and 450 (Bearwood and West Bromwich) stop nearby.

WIGAN ATHLETIC

2010/11 OVERVIEW

Final position: 16th, Premier League
Best cup runs: QF, League Cup; R4, FA Cup
Player of season: Ali Al-Habsi
Top scorer (all): 10, Charles N'Zogbia

ALL-TIME RECORD

(League matches only)

	PL	W	D	L
Home:	6	4	2	0
Away:	6	3	2	1
Overall:	12	7	4	1

LEADING SCORERS (LEAGUE)

LFC players v Wigan Athletic	Goals
Dirk Kuyt	5
Fernando Torres	3
Craig Bellamy	2
Yossi Benayoun	2
Peter Crouch	2

CLUB DETAILS

Nickname: The Latics
Ground: DW Stadium,
capacity 25,138
(10/11 away allocation 4,072)
Manager: Roberto Martinez (app. 15/06/09)
Major signings: David Jones, Ali Al-Habsi,
Shaun Maloney, Albert Crusat
Year formed: 1932

USEFUL INFORMATION

Website: www.wiganlatics.co.uk
Address: DW Stadium, Robin Park,
Newtown, Wigan WN5 0UZ
Switchboard: 01942 774000

TRAVEL INFORMATION

By Car (from Anfield): 21 miles/30 minutes.
By Train: Wigan Wallgate and Wigan North Western are a 15-minute walk. From either station head under the railway bridge and keep to the right – following the road (A49) for 10 minutes.
By Bus: No particular route, as the venue is within easy distance of the station.

WOLVERHAMPTON WANDERERS

2010/11 OVERVIEW

Final position: 17th, Premier League
Best cup runs: R4, FA Cup & League Cup
Player of season: Matt Jarvis
Top scorer (all): 12, Steven Fletcher

ALL-TIME RECORD

(League matches only)

	PL	W	D	L
Home:	46	30	7	9
Away:	46	15	10	21
Overall:	92	45	17	30

LEADING SCORERS (LEAGUE)

LFC players v Wolves	Goals
Roger Hunt	9
Kenny Dalglish	5
Sam Raybould	5
Jack Balmer	4
Harry Bradshaw	4
Gordon Hodgson	4

CLUB DETAILS

Nickname: Wolves
Ground: Molineux, capacity 28,565
(10/11 away allocation 2,577)
Manager: Mick McCarthy (app. 21/07/06)
Major signings: Roger Johnson, Jamie O'Hara
Year formed: 1877

USEFUL INFORMATION

Website: www.wolves.co.uk
Address: Waterloo Road, Wolverhampton,
West Midlands WV1 4QR
Switchboard: 0871 222 2220

TRAVEL INFORMATION

By Car (from Anfield): 88 miles/1 hour 35 minutes.
By Train: The stadium is a 15-minute walk from Wolverhampton station. Follow the Ring Road, walking down the side of the Chubb buildings. At the crossroads you will see the stadium on your left.
By Bus: The 503 and 504 from stand R in the city centre bus station stop at the stadium – this is opposite the railway station, in easy walking distance.

KENNEDY A 15

OFFICIAL CLUB SUPERSTORE
LIVERPOOL F.C.

MELWOOD TRAINING GROUND

RESPECT

Respect Our Neighbourhood
Week of Action
For full details of the Week of Action go to:
www.liverpool.gov.uk/citysafe
or telephone: 0151 233 3001

TICKETS

ADDRESS

Ticket Office,
PO Box 204,
Liverpool
L69 3JF

TELEPHONE NUMBERS/WEBSITE

0843 170 5555 (24-Hour Ticket Information & Booking Line)
++44 (0)151 907 9399 (International)
www.liverpoolfc.tv/tickets

TICKET OFFICE HOURS

Monday-Friday 8.15am-3.45pm
Matchdays 8.15am to kick-off (weekday), 9.15am to kick-off (weekend)
Non Match Saturdays 9.15am-1.00pm

PRICES

	Category A	Category B	Category C
Kop			
Adult	£45	£42	£39
Over 65	£34	£31.50	£29.50
Disabled and Visually Impaired	£34	£31.50	£29.50
Personal Assistants	FREE	FREE	FREE
Main Stand			
Adult	£48	£44	£42
Over 65	£36	£33	£31.50
Centenary Stand			
Adult	£48	£44	£42
Over 65	£36	£33	£31.50
Paddock Enclosure			
Adult	£48	£44	£42
Over 65	£36	£33	£31.50
Disabled and Visually Impaired	£36	£33	£31.50
Personal Assistants	FREE	FREE	FREE
Anfield Road			
Adult	£48	£44	£42
Over 65	£36	£33	£31.50
Combined 1 Adult/1 Child (16 or under)	£63	£59	£57
Disabled and Visually Impaired	£36	£33	£31.50
Personal Assistants	FREE	FREE	FREE

CATEGORY A MATCHES

Arsenal, Aston Villa, Chelsea, Everton, Manchester City, Manchester United, Tottenham Hotspur.

CATEGORY B MATCHES

Blackburn Rovers, Bolton Wanderers, Fulham, Newcastle United, Norwich City, QPR, Sunderland.

CATEGORY C MATCHES

Stoke City, Swansea City, West Bromwich Albion, Wigan Athletic, Wolverhampton Wanderers.

BUYING TICKETS – BARCLAYS PREMIER LEAGUE HOME GAMES

Adult and Junior LFC Official Members get priority access to all available tickets for Barclays Premier League home games.
Members will also be able to purchase tickets in advance for the 2011/12 season in two stages, July and November. For full details please go to **www.liverpoolfc.tv/tickets/lfc-members-tickets**

TICKETS

BUYING TICKETS – BARCLAYS PREMIER LEAGUE HOME GAMES

In order to offer fans the best opportunity to apply for tickets, any tickets returned through the Ticket Exchange may also be available through Late Availability, so keep checking the online ticketing system as tickets may become available to purchase.

You can apply for tickets online at **liverpoolfc.tv** or via 0843 170 5555 (Overseas +44 (0)151 907 9399). Should tickets still be available following the initial sales, tickets can be purchased in person at the Ticket Office. For further details please visit **www.liverpoolfc.tv/tickets**

Please note: Postal applications are no longer accepted.

Disabled fans, please visit our Accessibility section on the website for details on applying for tickets – **www.liverpoolfc.tv/tickets/accessibility**

BUYING TICKETS – BARCLAYS PREMIER LEAGUE AWAY GAMES

Tickets to away games are only available to season-ticket holders, members and Fan Card holders, with priority given according to the number of Barclays Premier League away fixtures attended during the 2010/11 season.

For any available tickets following the advertised sales, further announcement will be made at **www.liverpoolfc.tv/tickets**

BUYING TICKETS – DOMESTIC CUP AND EUROPEAN GAMES

For information on cup and European games, please see the fixture's selling notice under 'Latest Ticket News' on **www.liverpoolfc.tv**

TICKET OFFICE INFORMATION

Ticket stubs should be retained as they may be required for future ticket allocation or in the event a match is abandoned.

For latest ticket information visit **www.liverpoolfc.tv/tickets**

ABOUT ANFIELD

ADDRESS

Liverpool Football Club
Anfield Road
Liverpool
L4 0TH

ABOUT

First used in 1884 to house Everton FC, the Reds have called Anfield their home since 1892. Originally owned by John Orrell, fellow brewer and friend John Houlding bought the ground in 1891, soon after Everton won the league title. His proposed increase in rent to Everton – some records state a four-fold increase on their original agreement with Orrell – was a key factor in seeing the club leave. With an empty ground and no team, Houlding formed his own club – and so Liverpool FC were born.

Their first match at Anfield saw a 7-0 victory over Rotherham Town on September 1 1892, with the first Football League match played a year later, the Reds seeing off Lincoln City 4-0 on September 8, 1893 in front of an estimated 5,000 spectators.

On its original inauguration in 1884 Anfield housed 20,000. Extensive redevelopment has seen Anfield hold upwards of 60,000, the stadium's record attendance of 61,905 coming against Wolves on February 2, 1952.

The ground, which hosted European Championship games in 1996 and is rated a 4-star stadium by UEFA, holds 45,522 – with this figure taking into account the Press and disabled areas and all seating, some of which is not used due to segregation. Anfield, or a new stadium, is due to host games during the 2015 rugby union World Cup.

THE KOP GRANDSTAND

Built in 1906, after the Reds won the league championship for a second time. It was named 'The Spion Kop' after a South African hill in Natal which was the scene of a bloody Boer War battle. In 1928 it was rebuilt and a roof was added, with the capacity reaching close to 30,000 – the largest covered terrace in the Football League at that time. It was rebuilt in summer 1994 to its current splendour after an emotional send-off against Norwich City at the end of the 1993/94 campaign.

CENTENARY STAND

The original Kemlyn Road Stand incorporated a barrel roof and was fronted by an uncovered paddock. It was demolished in 1963 to make way for a new cantilever stand. In 1992 a second tier was added, and the stand was renamed to mark the club's 100th anniversary.

MAIN STAND/PADDOCK

The original structure was erected in the late 19th century, a 3,000-capacity stand with a distinctive red and white tudor style with the club's name in the centre. In 1973 it was redeveloped, with a new roof and officially opened by HRH the Duke of Kent. Seats were added to the Paddock in 1980.

ANFIELD ROAD STAND

In 1903 the first Anfield Road stand was built. Once a simple one-tier stand which contained a covered standing enclosure (the roof was first added in 1965), it was demolished to make way for a two-tier development in 1998 – the stand having been originally altered to accomodate multi-coloured seating in the early 1980s.

GETTING TO ANFIELD

HOW TO GET THERE - BY CAR

Follow the M62 until you reach the end of the motorway. Then follow the A5058 towards Liverpool for 3 miles, then turn left at the traffic lights into Utting Avenue (there is a McDonald's on the corner of this junction). Proceed for one mile and then turn right at The Arkles pub for the ground. It is recommended that you arrive at least 2 hours before kick-off in order to secure your parking space. Otherwise, you can park in the streets around Goodison Park and walk across Stanley Park to Anfield, or you can park in a secure parking area at Goodison.

HOW TO GET THERE - BY TRAIN

Kirkdale Station is the closest to Anfield (about a mile away), although Sandhills Station the stop before has the benefit of a bus service to the ground (Soccerbus). Both stations can be reached by first getting a train from Liverpool Lime Street (which is over 3 miles from the ground) to Liverpool Central (Merseyrail Northern Line), and then changing there for trains to Sandhills (2 stops away) or Kirkdale (3 stops). Note: only trains to Ormskirk or Kirkby go to Kirkdale station. A taxi from Liverpool Lime Street should cost between £5 and £7.

HOW TO GET THERE - SOCCERBUS

There are frequent shuttle buses from Sandhills Station to Anfield for all Liverpool home Premier League and cup matches. Soccerbus will run for 2 hours before each match (last bus from Sandhills Station is approximately 15 minutes before kick-off) and for 50 minutes after the final whistle (subject to availability). You can pay as you board the bus. Soccerbus is FREE for those who hold a valid TRIO, SOLO or SAVEAWAY ticket, or a Merseytravel Free Travel Pass. Please note: Soccerbus is now wheelchair accessible.

HOW TO GET THERE - BY BUS

Take a 26 (or 27) from Paradise Street Bus Station or a 17B, 17C, 17D or 217 from Queen Square bus station directly to the ground. The 68 and 168 which operate between Bootle and Aigburth and the 14 (from Queen Square) and 19 stop a short walk away.

HOW TO GET THERE - BY AIR

Liverpool John Lennon Airport is around 10 miles from the ground, and taxis should be easily obtainable. Alternatively, you can catch the 80A bus to Garston Station and change at Sandhills for the Soccerbus service.

HOW TO GET THERE - ON FOOT

From Kirkdale Station, turn right and then cross the railway bridge, where you will see the Melrose Abbey pub. Walk past up Westminster Road for around 1/3 of a mile before you arrive at the Elm Tree pub. Follow the road around the right-hand bend and then turn left into Bradwell Street. At the end of the road you will come to County Road (A59). Cross over at the traffic lights and then go down the road to the left of the Aldi superstore. At the end of this road you will reach Walton Lane (A580). You should be able to see Goodison Park on your left and Stanley Park in front of you. Cross Walton Lane and either enter Stanley Park, following the footpath through the park (keeping to the right) which will exit into Anfield Road. As an alternative to going through Stanley Park, bear right down Walton Lane and then turn left down the road at the end of Stanley Park to the ground.

TO CHECK BUS AND TRAIN TIMES (8AM-8PM, 7 DAYS A WEEK):

Traveline Merseyside	0871 200 22 33
Soccerbus	0151 330 1066

STADIUM & LEGENDS TOUR

ABOUT

The LFC Stadium Tour is a must for any LFC fan and visitor to the city.

Anfield is one of the oldest and most famous football grounds in the world. Originally the home of Everton Football Club between 1884 and 1892, Anfield has long since become synonymous with Liverpool Football Club and the amazing success achieved by the Reds.

Over the years, some of football's greatest names have graced the hallowed turf and contributed to some of the most memorable matches ever played.

ANFIELD STADIUM TOUR

Take an Anfield Stadium Tour and gain exclusive behind the scenes access to one of the world's true sporting cathedrals.

- Watch and learn as our passionate tour guides provide fascinating insights into Anfield's celebrated past and Liverpool FC's bright future.
- Follow in the footsteps of legends like Shankly, Paisley and Dalglish in a stadium steeped in glory.
- Enjoy an interactive experience in the Anfield Press Room.
- Take a look at the views pitch-side, from the best seats in the stadium.
- Sit in the same dressing room as modern-day icons, Gerrard, Carroll, Suarez and Carragher.
- To the backdrop of spine-tingling sound effects, walk down the tunnel, touch the world famous "THIS IS ANFIELD" sign and emerge to the roar of the Anfield faithful.
- Marvel at the Spion Kop – the most illustrious terrace in world football.

Price (includes LFC Museum entrance):

Adults	£15
Children	£9
Family ticket	£41 (2 adults and 2 children)

Open every day from 9am onwards, running later during summer and finishing earlier in winter. Visit **www.liverpoolfc.tv/tours** for latest information.
Treat yourself and the family to an unforgettable experience. Book online now at
www.liverpoolfc.tv/tours or call 0151 260 6677. Stadium Tours can also be bought as a gift voucher either online or in any of our LFC Official Club Stores.

LFC LEGENDS TOUR

This nostalgic stadium tour with an LFC legend takes you behind the scenes at Anfield and provides insight and dressing room tales never told before.
Visit the first-team dressing room and find out how things have changed, whilst reminiscing on the memories and highlights – hearing at first hand what playing at Anfield meant to them.
Go down the tunnel to the sound of the crowd and touch the famous "This Is Anfield" sign, before taking your seat in the dugout to hear how they received their instructions from the touchline.
Hear what affect the roar from the world-famous Kop had on the players with tales of their greatest goal scored, defence-splitting pass or crunching tackle before you finish off with a fun and entertaining question and answer session.
Taking a stadium tour with an LFC legend is a truly unique experience. To book visit
www.liverpoolfc.tv/tours or call 0151 260 6677.
Legends Stadium Tours can also be bought as a gift voucher either online or in any of our LFC Official Club Stores.

Price:

Adults	£35
Children and Concessions	£18

MUSEUM TOUR

LIVERPOOL FC MUSEUM

The Liverpool FC Museum captures the glory and catalogues the success of one of Britain's most successful football clubs. Amongst many other notable collections it is home to 5 European Cups, including the original trophy won for the fifth time against AC Milan in 2005.

Soak up the history and memories of the many legends to have worn the famous red strip, relive many of our famous triumphs and get lost in the nostalgia.

Price:

Adults	£6
Children	£4
Family ticket	£18
(2 adults and 2 children)	

Opening times:
9am-5pm (with last admission at 4pm).
Matchdays – Last admission is 1 hour before kick-off.

Please note, when we have later tours the museum will remain open.

For latest information and to book to visit:
Please see www.liverpoolfc.tv/tours or call 0151 260 6677.

Mini stadium tours:
Before some home games when we are preparing the stadium, there are restrictions with some of the areas we can visit. These tours will still give you limited access to the stadium and the LFC Museum (at a reduced cost). Visit our website for details.

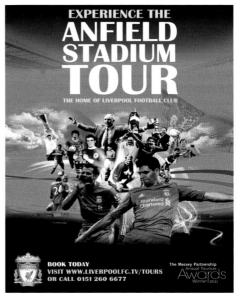

THE ANFIELD EXPERIENCE

Liverpool Football Club offers you the perfect opportunity to treat yourself – or anybody else – to a choice of two exclusive VIP days. These can be purchased either as an open voucher, giving you the flexibility to redeem the day over the next nine months, or on a specific date.

The stadium tour takes you behind the scenes at Anfield, visiting the dressing rooms, down the tunnel to the sound of the crowd, a chance to touch the famous "This Is Anfield" sign and sit in the team dugout. A knowledgeable tour guide will tell you about the historic Anfield Stadium and escort you on to The Kop – the most famous terrace in world football.

You'll enjoy a luxurious three-course lunch in one of our executive boxes overlooking the pitch – and expect one of our legends to drop in and make a special personal appearance.

Before you leave join the rest of the guests for a fun question and answer session with your Liverpool legend. A great day out for all Liverpool fans!

THE ULTIMATE ANFIELD EXPERIENCE

The Ultimate Anfield Experience is a once-in-a-lifetime opportunity which starts at Anfield with a meet and greet from LFC legends and a footballer's breakfast, before going to the LFC Academy to train with the Legends and Academy coaches.

You'll then enjoy a delicious 3-course meal at Anfield in one of our hospitality suites, have a question and answer session with the legends, followed by a guided Stadium Tour and Museum visit.

You'll be spending a day at the club you love...meeting past greats, collecting autographs and accessing areas of Liverpool FC that few fans are privileged to see.

It's a real once-in-a-lifetime VIP experience.

For more information and to book visit **www.liverpoolfc.tv/anfieldexperience** or call **0151 263 7744**.

REDS GALLERY AT THE BLUECOAT

Visit Liverpool FC's new 'The Reds Gallery at the Bluecoat' situated at the Bluecoat; Liverpool's historic and creative hub.

Take a trip down memory lane and reminisce over managers, players and moments in time that have helped shape the history of one of Britain's most successful clubs.

Since May 2011, the free-to-enter gallery has been a showcase for a series of exclusive photographic exhibitions, which includes iconic LFC images, commissioned pieces as well as alternative images influenced by acclaimed artists and award-winning photographer Steve Hale, who followed the Reds for over 30 years.

Visitors can purchase images on show at the gallery when they visit or can purchase them online at **www.redsgallery.tv**

For more information on what exhibitions are running up to the summer of 2012 visit **www.liverpoolfc.tv/redgallery**

THE BOOTROOM SPORTS CAFE, ANFIELD

Liverpool FC's Boot Room Sports Cafe offers a unique, fun and family-orientated experience.

The restaurant has been created with LFC fans in mind and boasts private booths and TV screens showing live sports. It also has a selection of club memorabilia on display and activities to keep children entertained.

A freshly prepared menu includes favourites including steaks, burgers, stone-baked pizzas and pasta dishes. Youngsters are catered for with a special Mini Boot Room menu, signature fruit cocktails and are invited to make their own pizzas with the help of a trained chef. They can also use the popular ice cream machine in the specially-designed kids' area.

Opening Times:
11am–11pm Thursday–Saturday.
11am–6pm Sunday-Wednesday (Except Matchdays).

For general reservations book online at **www.liverpoolfc.tv/bootroom** or call **0151 906 1892**.

Kid's parties, private parties, business events and functions can be catered for. For more information call **0151 906 1892**.

OFFICIAL WEBSITE

ABOUT

Anfield may be the world-famous home of Liverpool FC but when it comes to visiting the club online, there's only one place called 'home' and that's **www.liverpoolfc.tv**

Launched in April 2001, the official website of Liverpool Football Club has proved an incredible success for the Reds and is now one of the most popular sports sites on the web.

Within 12 months of launch the website (which is run by passionate supporters employed by the club) was recognised as the most visited football club website in the world – with fans from 139 countries viewing 13.3 million pages a month.

Today, these figures seem small in comparison to the records set over the last year.

In January 2011 liverpoolfc.tv broke the 100 million page impression barrier for the first time as 5.6 million fans logged on to hear news of Kenny Dalglish's dramatic return and transfer news about Fernando Torres, Luis Suarez and Andy Carroll. One article about Torres was viewed by 635,443 people – a record which still stands.

However, in July 2011 the club's official website again smashed the record once again as fans flocked to the site to check out the latest transfer rumours, news of new signings, exclusive player video diaries and live video coverage of all our pre-season games.

And it's not just breaking news that draws the numbers. With premium video content on LFC TV Online and a new social media platform called The Kop, Kopites are spending longer than ever with the club online.

LFC TV ONLINE

ABOUT

LFC TV Online is the club website's on-demand, premium content video service, allowing fans to:

- Watch LFC TV, the club's TV channel, LIVE or catch up with the best bits, at your leisure;
- Watch pre-season matches LIVE;
- Enjoy web-friendly and bite-sized videos of the best LFC video content anywhere;
- LIVE match commentary;
- Goal clips and video highlights of all our Premier League and cup matches;
- Live coverage of Liverpool Reserves;
- Live Academy games;
- Exclusive video interviews with players, managers and legends;
- The only place to watch every pre-match Reds press conference – IN FULL;
- Relive KOP classics – live and breathe Liverpool's history;
- Down the tunnel interviews post-match;

Watch what you want, where you want and when you want!

Visit **www.liverpoolfc.tv/video**

LFC TV

ABOUT
Launched in 2007, LFC TV is the most watched football club channel in Britain. Here are 10 reasons why you should tune in today...

1. It's the only place where you can watch every single minute of every single Barclays Premier League match Liverpool play this season. Liverpool's Saturday matches are available to watch in full from 6pm on Sunday while all other Reds league games can be watched on midnight of the same day they are played.

2. It's the only channel where you can watch the next generation of Liverpool's up-and-coming stars live on TV. Every Reserve game Liverpool play in 2011/12 will be shown live on LFC TV while, for the first time ever, we'll also be showing the majority of the Liverpool U18 side's home fixtures live.

3. When the players speak, they speak to LFC TV. Every week, LFC TV heads down to the club's training ground Melwood to interview the players and when a new player signs for the club, he conducts his first interview exclusively with LFC club media.

4. If you've got something to say, LFC TV wants to hear from you. Liverpool supporters are famous the world over for being football's most knowledgeable fans and on LFC TV, we're keen to hear what you think about the issues that matter. For 'You're on LFC TV' (Mondays nights) and after every away match, we'll be opening the phone lines so fans everywhere can get involved.

5. If goals are your thing, you'll love LFC TV. We show more Liverpool goals every day than any other channel shows in an entire year! Whether it's 'Goal Rush', a short, sharp burst of goals, 'Goals, Goals, Goals', where a spin of the wheel determines what strikes get featured or 'Goal of the Month', you won't have to wait long to get your daily fix.

6. Can't get a ticket on match day? Well, from this season, LFC TV will be bringing all the famous Anfield atmosphere right into your front room every time Liverpool play at home. For the first time ever, we'll be broadcasting live from Anfield on a match day with the best build-up coverage and post-match reaction available anywhere.

7. Can't wait until 5pm for your daily news fix courtesy of our LFC Now show? Well now you can stay in touch with all the latest breaking news from not just LFC but also around the Premier League with our brand new interactive on-screen ticker service at 10am and 2pm each week day.

8. Fancy a less serious look ahead to the weekend game? Join us for 'Friday Night Live'. Filmed live in the LFC TV lounge at 6pm every Friday, it's a show where we could make you the star – if you've submitted a video to The Kop section of the official website. We'll also be taking your calls, texts, emails and tweets as we build up to the big game.

9. If nostalgia is your thing, we've never been shy about celebrating the players, games and goals that have made Liverpool Football Club what it is today. From the glory that was Rome in 1977 to that unforgettable night at the Ataturk in 2005, we've got every magical moment covered.

10. And one final reason to tune in – it's free! Yes, you did read that right – LFC TV is 100% free to watch if you're on Sky (also available via the XL package on Virgin). How many other Barclays Premier League clubs provide their fans with a free TV channel seven days a week? Er, none. So, what are you waiting for? Tune into LFC TV today.

LFC TV can be viewed on Sky Channel 434 or Virgin Media Channel 544.
Alternatively, watch online via LFC TV Online (**www.liverpoolfc.tv/video**)

CLUB STORES

Selling everything from the new replica kits to the latest toys and games, the club stores provide supporters with a wealth of souvenirs. With the new adidas range having been unveiled, there is a wealth of choice for the 2011/2012 season.
Addresses and contact details are as follows:

WILLIAMSON SQUARE OFFICIAL CLUB STORE

11 Williamson Square, Liverpool, L1 1EQ
United Kingdom
Tel +44 (0)151 330 3077
Opening times: Mon-Wed 9am - 5.30pm;
Thursday 9am - 7pm; Fri-Sat 9am - 5.30pm;
Sundays 10am - 4pm. **The store will have varying opening hours on matchdays, depending on KO times. Please call for details.**

ANFIELD OFFICIAL CLUB STORE

Telephone +44 (0)151 264 2368
Opening times Mon-Sat 9am - 5pm;
Sundays 10am - 4pm.
The store will have varying opening hours on matchdays, depending on KO times. Please call for details.

CHESTER OFFICIAL CLUB STORE

48 Eastgate Street, Chester, CH1 1LE
United Kingdom
Tel +44 (0)1244 344 608
Opening times: Mon-Sat 9am - 5.30pm;
Sundays 10am - 4pm.

LIVERPOOL ONE SUPERSTORE

7 South John Street, Liverpool, L1 8BU
United Kingdom
Tel +44 (0)151 709 4345
Opening times: Mon-Fri 9.30am - 8pm;
Saturdays 9am - 7pm;
Sundays 11am - 5pm.

BELFAST OFFICIAL CLUB STORE

9 Castle Lane, Belfast, BT1 5DA
Northern Ireland
Tel 00 44 (0)28 9031 9341
Opening times: Mon-Wed 9.30am - 6pm
Thursday 9am - 9pm
Fri-Sat 9.30am - 6pm;
Sundays 1pm - 5pm.

ONLINE STORE

www.liverpoolfc.tv/store

ORDERING BY PHONE

(UK) + 44 (0)151 907 9500
(International calls) 0843 170 1892
**Lines open (subject to change): Monday-Friday 8.00am - 7.00pm
Saturday 9.00am - 5.00pm
Sunday 10.00am - 4.00pm**
LFC Official Members receive 10% retail discount both in store and online

OFFICIAL PUBLICATIONS

Official Matchday Programme

The award-winning 84-page souvenir matchday publication is available every Anfield matchday, providing a wealth of features and information for fans. Exclusive interviews with players and management, club news, columns, quizzes, facts and statistics remain at the forefront of the publication, while other features include The Kop, Behind The Glass, Outside Anfield, Where Once We Watched, Just Can't Get Enough, Red Carpet and Kids' Zone.

How to subscribe

Phone: 0845 143 0001 (Monday-Friday 9am-5pm)
Website: www.liverpoolfc.tv/match/magazine
(Also available in braille and other formats – contact community department on 0151 264 2316 for details)

LFC

Established as the only weekly publication produced by a Barclays Premier League club in 2002, the popular club magazine informs and entertains fans of all ages. Packed with content and analysis, the magazine offers interaction with fans and liverpoolfc.tv. Going behind the scenes at Melwood, we speak to the stars while offering the very best match previews, reports, on-field action, interviews and statistics – while columnists Alan Hansen, and manager Kenny Dalglish deliver their expert opinion.

How to subscribe

Phone: 0845 143 0001 (Monday-Friday 9am-5pm)
Website: www.liverpoolfc.tv/match/magazine

The Liverpool FC Family Tree

Ever wondered how Liverpool FC became so unique? Our Anfield family roots provide the answer. The LFC magic is made up of many different people and places. This book takes you on a colourful journey of discovery – through eight unique excursions, linking the Anfield past and present. It is guaranteed to unearth some fascinating secrets about LFC loved ones. Just like researching your own family, this book will inspire you, make you laugh, provoke emotion and ultimately fill you with pride.

How to order

Phone: 0845 143 0001 (Monday-Friday 9am-5pm)
Website: www.liverpoolfc.tv/store

LIVERPOOL FC MOBILE ZONE

ABOUT

The Liverpool FC Mobile Zone is your one-stop shop for all the latest apps, ringtones, animations, wallpapers and videos from Anfield.

With regular updates to this popular area on **www.liverpoolfc.tv**, we have a wide array of the latest downloads to give you the chance of bringing your favourite club straight to your mobile phone.

LFC APP STORE

The Club has an array of mobile applications on offer for a number of handsets. Check out the latest selection at **www.liverpoolfc.tv/mobile/app-store**
Some of our most popular apps are:

LFC MATCH & NEWS CENTRE

Kopites can follow the team wherever they go with the official app from Liverpool FC. Whether it's breaking news, exclusive interviews, in-game scores or commentary that you're after, you won't miss a thing with this innovative application.

PENALTY SHOOTOUT

Pit your skills against a Liverpool FC goalie in front of The Kop! Featuring Classic Penalty Mode, Time Attack Mode and Target Mode. 20 Game Center Achievements to unlock and 3 Game Center Leaderboards to compete in.

More applications will be launched throughout the season on a variety of handsets so keep checking back for the latest.

MOBILE MEMBERSHIP

You can now download as many wallpapers and videos as you like with LFC Mobile Membership. For £1.50 a week, you will have access to match action, features, interviews and the latest news videos plus wallpapers of your favourite players and the famous crest.
Text CLUB to 61718 for info. Text will cost standard network rate and your phone must be WAP enabled to receive the service.

TEXT ALERTS AND DOWNLOADS

Whether it's news of the latest goal to your mobile or a You'll Never Walk Alone ringtone, we've got it all.

Text Alerts: Choose from goals, teamsheets, latest news and more straight to your mobile as it happens.

Downloads: Animations of your favourite players, ringtones to get your phone jumping and wallpapers of the team in action. Show your allegiance to the Reds on your mobile...

INTERNATIONAL FOOTBALL ACADEMY
SOCCER SCHOOLS

ABOUT

Take your natural skills onto the next level...

This 3-day specialist programme for both outfield players and goalkeepers is designed to develop the potential of every child that attends by enhancing their confidence and improving their skills, whilst ensuring they are fun and rewarding in every sense.

It is available to children of all abilities from the ages of 5 to 14 – from beginner to superstar! By taking part you'll benefit from:

- Professional and dedicated coaching from Academy staff in all areas of the game;
- Expertly designed practices, activities and skill sessions;
- Learning new tactics and techniques;
- Improving your ball skills, passing, balance and co-ordination;
- Mini-tournaments and penalty shoot-outs.

And who knows? If our coaches spot your talent you could be the next Academy protégé to make it through to the first team.

So whether you want to show off your skills or improve your techniques, why not take the opportunity to play like your heroes and book your place.
For more information or to book please visit **www.liverpoolfc.tv/soccerschools**

MEMBERSHIP

ABOUT

LFC Official Membership for 2011/12 is bigger and better than ever, and gets fans even closer to the club. With three different types of membership, you're sure to find one that's suitable for you. To join visit **liverpoolfc.tv/membership** or call 0843 170 5000. The benefits you'll receive are:

LFC OFFICIAL ADULT MEMBERSHIP – ONLY £29.99

- Priority access to all available tickets for Barclays Premier League home games and the opportunity to purchase tickets in advance for the 2011/12 season in two stages; July and November;
- Members-only monthly e-newsletter with exclusive and unseen interviews with players, competitions and offers;
- No web fees when purchasing tickets online in the members ticket sale;
- An exclusive membership pack containing an Official Membership Card, limited edition book and LFC pen;
- 3 months free trial to LFC TV Online;
- 10% off retail in our online shop and in any official LFC club store;
- Up to 40% off LFC subscriptions and official books;
- 20% off Liverpool FC Experience Days;
- 10% off images in 'The Reds Gallery at the Bluecoat';
- 10% off food in the Boot Room Sports Cafe, Anfield, and a bottle of champagne on your birthday, when 4 or more dine (over 18s only);
- Club discounts, partner offers and more...

LFC OFFICIAL JUNIOR MEMBERSHIP – ONLY £14.99

- Priority access to all available tickets for Barclays Premier League home games and the opportunity to purchase tickets in advance for the 2011/12 season in two stages; July and November;
- The chance to be an LFC Mascot and walk out onto the pitch with their heroes;
- The chance to attend an exclusive Junior Member's Soccer School at the LFC Academy;
- Junior Members-only monthly e-newsletter, with interviews with all their favourite players, competitions and offers;
- An exclusive Membership pack containing an LFC Official Membership Card, kitbag, stationary set, signed player cards and certificate;
- 3 months free trial to LFC TV Online;
- 10% off retail in our online store and in any official LFC club store;
- Up to 40% off LFC subscriptions and official books;
- 20% off Liverpool FC Experience Days;
- 10% off images at 'The Reds Gallery at the Bluecoat';
- 10% off food in the Boot Room Sports Cafe, Anfield, and they'll eat free on their birthday!

MEMBERSHIP

LFC OFFICIAL INTERNATIONAL MEMBERSHIP – ONLY £18.99

- Members-only monthly e-newsletter containing unseen film, footage, news and interviews from the manager and players;
- Team news and notes from the manager and captain sent before all Barclays Premier League home games;
- 3 months free trial to LFC TV Online, providing you with premium content on the LFC website;
- An exclusive membership pack containing an official membership card, USB stick with 'Members only' content and footage, plus an LFC pen;
- 10% off retail in our online store or in any official LFC club store;
- Up to 40% off LFC subscriptions and official books;
- 20% off Liverpool FC Experience Days;
- 10% off images at 'The Reds Gallery at the Bluecoat';
- 10% off food in the Boot Room Sports Cafe, Anfield, and a bottle of champagne on your birthday (over 18s only);
- Club discounts, partner offers and more...

Become an LFC official member today.
To join visit **liverpoolfc.tv/membership** or call 0843 170 5000.

LFC IN THE COMMUNITY

ABOUT

LFC Community department vision is 'To Serve our Community with Excellence'.
Liverpool Football Club achieved Business in the Community's **CommunityMark** in 2009.
The CommunityMark is a national standard that recognises companies that are the best investors in their communities.
It is a robust, strategic and independently assessed standard only achieved by 38 companies in the UK. The Club benchmarks all of its community activities by this standard of excellence and seeks to fulfill the CommunityMark standards in all of its programmes.

EDUCATION

- The **Truth 4 Youth** programme delivers social messages to both primary and senior schools such as: Ban the Bully, Rule out the Racist, Drop the Drugs, Shoot Goals not Guns, say No to Knife Crime, health is Wealth Love is Infectious, More important then being a Good Footballer is being a Good Person and You'll Never Walk Alone.
- **Tactics 4 Families** is an education programme to children in school years 4-6 and their families, delivering classroom and sports sessions as well as a parent/carer session. The programme is specifically designed using the principles of football to cover key messages about family life.
- The newly-refurbished LFC Education Centre **Reducate** is designed to improve skills in key areas such as reading, writing, speaking and listening. Working individually, in pairs and in teams children enjoy a vast range of learning opportunities using all of the new ICT equipment and working with exceptional and enthusiastic students from the three Universities of Liverpool.
- **SweeperZone** is an environmental project whereby 25 young people from local schools, organisations and resident groups work around the stadium on match days collecting litter. The project has being running for several years now and helps support local resident living around the stadium.
- The **Young Person of the Year Award** is a prestigious annual event that commends local young people for their courage, compassion or care towards others in their community.
- **Goals 4 All** programme brings together several of the established Community Department projects, in order to create a full days' experience for local school children and Community Groups.

SOCIAL INCLUSION

- LFC provides football opportunities for impairment specific disabilities through its **Respect 4 All** centre. Football sessions run four nights a week for children and adults with physical disabilities, blind and visually impaired, learning difficulties and wheelchair users. In addition the Ability Counts teams train each week and compete in regional tournaments every month.
- The **Equality 4 All** project delivers evening coaching sessions to young people around the city from ethnic and excluded backgrounds, working in areas such as Toxteth, Kensington, the City Centre, Wavertree, Kirkdale and Vauxhall. The project seeks to integrate the diverse communities of our city regardless of ethnicity, gender, background, sexuality, religion or ability.
- The **KICKZ** programme is late night football for 12–18 year olds. The programme works in partnership with Everton FC and Merseyside Police.
- The **Social Academy** project works with local homeless people by improving their life skills using football as an engagement tool. The participants enrol on an eight-week 'LFC Introduction to Coaching Football' course, with a view to going on to complete their Level 1 coaching badge.

LFC IN THE COMMUNITY

SOCIAL INCLUSION

- **Goals 4 Girls** is aimed towards girls and young women around the city, delivering messages on female specific issues such as diet, peer pressure, sexual health, image consciousness and bullying. The project also offers coaching sessions in a variety of sports to its participants.
- Working in partnership with the **Princes Trust** on their TEAM project which is a 12-week personal development course. LFC provide a fitness session, work placements and a health and nutrition workshop.

PHYSICAL ACTIVITY

- Each week **LFC coaches** run sessions in 35 mainstream schools and 14 special needs schools across Liverpool. Coaching is also delivered at after-schools sessions, sports centres and summer and half-term football camps.
- The **PL4Sport** programme delivers multi-sports activities in badminton, judo, volleyball, table tennis and netball, and is linked with the 2012 Olympics. The project seeks to offer more sporting opportunities and assists in the transition from school sports clubs to community clubs.

HEALTH

- The **Action for Health** programme encompasses health and lifestyle initiatives managed by the club and delivered with community agencies, Liverpool PCT and Liverpool City Council.
- Specific initiatives include a Men's Health programme, healthy lifestyle and positive mental health for the over 50s, a 'Drop a Shirt' size weight management project and ongoing support to the 2020 Decade of Health and Wellbeing in Liverpool.
- LFC is a member of the European Healthy Stadia Network. Good practice includes offering health checks to employees and introducing a **Cycle2Work** scheme.

LFC IN ANFIELD

- Liverpool FC is a key partner in the continuing regeneration of the Anfield neighbourhood and the wider communities across north Liverpool. It is the objective of the Club to support the Voluntary sector groups and public agencies in tackling the various social and economic problems.
- This commitment to the regeneration of the neighbourhood is no more apparent than the Club's £10m investment towards the restoration of Stanley Park and the Isla Gladstone Conservatory. As well as helping the City Council to secure other public monies that assisted the building or renovation of four key community centres, as well as the introduction of improved highways infrastructure.

SUPPORT FOR OTHER CHARITIES

- LFC communicates with its huge national and international fan base, with thousands of letters being answered each year.
- The department receives a huge volume of requests for charitable support and every request is responded to by this section. We give support to registered charities and worthy causes. Last season we sent over 10,000 positive responses
- LFC makes wishes come true for our fans who are dealing with a serious/terminal illness. We arrange for our special guest to come to Melwood to meet and greet the players.

INTERNATIONAL COMMUNITY WORK

- Working with Oxfam, FOMO, The Red Cross, International Needs and various missionaries LFC donates hundreds of kits to third-world countries.
- LFC handed over thousands of match-worn kits and club memorabilia to the British Red Cross to help raise funds for their Japan Tsunami Appeal.

REDUC@TE

ABOUT

The new Liverpool Football Education Centre is located above the ticket office at the Kop end of the famous Anfield Stadium. Staff at the centre deliver high quality educational packages in an inspirational environment to students across Liverpool and additionally the facility is available for schools from outside the city and for local community groups.

Holiday programmes are also available for children and further information is available on the community section of the LFC website. Since the new centre opened in October 2010 young people have enjoyed the numerous learning opportunities on offer including Maths Days, Language Days and Rewards and Achievement Days. Contact details for bookings and enquiries are as follows:

Centre manager: Keith White **07736 382795**

Centre Phone Number: **0151 906 1835**

Email centre manager: **krwhite.lfc.study@talk21.com**

Email the centre: **keith.white@liverpoolfc.tv**

OFFICIAL SUPPORTERS CLUB BRANCHES

ABOUT

Liverpool Football Club has just over 200 official supporters clubs all over the world in over 50 different countries. Our official supporters club branches provide a valuable service to loyal Liverpool Football Club supporters living in the local area. The supporters clubs also provide an excellent way of meeting fellow supporters who are devoted to following Liverpool Football Club, wherever they live in the world. All registered branches are listed on **www.liverpoolfc.tv**

LIVERPOOL DISABLED SUPPORTERS' ASSOCIATION

AIMS AND OBJECTIVES

To act in partnership with Liverpool Football Club to promote inclusiveness for the disabled fans of the club, the disabled fans of visiting clubs as well as those individuals who support disabled people and those with impairments.

This association recognises that all fans should have an equal opportunity to participate in an enjoyable matchday experience and that people with disabilities and/or impairments must have their interests recognised and promoted by LFC with equal status to that of all other Liverpool fans.

CONTACT DETAILS

Disability liaison officer Colin McCall continues to develop the LDSA, acting as a link between the club and its supporters. The LDSA committee is made up of 10 members who are all Liverpool supporters and they meet once a month with the liaison officer to discuss disability issues at LFC.

If you would like any more information about the LDSA then please email **LDSA@liverpoolfc.tv** or write to: **LFC, 10th Floor, 20, Chapel Street, L3 9AG.**

OFFICIAL CLUB PARTNERS

Standard Chartered
www.standardchartered.com

adidas
www.adidas.com/football

Carlsberg
www.carlsberg.com/#/football/lfc

Thomas Cook
www.thomascooksport.com/liverpoolfc

188Bet
www.188promo.com/liverpool

Jack Wolfskin
www.jack-wolfskin.com/en/

LFC Credit Card
www.liverpoolfc.tv/corporate/lfc-credit-card

Maxxis
www.maxxis.co.uk

Lucozade Sport
www.lucozade.com

Visit Spain
www.spain.info

2012	Jan	Feb	March	April	May	June
Monday						
Tuesday					1	
Wednesday		1		2	2	
Thursday		2	1		3	
Friday		3	2		4	1
Saturday	1	4	3		5	2
Sunday	2	5	4	1	6	3
Monday	3	6	5	2	7	4
Tuesday	4	7	6	3	8	5
Wednesday	5	8	7	4	9	6
Thursday	6	9	8	5	10	7
Friday	7	10	9	6	11	8
Saturday	8	11	10	7	12	9
Sunday	9	12	11	8	13	10
Monday	10	13	12	9	14	11
Tuesday	11	14	13	10	15	12
Wednesday	12	15	14	11	16	13
Thursday	13	16	15	12	17	14
Friday	14	17	16	13	18	15
Saturday	15	18	17	14	19	16
Sunday	16	19	18	15	20	17
Monday	17	20	19	16	21	18
Tuesday	18	21	20	17	22	19
Wednesday	19	22	21	18	23	20
Thursday	20	23	22	19	24	21
Friday	21	24	23	20	25	22
Saturday	22	25	24	21	26	23
Sunday	23	26	25	22	27	24
Monday	24	27	26	23	28	25
Tuesday	25	28	27	24	29	26
Wednesday	26	29	28	25	30	27
Thursday	27		29	26	31	28
Friday	28		30	27		29
Saturday	29		31	28		30
Sunday	30			29		
Monday	31			30		
Tuesday						

July	Aug	Sept	Oct	Nov	Dec	
			1			Monday
			2			Tuesday
	1		3			Wednesday
	2		4	1		Thursday
	3		5	2		Friday
	4	1	6	3	1	Saturday
	5	2	7	4	2	Sunday
	6	3	8	5	3	Monday
	7	4	9	6	4	Tuesday
	8	5	10	7	5	Wednesday
	9	6	11	8	6	Thursday
	10	7	12	9	7	Friday
	11	8	13	10	8	Saturday
	12	9	14	11	9	Sunday
	13	10	15	12	10	Monday
	14	11	16	13	11	Tuesday
	15	12	17	14	12	Wednesday
	16	13	18	15	13	Thursday
	17	14	19	16	14	Friday
	18	15	20	17	15	Saturday
	19	16	21	18	16	Sunday
	20	17	22	19	17	Monday
	21	18	23	20	18	Tuesday
	22	19	24	21	19	Wednesday
	23	20	25	22	20	Thursday
	24	21	26	23	21	Friday
	25	22	27	24	22	Saturday
	26	23	28	25	23	Sunday
	27	24	29	26	24	Monday
	28	25	30	27	25	Tuesday
	29	26	31	28	26	Wednesday
	30	27		29	27	Thursday
	31	28		30	28	Friday
		29			29	Saturday
		30			30	Sunday
					31	Monday
						Tuesday

OTHER USEFUL CONTACTS

The Premier League
30 Gloucester Place,
London W1U 8PL
Phone: 0207 864 9000
Email: **info@premierleague.com**

The Football Association
Wembley Stadium,
PO Box 1966,
London SW1P 9EQ
Phone: 0844 980 8200

The Football League
Edward VII Quay, Navigation Way,
Preston PR2 2YF
Email: **fl@football-league.co.uk**

Professional Footballers' Association
2 Oxford Court,
Bishopsgate,
Off Lower Mosley Street,
Manchester M2 3WQ
Phone: 0161 236 0575
Email: **info@thepfa.co.uk**

Hillsborough Family
Support Group
c/o Liverpool FC,
Anfield Road,
Liverpool L4 0TH
Email: **hfsg@worthside.co.uk**

Published in Great Britain in 2011 by: Trinity Mirror Sport Media, PO Box 48, Old Hall Street, Liverpool, L69 3EB

ISBN: 1 9068 0278 3
978 1 9068 0278 3

Photographs: PA Photos, Trinity Mirror, Liverpool FC & AG Ltd
Printed and finished by KINT Ljubljana